Heroic Nature

N. Poussin, *St. John on Patmos*

HEROIC NATURE

Ideal Landscape in English Poetry
from Marvell to Thomson

JEFFRY B. SPENCER

———•◦•———

Northwestern University Press
Evanston   1973

TO JEAN HAGSTRUM

Contents

Acknowledgments

My most profound debt is owed to that distinguished teacher, scholar, and critic to whom this book is dedicated. I also wish to thank Professors Olan A. Rand and Albert R. Cirillo for reading my manuscript, which has benefited from their suggestions. I am grateful to the staffs of Deering Library at Northwestern and the Newberry Library, Chicago; the Huntington and the Clark libraries in California; the Bodleian Library, Oxford; and the Fitzwilliam Library, Cambridge. For special favors I am indebted to Mr. Edward Croft-Murray, Keeper, Department of Prints and Drawings, the British Museum, and to Dr. Isabel Henderson of the National Library of Scotland. Those at the Northwestern University Press who have worked with me on preparing the manuscript have been helpful and kind. Mr. Ralph Carlson, Mrs. Joy Neuman, and Ms. Elizabeth Stout deserve my gratitude. Mrs. Marge Homan meticulously typed the manuscript. Jeanne D. Kennedy prepared the index.

My oldest debt is to my husband David, who first taught me to love the eighteenth century and who has sustained my spirits, supported my endeavors, and criticized my work with invariable good humor and unfailing tact.

Introduction

The present emphasis on the visual and pictorial in literary criticism grows logically enough out of the preoccupation with the image which has characterized so many modern textual studies of poetry. It has gained impetus from the comparatively recent concern with interdisciplinary studies in the arts. The latter reflect the contemporary movement away from the kind of critical fragmentation that sometimes resulted from too much emphasis on the uniqueness of each poem's microcosmic world. Comparatist or contextualist studies represent, in part, the return to a consideration of the poem as a cultural artifact, as a repository for the ideas both thematic and stylistic which characterize particular historical periods as well as reflect individual artistic sensibilities.

Taking this larger view makes an investigation of ideal landscape in seventeenth- and eighteenth-century poetry a study in the development of a metaphor, the durability inherent in a myth, and the variations possible to an apparently inflexible and stylized poetic genre. Because these landscapes are essentially allegorical, they are equivalences on a mythic or metaphoric level of certain contemporary preoccupations, anxieties, and desires, whether these are political, religious, or simply aesthetic. The allusiveness they gain through the evocation of a rich tradition is strengthened by the visual dimension they possess, reflecting, as they do, the old congeniality of the "sister arts." The nature and force of their pictorial impact can, I believe, be felt by readers of today perhaps more than at any time since their creation. There is evidence that our own poetic perceptions in the last half of the twentieth century are much more visually oriented than they were in the first half, when with Mr. Eliot we were discovering affinities with the intellectual, abstract, and seldom pictorial metaphysical poets, whose witty conceits and verbal pyrotechnics now seem less congenial to our literary sensibilities than they did to poets of the twenties and thirties. On a more popular level, the influence of films and television upon our society has made us conscious anew of what Coleridge, in the *Biographia,* called "the despotism of the eye." The alliance between contemporary cinematic art and the French new-wave novel may soon prompt a Latinist to rephrase the old tag, *ut pictura poesis,* in order to describe the modern manifestation of the continuing relationship between the verbal and the visual arts.

Once we become attuned to the sort of visual sensitivity displayed by poets of the Restoration and Augustan periods, we can evaluate the nature poetry of the age more perceptively, noting that it is often vivified as well as structured by an intrinsic pictorialism that is strongly thematic rather than simply decorative. This pictorial quality is at first incipient in the work of poets of the middle and later seventeenth century, reflecting the comparatively slow response of the English people to the visual arts; it only reaches full development in the poetry of Augustans like Pope and Thomson. By no means, however, does it originate with them, as scholars of an earlier generation appear to have assumed.[1] The tradition of *ut pictura poesis,* extending back to Simonides, then echoed by Horace, and later reiterated during the Renaissance, was, by the seventeenth century, an unassailably entrenched critical doctrine. In England, however, aesthetic theory was not knowledgeably reinforced by literary practice until poets began to acquire a greater understanding of the traditions of Western painting. We can observe a growing familiarity with the visual arts

1. See especially Elizabeth Wheeler Manwaring, *Italian Landscape in Eighteenth-Century England* (London, 1925).

during the seventeenth century, the first period in which English writers demonstrated a sustained interest in literary pictorialism. Such an interest presupposes at least a rudimentary acquaintance with great works of art and an acceptance of the concept of painting and poetry as sister arts.[2] The extent to which this relationship between the arts is imaginatively pursued depends, of course, upon the degree of artistic sophistication possessed by each poet whose work in some manner recalls the tradition of literary pictorialism.

All of the verbal landscapes to be examined in this study can be labeled pictorial in the sense defined above. That is, they reflect a recognized aesthetic doctrine, and they resemble painted landscapes in certain specific ways—their imagery is often indebted to iconographical conventions familiar to Renaissance art; the deliberate slowing of poetic movement is attempted, in order to achieve an effect of stasis; and, especially in the poetry of Pope and Thomson, the natural scene reveals the techniques of painterly composition in its very structure, usually proceeding in its design from foreground to more distant views. The poets whose work constitutes the present study are not equally pictorial, nor are they pictorial in identical ways. Their relationship to the tradition varies; in the case of Milton, for example, it is subtle and indirect, while in the case of Dryden, his contemporary, it is repeatedly acknowledged. As prolegomenon to an investigation of the poetic landscapes themselves, it would be useful, therefore, to determine the degree to which each poet responded to the tradition of literary pictorialism, so that we may more effectively assess the nature of that response in the chapters that follow, beginning with Andrew Marvell.

2. Other characteristics that distinguish the literary pictorialist may include a predilection for occasionally composing iconic verse, the tendency to associate with artists and connoisseurs, and the habit of using certain poetic techniques (i.e., slowing the movement of descriptive verse passages to achieve a feeling of stasis) that help to gain a pictorial effect. These marks of literary pictorialism have been described by Jean Hagstrum. See "The Sister Arts: From Neoclassic to Romantic," in *Comparatists at Work*, ed. Stephen G. Nichols, Jr., and Richard B. Vowles (Waltham, Mass., 1968), pp. 172–73.

Marvell's knowledge of the visual arts, though exhibited informally, seems to have been extensive. His poetry is sprinkled with offhand references to a "landskip" or a portrait, a statue or a *"Basso Relievo";* he can drop a name like Lely or Rubens and mention in passing the Mexican vogue for "painting" with brightly colored feathers or the great art collection that Charles I bought from the Duke of Mantua. He probably knew Edward Norgate's important early study, *Miniatura,* owned by Lord Fairfax and dedicated to his daughter (and Marvell's pupil) Mary.[3] He can claim in "The Gallery" to have transformed his soul into a picture salon in which his mistress is memorialized in several guises, here as an "Inhumane Murtheress," there as a "tender Shepherdess," or, alternatively, in attitudes familiar to students of Renaissance iconography, as Aurora or Venus. Marvell wrote several satiric poems advising mythical painters how to depict kings' mistresses and venal courtiers; though this form was a Restoration commonplace for satirical poetry, the writer employed many a confident reference to pictorial technique in using it.[4] He displayed an appreciative eye for the design of funerary sculpture, achieving, in "The Nymph Complaining for the Death of her Fawn," an effect that is both elegiac and witty.

> First my unhappy Statue shall
> Be cut in Marble; and withal,
> Let it be weeping too: but there
> Th' Engraver sure his Art may spare;
> For I so truly thee bemoane,
> That I shall weep though I be Stone:
> Until my Tears, still dropping, wear

3. Rosalie Colie, *"My Ecchoing Song": Andrew Marvell's Poetry of Criticism* (Princeton, 1970), p. 194.

4. Earl Miner discusses several iconographic and compositional conventions deriving from paintings, engravings, and political cartoons which provide visual analogues to the Instructions to Painters poems, especially those known to be by Marvell. See "The 'Poetic Picture, Painted Poetry' of *The Last Instructions to a Painter,*" in *Andrew Marvell: A Collection of Critical Essays,* ed. George deF. Lord (Englewood Cliffs, N.J., 1968), pp. 165–74.

My breast, themselves engraving there.
There at my feet shalt thou be laid,
Of purest Alabaster made:
For I would have thine Image be
White as I can, though not as Thee.[5]

Marvell's four years abroad, where he might be expected to
have acquired this easy expertise with painters and their craft,
is a well-documented part of his biography. Pierre Legouis
quotes a letter of Milton's (1652/3) which refers to Marvell's
having "spent four years abroad in Holland, France, Italy, and
Spain to very good purpose . . . and the gaining of these four
languages." [6] Whether he traveled to the Continent to escape
the Civil War at home or to accompany as tutor some unknown
young gentleman on the Grand Tour cannot be ascertained. We
do know he wrote a verbal "caricature" of "Dutch women
'Reeking at *Church* over the Chafing-Dish' "; memorialized,
with a crudely unflattering poem to Richard Fleckno, a visit in
Rome (between 1645 and 1647); and in Spain studied fencing
and attended a bullfight.[7] One may rather confidently conclude
from this collection of miscellany that any sort of innate visual
sensitivity coupled with a leisurely four-year tour of those
countries where, in the seventeenth century, the painters' craft
flourished most notably, might well combine to equip the
youthful Marvell with a much greater knowledge of the visual
arts than most Englishmen of his century possessed. Not unexpectedly this knowledge is reflected in Marvell's poetic depictions of nature, the most constant and popular theme of his
important lyric poetry.

John Milton's travels on the Continent, though less pro-
tracted and extensive than those of Marvell, were among the
youthful experiences that contributed most tellingly to "the
growth of a poet's mind." Milton scholars and biographers have

5. *The Poems and Letters of Andrew Marvell,* ed. H. M. Margoliouth, 2 vols. (Oxford, 1927). All subsequent citations to Marvell's
poetry will be to the first volume of this edition.
6. *Andrew Marvell, Poet, Puritan, Patriot* (Oxford, 1965), p. 9.
7. *Ibid.,* pp. 11–12.

exhibited a universal tendency to linger long over records of the Italian journey in the *Defensio Secunda*.[8] Milton made friends in Italy—many of them influential and artistic—visited the Vatican and saw the rare manuscripts in its library, and twice called at the Barberini Palace, the best-known "center for the performing arts" in Rome. He traveled to Florence; in September of 1638 he probably saw a performance of Andreini's biblical drama *L'Adamo*. In Naples he became acquainted with Manso, the patron of Tasso and Marino, and wrote a Latin poem, *Mansus,* linking himself, in anticipation, to these epic predecessors.

Certainly Milton's greatest achievements were to be the works composed after the Italian period, when he returned to his poetic vocation with a new confidence and sense of direction. Curiously, when writing about the stimulation that Italy afforded him, Milton failed to mention the visual arts, an omission which has perplexed both artists like Jonathan Richardson, who found his descriptions strikingly visual,[9] and eminent literary critics like Samuel Taylor Coleridge, who knew he was surrounded by the splendors of Italian Renaissance and baroque art almost wherever he went. The section of David Masson's vast nineteenth-century biography dealing with the Italian journey hypothesizes that in his travels Milton must have seen

8. Helen Darbishire, in an introduction to her edition of five early biographical sketches of Milton, suggests that "the visit to Italy bulks large because Milton himself set so high a value on it." See *The Early Lives of Milton* (London, 1932), p. lvii.

9. Milton's work had an extraordinary impact upon painters. Richardson, in *Explanatory Notes on Paradise Lost* (see Darbishire, *Early Lives*), found about forty-five "pictures" in Milton's epic— verbal "landscapes," "portraits," and "history paintings"—which he compared to works by Raphael, Guido, Correggio, Titian, and the whole pantheon of Italian Renaissance and baroque artists enshrined in eighteenth-century tastes. Henry Fuseli devoted ten years of his life (1790–1800) to his ill-fated Milton Gallery; his friend William Blake copiously illustrated the major poems; and J. M. W. Turner both attempted illustrations for the poems and "quoted" Milton in his own landscape art. A study of Milton's influence upon the visual arts is the subject of Marcia R. Pointon's recent book, *Milton and English Art* (Toronto, 1970).

a "bewildering wealth of statues, paintings, carvings, and bronzes." [10] Yet neither Masson nor, later, more scholarly researchers can offer documented evidence that Milton ever commented on specific works, though speculations about suggestive affinities between Italian art and architecture and the "spatial quality" of Milton's epics have abounded.[11] The English poet's visits to the Barberini Palace are the surest indication on record of Milton's undoubted exposure to his age's significant achievements in the visual arts. Both the artists represented and the subjects displayed at the time of his visit are interesting. The left wing of the palace was decorated with wall paintings of the Creation, Adam and Eve, Eden, and the Expulsion. Rooms were filled with works by Leonardo, Raphael, Tintoretto, Caravaggio, and "almost every great painter of the Renaissance." [12] E. K. Waterhouse refers to Pietro da Cortona's work on the

10. *The Life of John Milton,* 7 vols. (London, 1881), I, 770. Harry Morris supports Masson by offering a specific instance of Milton's debt to Italian art. Morris has shown that paintings seen on the Italian journey appear to have influenced the description of angels in Milton's work. Unlike other English poets (Chaucer, Spenser), Milton describes his angels with "iconographical correctness," implying "an acquaintance with the visual arts" gained abroad. Morris cites angels in works by Carpaccio, Fra Angelico, and Ambrogio Lorenzetti in Venice, Florence, and Siena respectively, also pointing out illuminated manuscripts of the thirteenth to fifteenth centuries which Milton may have seen in Paris. See "Some Uses of Angel Iconography in English Literature," *Comp. Lit.,* X (1958), 43.
11. An emphasis upon the spatial and visual qualities of Milton's imagery has characterized much of the work done on his poetry by scholars of the last two decades. Jackson Cope's belief that *Paradise Lost* is a "spatial poem" (*The Metaphoric Structure of Paradise Lost* [Baltimore, 1962], p. 34) reiterates similar judgments by Marjorie Hope Nicolson and Isabel MacCaffrey. The latter asserts that "Milton experienced the world of his epic architecturally, in terms of mass and space. The modulation of time into spatial effects . . . is the result." (See *Paradise Lost as "Myth"* [Cambridge, Mass., 1959], pp. 76–77.) Roy Daniells calls attention to Milton's "manipulation of space," likening the structure of his poetry to mannerist and baroque architectural forms (*Milton, Mannerism and Baroque* [Toronto, 1963]).
12. John Arthos, *Milton and the Italian Cities* (London, 1968), p. 75.

ceiling of the Great Salon as "the most breathtaking achievement of Roman Baroque painting." [13] The work was done between 1633 and 1639; at the time of Milton's visit, it was nearly completed and was almost certainly the setting for the famous musical evening long remembered by the poet, an occasion highlighted by the performance of a new opera (probably by Rospigliosi) with stage designs by Bernini.[14]

Whether or not Milton responded consciously to examples of the visual arts all about him in Italy, he could well have absorbed a pictorial tendency through the aesthetics of the period. Those who theorized about literature, however else they differed, had one common ground of agreement that had, by the 1630s, already become something of a cliché: poetry and painting were "sister arts"; it was proper and natural for one to resemble the other. The Italian poets were especially insistent on this point. Tasso described the epic poet as "a maker of images in the guise of a speaking picture." [15] Andreini, attempting to justify the use in poetic drama of actors to represent allegorical personifications or abstractions, reasons thus in the Preface to *L'Adamo* (1613):

> But, if it is permitted to the painter, who is a dumb poet, to express by colours God the Father under the person of a man silvered by age, and to describe under the image of a white dove the purity of the Spirit, and to figure the divine messengers or Angels, in the shape of winged youths; why is it not permitted to the poet, who is a speaking painter, to represent in his theatrical production another man and woman besides Adam and Eve, and to represent their internal conflicts through the medium of images and voices entirely human? [16]

Poets like Andreini who considered themselves "speaking painters" found precedents in the visual arts for techniques

13. *Italian Baroque Painting* (London, 1962), p. 49.
14. Carl Friedrich, *The Age of the Baroque* (New York, 1952), pp. 86–87.
15. "Discourses on the Heroic Poem," in *Literary Criticism,* ed. Allan Gilbert, 2 vols. (New York, 1940), I, 476.
16. Quoted in Arthos, *Milton and the Italian Cities,* p. 30.

which could be adapted to the verbal arts. The use in baroque art, for instance, of events and personages from classical mythology to represent allegorically certain historical occurrences or religious beliefs added a deeper level of significance to the pictures of Hercules, Venus, or Jove which adorned the walls and ceilings of Italian palaces during the age of the baroque. The emblem and *impresa* which suggested (openly in the case of the first and cryptically in the case of the second) a moral or intellectual concept often lent new vigor and concrete power to personified abstractions in poetic images.

The qualities inherent in Milton's "grand style" suggest that the English poet might have understood Tasso's emphasis on *asprezza* ("roughness"), which includes the use of a deliberately complex diction, an unevenness of rhythm, and a slowing of metrical pace. It is designed to give the impression of weighty grandeur to the heroic poem, attempting to approximate on a verbal level the monumentality of baroque painting. During the seventeenth century, both verbal and visual arts prized the *difficulté vaincue,* that self-imposed challenge to transcend the ostensible limitations of a given medium. The painter or sculptor often displayed this quality in his work by achieving a sense of movement or a floating lightness of form; Bernini's *Daphne and Apollo* is a well-known example. Conversely the poet, working in a supposedly temporal mode, could display his control over his medium by experimenting with methods of obtaining stasis, of suspending the action or narrative for a pictorial descriptive passage as timeless in effect as a painting. Both sister arts strove as well to exploit all the dramatic possibilities inherent in such scenes. Theme and subject in an age of grandeur tended to be both lofty and dramatic, filled with a splendid theatricality and pitched at the level of highest emotional intensity.

The work of Milton's younger contemporary, John Dryden, reveals a similar intermingling of classical and baroque styles, though Dryden's pictorialism is more studied than Milton's, and his familiarity with the visual arts is displayed with a complacent connoisseurship that anticipates the Augustans. Dryden often uses figurative language taken from painting,[17] mentions painters by name,[18] and proclaims the orthodoxy of his taste by being especially appreciative of Raphael in painting and of Vitruvius in architecture.[19] We know that he interrupted his task of translating Vergil to spend two months on an English version of Dufresnoy's "De arte graphica," even writing an interesting, if hasty and discursive, preface to accompany the translation. Considering himself unsuited for such work because "not sufficiently versed in the terms of art," he nevertheless yielded to the urgings of "many of our most skillful painters, and other artists" who volunteered to assist him.[20] Dryden was also thoroughly familiar with the trite but still unquestioned concept of poetry and painting as sister arts, first quoting the *ut pictura poesis* tag from Horace in 1668,[21] long before the Dufresnoy translation and preface of 1695, and recalling the theory repeatedly in both his poetry and prose.[22]

Although Dryden never traveled abroad and was born too late to enjoy the great art collections dispersed after the death of Charles I, he nonetheless demonstrates a more knowledgeable acquaintance with art and artists than any poet of his age. In the latter half of the seventeenth century, it was no longer

17. See, e.g., an early example (1660) from "To Sir Robert Howard," ll. 71–80. Unless otherwise noted, all references to Dryden's poetry will be from the *Poems*, ed. James Kinsley, 4 vols. (Oxford, 1958).

18. See, e.g., Holbein, Rubens, Van Dyck, Raphael, Titian, Correggio, Michelangelo, A. Carracci, N. Poussin, in "A Parallel Betwixt Painting and Poetry," in *Of Dramatic Poesy and Other Critical Essays*, ed. George Watson, 2 vols. (London, 1962), II, 182, 187, 189. All further references to the essays will cite this edition.

19. On Raphael, see "To Sir Godfrey Kneller," ll. 57–64 and l. 98, as well as "To My Dear Friend Mr. Congreve," ll. 39–40; on Vitruvius, see "To Congreve," ll. 13–19.

20. "A Parallel," pp. 182–83. For a detailed discussion of Dufresnoy's treatise, its embodiment of the *ut pictura poesis* concept, and its implications for Dryden, see Jean H. Hagstrum, *The Sister Arts* (Chicago, 1958), pp. 174–76.

21. "A Defense of An Essay of Dramatic Poesy," Watson, *Of Dramatic Poesy*, I, 114.

22. Mark Van Doren says that Dryden "draws the parallel, with applications of his own, no fewer than twenty times; and he often extends it" (*John Dryden* [Bloomington, 1963], p. 52).

necessary to go to Italy in order to view numerous examples of landscape painting, both topograhical and ideal. Walpole's *Anecdotes* mentions a dozen landscapists, native and foreign, well known during the reign of Charles II.[23] Though Dryden's grasp of painting's technical aspects and his close acquaintance with significant original works of the Italian Renaissance pantheon were certainly limited, he occupies a pivotal position both historically and in this study. On one side are his older contemporaries Milton and Marvell, who reflect the period of the Puritan interregnum in their lack of sympathetic interest in painting and painters, and, on the other hand, there are the Augustans, Pope and Thomson, who exemplify in their work the virtuosity and expertise in the visual arts expected of eighteenth-century men of taste.

The essentially pictorial quality of Dryden's imagination, while certainly attributable in part to an innate response, was also affected by the age's preoccupation with the "Lordship of the eye" in both science and the arts.[24] Dryden's long tenure as a dramatist—he was the author of almost thirty plays, the greater number written between 1663 and 1683—must also have contributed significantly to the formation of his spatial and pictorial awareness. It is especially useful to conjecture in what ways Dryden's heroic plays helped to develop his visual sensitivity. Exotic settings, opulent costumes, and an emphasis on spectacle were inherited from both masque and opera; it is appropriate to remember in this context a transitional figure like William Davenant who began as a masque writer and whose later "operas" were simply heroic dramas with enough music added to exempt them from Cromwell's proscription of plays. Dryden's own work includes an opera, *The State of Innocence*, published in 1677, and a masque, probably his last literary effort, which was written early in 1700 for a revival of Fletcher's play, *The Pilgrim*. In all three forms—masque, opera, and

23. For a comprehensive modern survey, see Henry and Margaret Ogden, *English Taste in Landscape in the Seventeenth Century* (Ann Arbor, 1955).
24. See Sir Henry Wotton, "The Elements of Architecture," *Reliquiae Wottonianae* (London, 1651), p. 204.

heroic play—the action is static; lengthy speeches or songs freeze the movement on the stage into a series of tableaux that catch and hold the dazzling splendor of the moment before relinquishing it to return to a temporal progression.[25]

When Dryden turned to other forms—prose as well as poetry—his pictorialist eye continued to function. Even his similes illustrate in brief the diversity of his literary landscapes, from the homely familiarity of the hunter's spaniel coursing to and fro across a field (Preface to *Annus Mirabilis*) to the cosmic grandeur of the starry heavens in the opening lines of *Religio Laici*. As a portraitist, in either satiric or panegyric vein, he has no equal but Pope. Dryden's depiction of Charles II as King David attempts the same effects as the great baroque portraits of seventeenth-century monarchs by artists like Philippe de Champaigne, whose portrait of Charles II hangs in the Cleveland Museum: the poet, like the painter, has caught and held in balance both the all too human individuality of his subject and the concept of divine right which allowed majesty to transcend humanity without denying it. Though some of Dryden's personifications and mythological portraits, especially in the translations and *Fables,* may reflect a familiarity with emblem books, they are not, for the most part, truly emblematic, being personae from verbal and visual allegories, most often used decoratively rather than didactically. Marvell's use of emblematic techniques is both more frequent and more traditional than that of Dryden.

It is chiefly the miscellaneousness of Dryden's descriptions that distinguishes his literary pictorialism from that of his Augustan successors, who acquired the one skill he almost invariably fails to demonstrate—the facility for painterly composition, the management of the various planes in a landscape and the means whereby the eye is led from foreground details to more distant vistas. Helping to account for this change was the age's growing connoisseurship in the visual arts, a phenomenon likely to encourage an intelligent amateur like young Alexander Pope to develop into something of a virtuoso.

25. See, e.g., Jean Hagstrum's analysis of *All for Love* in *The Sister Arts,* pp. 184–90.

Pope's poetry reflects the influence of the visual arts more intimately and more pervasively than does Dryden's. Unlike his great predecessor, Pope had actually been a painter: a thorough understanding of technique accompanies his background of critical theory, and the younger poet is more likely to draw on his store of technical skills than on his theoretical knowledge. Like Dryden, he uses analogies from the sister art and references to its practitioners and procedures, but Pope's debt to painting goes beyond such comparative superficialities.[26] Pope was evidently the first to use the word *picturesque* in the sense of "like a picture" or "fit to be the subject of a picture," [27] but, more important, he ultimately employed painting techniques in his poetic structure and imagery with the same kind of sophisticated and imaginative verve that modern writers like Mann and Huxley display in adapting musical techniques—the leitmotiv or symphonic structure—to the form of their novels.

Such expertise betokens long apprenticeship. Pope sketched from boyhood, and by his twenties he had apparently acquired a measure of facility, at least in the opinion of his friends. His year of study with the painter Charles Jervas, which began in 1713, is a well-documented chapter in his life, as is the pleasure he derived from this artistic activity. Joseph Spence records Pope's being asked the question, "Which, Sir, gives you the most pleasure, poetry or painting?" His answer may have surprised his contemporaries only slightly less than it does us: "I really can't well say, both of them are so extremely pleasing." [28] An affectionate memorial to the hours spent under the tutelage of Jervas survives in Pope's *Epistle to Mr. Jervas,*

26. As an example of the ease and frequency with which Pope refers to painting, even when writing about another subject entirely, see *An Essay on Criticism,* ll. 21–25, 171–74, 293–96, 484–93, 701–4. Among the painters he mentions by name in various works are Raphael, Guido Reni, Annibale Carracci, Correggio, Paul Brill, Titian, Dürer, Antonio Verrio, Rubens, Giulio Romano, and Salvator Rosa.

27. Norman Ault, *New Light on Pope* (London, 1949), p. 80.

28. *Anecdotes, Observations and Characters of Books and Men,* ed. James M. Osborn, 2 vols. (Oxford, 1966), I, 46.

which accompanied a copy of Dryden's translation of Dufresnoy. Recalling the *ut pictura poesis* tradition acknowledged by their predecessors, Pope records his and Jervas' allegiance to the same aesthetic philosophy:

> Smit with the love of Sister-arts we came,
> And met congenial, mingling flame with flame;
> Like friendly colours found them both unite,
> And each from each contract new strength and light.[29]
>
> [ll. 13–16]

Pope's taste, like that of Jervas, though classical and Roman for the most part, was wide enough to embrace the Venetians and even, on occasion, the followers of Caravaggio. He was also more affected then he knew, perhaps, by the modification of baroque styles dictated by contemporary taste and exemplified in various aspects of the work of rococo artists like Hogarth and Watteau. At the same time the decorative talents of older painters of the Augustan age like Sir James Thornhill, who succeeded the Italian Antonio Verrio as chief court painter, proved that the baroque style was still vital in eighteenth-century England. As in Dryden's day, such eclecticism was the rule more than the exception. The severely geometrical Palladian mansion set in a natural English garden landscape full of serpentine paths winding through agreeably "wild" terrain may well serve as a visual metaphor for the tastes of the age.[30]

Though, like Dryden, Pope never traveled abroad, he enjoyed the art collections of wealthy friends such as Burlington, and he eagerly accumulated copies and prints to study. A few

29. *Works*, Twickenham ed., 11 vols. (London and New Haven, 1954–67), Vol. VI. All subsequent citations to Pope's poetry will refer to this edition.

30. The purity of even the English Palladian style has been questioned by Rudolf Wittkower who describes the way in which the window treatment of the architects of the Burlington circle often reflected the style of Palladio's mannerist phase or the work of less conservative imitators. See "Pseudo-Palladian Elements in English Neo-Classical Architecture," *JWCI*, VI (1943), 154–64.

extravagant lines to Kneller (written c. 1719) survive, revealing his delight in the painter's gift to him:

To Sir Godfrey Kneller, On his painting for me the Statues of Apollo, Venus and Hercules [31]

What God, what Genius did the Pencil move
When KNELLER painted these?
'Twas Friendship—warm as *Phoebus,* kind as Love,
And strong as *Hercules.*

Kneller and Jervas were not Pope's only painter friends; he also knew both the older and the younger Jonathan Richardson. Through Lord Burlington, Pope was acquainted with the clever, versatile William Kent, a painter whose facile talents catered to the tastes of the age in areas as disparate as landscape gardening and costume design. Pope expressed approval of Peter Tillemans (1684–1734), the topographical painter and friend of John Gay, and also praised John Wootton (c. 1678–1765), who was associated with William Kent as an illustrator, though he was largely a painter of sporting scenes. Wootton had won his reputation as a serious artist in the 1720s by imitating Gaspard Poussin and Claude Lorrain after returning from an educative trip to Italy.[32] Such a lusterless group of painters, however, can be given only limited credit for helping to form or direct Pope's taste. From them he learned genres, styles, and techniques which he often adapted to literary purposes. While we may credit Charles Jervas both with helping to develop his young friend's eye and with contributing to his training in the technical intricacies of the painter's craft, Pope's most important gifts were largely intrinsic, notably his feeling

31. These statues were the Apollo Belvedere, the Venus de' Medici, and the Farnese Hercules. The grisaille paintings by Kneller were bequeathed by Pope to Lord Bathurst in 1744.

32. E. K. Waterhouse credits Wootton with the introduction of "Gaspardesque landscape into the British tradition" in the second decade of the century. See *Painting in Britain, 1530–1790,* The Pelican History of Art (Harmondsworth, Middlesex, 1954), p. 106.

for color and light and his ability to harmonize painterly imagery with a rich variety of poetic moods.

Like Pope, his contemporary, James Thomson combined an innate visual sensitivity with an educated taste in the arts of painting and sculpture. The extent to which his pictorial poetry influenced artists both of his own and of later ages recalls his predecessor, John Milton. Though William Kent had never designed a landscape before illustrating *The Seasons* for the subscription edition of 1730, Douglas Grant may be exaggerating only a trifle when he suggests that Kent learned some essentials of his trade from Thomson's poem.[33] Certainly Thomson's pictorial quality was immediately recognized, making *The Seasons* "for more than one hundred and fifty years the most illustrated poem in the English language." [34]

It might be possible to dismiss seemingly hyperbolic tributes by his contemporaries to Thomson's painterly gifts as typical effusions of a period dominated overmuch by visual stimuli, were it not for equally strong testimonials to his pictorialism by painters of undisputed stature whose major works were largely produced in the succeeding age. Both Constable and Turner painted landscapes to which they affixed lines from *The Seasons,* as though to acknowledge the source of their inspiration; Turner especially left no doubt of his own debt to Thomson. Jack Lindsay, who has edited Turner's poems (among which are four on Thomson), believes that the poet "had a formative influence, guiding the artist in his conception of what constituted a landscape emotionally and artistically significant." [35] Turner's exhibition at the Royal Academy in 1798, when he was twenty-three, displayed ten pictures, four of which were accompanied by verse-quotations from *The Seasons,* while a

33. *James Thomson: Poet of "The Seasons"* (London, 1951), pp. 223–24.

34. Ralph Cohen, *The Art of Discrimination* (Berkeley, 1964), p. 250. Cohen quotes copiously from eighteenth-century writers and critics who remark upon Thomson's painterly qualities. See, for example, pp. 178–79, 194–95, 206–7, 216.

35. J. M. W. Turner, *The Sunset Ship,* ed., with an essay, by Jack Lindsay (London, 1966), p. 11.

fifth cited lines from *Paradise Lost*.[36] Later in his career, the celebrated lectures on perspective presented to the Royal Academy again reveal the influence of Thomson's verse on Turner's philosophy and practice of art.

It is natural to wonder how a young Scots poet untutored in art and, in 1725, newly arrived in London should have become conversant with landscape painting quickly enough for the reader to perceive some pictorialist effects even in "Winter," published in March of 1726, and a great many more in "Summer," published the following year. Several Thomson scholars credit his boyhood environment in the wild, picturesque Scottish Border country with first rendering him sensitive to rural beauty.[37] Early he acquired a perceptive, sympathetic eye for natural scenery reminiscent of Wordsworth's in its depth and fervor. But perhaps of even more crucial importance in the evolution of *The Seasons* is Thomson's acquaintanceship with painters. Certainly we can attribute much of Thomson's early artistic education to the influence of the poet-painter John Dyer. Through his countryman David Mallet, Thomson met Dyer, probably in the spring of 1726, and, as Ralph Williams has shown, they soon became close friends, discussing poetry, painting, and the relationship between the two arts.[38] Dyer was a student of Jonathan Richardson, who stressed the *ut pictura poesis* tradition and held that a painter should "have the talents requisite to a good poet, the rules for the conduct of a picture being much the same with those to be observed in writing a poem." [39]

36. *Ibid.*
37. See Grant, *James Thomson: Poet*, p. 110. C. E. deHaas (*Nature and the Country in English Poetry* [Amsterdam, 1928], p. 100) and G. C. Macaulay (*James Thomson* [London, 1908], p. 2) also cite the influence of Thomson's childhood setting upon the formation of his visual imagination.
38. "Thomson and Dyer: Poet and Painter," in *The Age of Johnson, Essays Presented to Chauncey Brewster Tinker,* ed. Frederick W. Hilles (New Haven and London, 1949; reprint, 1964), pp. 210–11.
39. *An Essay on the Theory of Painting* (1715), p. 21. Cited in *ibid.*, p. 211.

Thomson also knew the Scots painter William Aikman, though he was not so close a friend as Dyer. Aikman, however, did paint Thomson's portrait (now in the Scottish Gallery, Edinburgh) in 1726, a significant year in the gestation of *The Seasons,* and Thomson, in turn, memorialized Aikman in a poem, "On the Death of Mr. William Aikman, the Painter," written in 1731. The poem dwells more on Aikman's virtues than on his talent; the only reference to painting is a pallid tribute to "Raphael's figures" and "Titian's colours," betraying the conventionality of the poet's taste. Thomson's artistic preferences were typically Augustan and oriented to the classical and ideal. A sale catalogue of his effects, sold at auction in May, 1749, lists eighty-three pictures and a large number of prints and engravings, the latter including works by Raphael, Guido, Correggio, Carlo Maratti, Annibale Carracci, Domenichino, and Poussin, as well as drawings by Castelli of the classical statues that Thomson admired and celebrated in *Liberty,* Part IV: the Venus de' Medici, the Fighting and the Dying Gladiator, Meleager, and Laocoön.[40]

In *Liberty,* Part IV, Thomson hails sculpture as the "elder" of its "sister art," painting, crediting the former with first exemplifying "correct design," "great ideas," "expression," and "the graceful attitude." In addition, he shows himself familiar with the legend of Zeuxis' Helen and the theory of ideal imitation,[41] with the preferred genres in painting, and with the succession of architectural orders. In Part I of the same poem, he refers to Michelangelo, Raphael, and Palladio, the most em-

40. For this list, see Macaulay, *James Thomson,* p. 74, and Hagstrum, *The Sister Arts,* p. 244.

41. In his picture of Helen, Zeuxis achieved the ideal of feminine beauty he sought by copying the physical perfections of not one but five Crotonian maidens selected as models. Such a procedure, which imitated nature but avoided individual imperfections, was approved by Socrates, Plato, and Aristotle. As Erwin Panofsky remarks, the story of Zeuxis was "repeated *ad nauseam*" in later ages—by Cicero and again by painters and aestheticians of the Renaissance, who also wished both to "follow nature" and to imitate the ideal. For a discussion of the place of Zeuxis' Helen in classical art theory, see Erwin Panofsky, *Idea,* trans. Joseph J. S. Peake (Columbia, S.C., 1968), pp. 15, 49, 58, 157, 161.

inent practitioners of the arts of sculpture, painting, and architecture, while in Part V he alludes to the Gobelin tapestries
(l. 518), mentions the landscape art of Pope and Bathurst, and
notes the architectural feats of Burlington at Chiswick and
Burlington House. Distinguishing among the schools of Renaissance painting in Italy, Thomson, in *Liberty*, Part IV, knowledgeably assigns the traditional excellences to each of the four
major groups he cites:

> In elegant design,
> Improving nature: in ideas, fair
> Or great, extracted from the fine antique;
> In attitude, expression, airs divine—
> Her sons of Rome and Florence bore the prize.
> To those of Venice she the magic art
> Of colours melting into colours gave.
> Theirs too it was by one embracing mass
> Of light and shade, that settles round the whole,
> Or varies tremulous from part to part,
> O'er all a binding harmony to throw,
> To raise the picture, and repose the sight.
> The Lombard school, succeeding, mingled both.[42]
>
> [ll. 232–44]

The passages in Thomson's poetry that describe actual works
of art reveal more than just the theoretical understanding
shown in the lines just quoted. Combined with the learning he
amassed through study and conversation was a discerning, appreciative eye for visual beauty, enormously stimulated by a
continental tour, taken when he was tutor to Charles Talbot,
in 1730–31. After reading the passages describing classical statuary in *Liberty*, Part IV, Patrick Murdoch, his friend and bi-
ographer, paid homage to the impact of Thomson's poetic
pictures. He asserted that the poet had studied these antique
sculptures "so minutely, and with so true a judgment, that in
some of his descriptions, in the poem of *Liberty*, we have the

42. *James Thomson, Poetical Works*, ed. J. Logie Robertson (Oxford, 1908; reprint, 1965). All subsequent citations of Thomson's
poetry will refer to this edition, and unless otherwise specified, quotations from *The Seasons* will be from the 1746 edition.

masterpieces there mentioned placed in a stronger light perhaps than if we saw them with our eyes." [43] Here Murdoch has singled out the most obvious general effect of Thomson's preoccupation with the visual arts: it is the infusion of *enargeia*, or a markedly pictorial vividness, into descriptive passages. [44] This quality characterizes much of the work of the five poets whose landscape poetry is studied in later chapters, although the degree of sophistication in the achievement of pictorial effects varies considerably from Marvell to Thomson. All five, however, possessed strongly visual imaginations that, while innate for the most part, were doubtless stimulated further by the age's acceptance of the doctrine of *ut pictura poesis*.

43. James Thomson, *Works*, ed., with a biographical sketch, by Patrick Murdoch, 2 vols. (London, 1762), I, xviii.
44. Throughout this study I will occasionally employ more or less familiar terms which are helpful in distinguishing certain kinds or degrees of pictorialism. These should be defined all together for the sake of clarity. *Enargeia* means pictorially vivid, visually striking in the manner of a picture. For a more extended discussion of *enargeia* and its use in literary criticism, see Hagstrum, *The Sister Arts*, pp. 11–12. *Ecphrasis* or *ecphrastic* is defined in its noun form by the *Oxford Classical Dictionary* as "the rhetorical description of a work of art." As such it is almost synonymous with a third term, *iconic*. The latter term is, however, the more common, and I will restrict its usage to refer to poems describing or celebrating actual works of art (i.e., Keats's "Ode on a Grecian Urn"). Less familiar and more variously defined is *ecphrasis*. Thomas Rosenmeyer, in a discussion of landscape in Greek literature, regards it as that effect "whereby an object is made to look like a pictorial imitation of that object" (*The Green Cabinet* [Berkeley, 1969], p. 192). *Ecphrastic* will be used less narrowly than *iconic*, designating something (a landscape or a detail from a landscape) which is not initially an art object but which, in the course of a visually striking description by a pictorial poet, *becomes* finally an object of art, specifically a verbal landscape. As such, an ecphrastic passage is one possessing a heightened *enargeia*.

Heroic Nature

Plate 1 N. Poussin, *Spring: The Earthly Paradise*

⌁ 1 ⌁

Heroic and Ideal

Landscape before 1650

By man's unwillingness to accept primal catastrophes like the end of the Golden Age or the loss of Eden the durability of landscape poetry may in part be explained. Whether compelled by nostalgia or beset by adversity, poets since Theocritus have lyrically praised natural beauty and the joys of rural retirement, persuading us that wisdom as well as pleasure may be derived from the cultivation of our gardens. The quest for an earthly paradise may end variously—in an enclosed garden or an eighteenth-century *ferme ornée,* almost any place where external nature submits to a measure of idealization. The Eden thus re-created has flexible boundaries. In one age it may be little more than a bower (all too often furnished with a new Eve), while in another time it expands to corroborate the Augustan thesis that all nature is a garden. Whatever its dimensions, it carefully preserves as orthodox the necessary dominance of nature over art. Ideal landscape, despite its mythic or legendary origins, is a heightened natural landscape, stripped of its imperfections and its ingredients rearranged to achieve a more aesthetically satisfying form.

The early emergence of such literary landscapes in Homer

and the pastoral poets, as well as the Old Testament, eventually resulted in a number of recognized types of ideal landscape in post-classical Western literature. These, in turn, came to be adapted and further refined by painters and emblematists of medieval and Renaissance Europe. Because the visual arts were later to be influential in revitalizing ideal landscapes in poetry, thus adding another chapter to this reciprocal relationship between the two arts, we must at this juncture briefly survey certain developments in landscape painting.

The Tradition of Ideal Landscape in Painting

Such ideal, or more properly idealized, literary landscapes alluded to above (the problems of definition will be dealt with subsequently) antedate those in the visual arts, largely because of the slow emergence of landscape as a separate genre in Renaissance painting. The classical frescoes involving landscape which have survived until our day suggest that the Greek stress on man himself subordinated nature to a level that was mostly decorative in art.[1] In Roman painting (one may instance the Odyssey landscapes in the Vatican Museum) examples of landscape endowed with significance and scope are more plentiful. The medieval artist, more concerned with the world to come than the one all about him, often used a landscape background in his religious paintings, but Lord Kenneth Clark has labeled the view of nature thus depicted "the landscape of symbols," [2] which testifies to medieval man's tendency to regard the objects of the natural world as significant mainly for their power to recall or represent the supernatural world. One such symbolic landscape which continued to be suggestively reinterpreted throughout Renaissance art and literature was the *hortus conclusus,* in which the enclosed garden provided both the setting for the virgin-mother Mary and a

1. Kenneth Clark, *Landscape into Art* (Boston, 1961), p. 1. Also see Benjamin Rowland, Jr., *The Classical Tradition in Western Art* (Cambridge, Mass., 1963), pp. 53–55.
2. *Ibid.,* p. 3.

symbolic equivalence for her.³ Mary, the new Eve,⁴ to whose *fiat* a fallen humanity owed its rebirth and redemption, could appropriately be pictured in a new paradise garden, this one deriving largely from the biblical Song of Songs which church fathers interpreted metaphorically as representing Christ's love for the church or for the individual soul and his union with them. This loving union was most perfectly typified in Mary. The pious practice of reinterpreting or revising for edification and instruction certain expressions of ostensibly "profane" love in art and literature can also be illustrated by a reference to the custom of Renaissance emblematists. Mario Praz has shown how widely known sixteenth-century love emblems, most commonly derived from classical literature, Ovid in particular, were redesigned for religious purposes and accompanied by scriptural texts referring to sacred or divine love. Once again, many of these emblems show Anima and Love, personifications of the soul and God, in a springlike garden setting. This appears to be an adaptation of a *locus amoenus* which originally formed the background for traditional representations of Cupid and Psyche.⁵ The garden, earthly paradise, or idealized pastoral retreat was, of course, much more frequently employed by artists as a setting for classical as well as Christian subjects from the time of the Renaissance. Mythological scenes, again especially those from Ovid, vied for popularity with heretofore much more com-

3. For a recent study of the *hortus conclusus* convention in medieval and Renaissance poetry, see Stanley Stewart, *The Enclosed Garden* (Madison, 1966).

4. The juxtaposition of Mary and Eve in a paradise or garden setting, often containing the Tree of Knowledge, is a fairly common subject in religious art since the medieval period. The iconography of such paintings has been studied in Ernst Guldan, *Eva und Maria, Eine Antithese als Bildmotiv* (Graz-Cologne, 1966).

5. Mario Praz, *Studies in Seventeenth-Century Imagery*, 2d ed. (Rome, 1964), pp. 145–46. Also see Samuel C. Chew, *The Pilgrimage of Life* (New Haven, 1962), pp. 189–90, 289. These emblems are the work of Fr. Herman Hugo, a Jesuit whose *Pia Desideria Emblemata* was published in Antwerp in 1628. Both Praz and Chew point out his debt to the Song of Songs as well as to classical sources.

monly chosen biblical subjects. A. Richard Turner, discussing the popularity of the pastoral form among Venetians in the early sixteenth century following the publication of Sannazzaro's *L'Arcadia,* points to Giorgione's *Sleeping Venus* (landscape by Titian) as an early achievement in art of the idealized Arcadian setting, again a *locus amoenus.*[6]

Though these two conventions, the *locus amoenus* and the *hortus conclusus,* by no means exhaust the varieties of ideal landscape, they are useful aids for helping to clarify what constitutes this type of landscape. The label itself was derived retrospectively from Renaissance and baroque artists and aestheticians concerned with the doctrine of imitation and the depiction of ideal beauty in representations of nature, both human and horticultural. The general term *ideal landscape* or *heroic landscape*—the two are used almost synonymously by most literary critics and art historians [7]—is employed, then, to describe an elevated, nonrealistic depiction of nature in literature and art which originated in classical antiquity, deriving ultimately, in part, from the Golden Age landscape of Hesiod and Vergil as well as from the Eden landscape in Genesis and the pastoral setting of the Song of Songs. Whether classical or Christian, however, the originals are places associated with deities and specially favored mortals, or they represent a remote time in the past, before the Fall, when all men lived in an Arcadian paradise. Such a landscape, considered the norm for Renaissance artists concerned with the ideal, was the only kind that, used in conjunction with figures, might "aspire to those higher kinds of painting which illustrate a theme, religious, historical or poetic," [8] in short, the sort of "history painting" which was to be considered the highest form of art until the

6. *The Vision of Landscape in Renaissance Italy* (Princeton, 1966), pp. 92–95.

7. H. W. Janson differentiates between Nicolas Poussin's more "heroic" landscapes, with their "rational clarity" and "austere beauty," and the correspondingly more "ideal" landscapes of Claude Lorrain, which "evoke the poetic essence of a countryside" and emphasize "its idyllic aspects" (*History of Art* [New York, 1962], p. 441).

8. Clark, *Landscape into Art,* p. 54.

Romantics' preference for pure landscape asserted itself. "The features of which it [this elevated landscape] is composed must be chosen from nature, as poetic diction is chosen from ordinary speech, for their elegance, their ancient associations and their faculty of harmonious combination. *Ut pictura poesis.*" [9] Lord Clark's comparison is well chosen; both poetic diction and ideal landscape depend upon artifice, upon nature improved by art, upon reality heightened to the ideal.

The contributions made by certain Renaissance and baroque painters to the development of ideal landscape subsequently trained the eye and formed the taste not only of their own successors but of many English poets of the seventeenth and eighteenth centuries, all of whom accepted the doctrine of *ut pictura poesis.* Some familiarity, therefore, with their pictorial pantheon, with the visual contexts within which they functioned, is a useful preliminary to the later portions of this study dealing with individual poets.

Ideal landscape dates from the early sixteenth century, and various elements of it were first discovered and employed by Venetian and Bolognese artists, some of whom later introduced it into Roman art. Among the Venetians was Giorgione (1477–1510), who associated near Castelfranco with a group of poets interested in an "Arcadian Movement"; he was inspired by them to attempt an Arcadian landscape, whose natural features were judiciously heightened to correspond with the painter's concept of ideal nature, deriving from classical sources. Such a landscape makes use of a regular pattern of dark trees and rock masses at the sides of the painting, framing the center of the picture and emphasizing the poetic mood engendered by the distances and open sky. These compositional details contribute to a sense of spatial order and imbue the pastoral setting with a formal dignity as well as a lyrical beauty. The effect is not realistic as in most northern landscapes, but rather idyllic and lofty. Even figures are often placed at the sides rather than the center of the picture, so that they blend with the landscape but never dominate it.

Giorgione's associate Titian (1477–1576) contributed to

9. *Ibid.*

ideal landscape especially through his careful rendering of trees and hills, again ideal rather than naturalistic, imitated by both Claude and Poussin. The Carraccis, from Bologna, preeminently Annibale (1560–1609) and his student Domenichino (1581–1641), introduced into Roman art in the first three decades of the seventeenth century mythological landscapes of larger scope, done in a mixture of classical and baroque styles that harmoniously blended compositional elements, consciously attempting to evoke a feeling for the antique. Northern artists working concurrently in Rome, especially Paul Brill and Adam Elsheimer, adapted their native landscape tradition to the new classical style; Brill's emphasis was on distances and larger prospects, Elsheimer's on the peculiar properties, both visual and emotional, of light on landscape and the romantic appeal of nocturnal landscapes. Elsheimer's style allegedly influenced, though not in identical ways, Rubens, Rembrandt, and Claude. The eclecticism inevitable in an art form deriving from such varied sources insured both the vitality and the versatility of ideal landscape. When it reached a kind of culmination in the work of Claude Lorrain (1600–1662) and Nicolas Poussin (1594–1665), the disparate elements—Venetian, Bolognese, Roman, and Northern—were coherently ordered to produce a harmonious whole. To be sure, the more "ideal" Claude emphasized emotive aspects, Elsheimer's feeling for light and Giorgione's lyricism, while Poussin's appreciation for antique grandeur and his geometric handling of space made him more indebted to the "heroic" style of Annibale Carracci and Domenichino. Both, however, persuasively communicate a mood of Vergilian ideality and Arcadian nostalgia.[10]

The painters we have been discussing were inevitably affected by their age's attempt to solve the knotty problem of ideal imitation and the role of the artist in defining it. Giovanni Pietro Bellori (1615–96), the friend of Nicolas Poussin, formulated a philosophy of art reflecting an idealized and ele-

10. A more lengthy discussion of the development of ideal landscape may be found in *ibid.*, chap. 4, and in the *Encyclopedia of World Art*, 15 vols. (New York, 1964), Vol. IX, sources which provided information for the above résumé.

vated concept of beauty in nature, yet one attempting "to reconcile imitation of nature with the expression of an ideal." [11] Bellori theorizes:

> The noble painters and sculptors imitate that first creator, and form in their minds also an example of superior beauty and, reflecting on it, improve upon nature until it is without fault of color or of line.
>
> This *Idea,* or we might say goddess of painting and sculpture, after opening the sacred curtains of the exalted genius of men like Daedalus and Apelles, unveils herself to us, and descends upon the marbles and canvases. Originating from nature, she rises above her origin and becomes herself the original of art; gauged by the compass of the intellect, she becomes the measure of the hand; and animated by the imagination, she gives life to the image. [12]

Although the phrase "originating from nature" suggests an influence more Aristotelian than Platonic, the tone of the first paragraph certainly appears significantly Platonic, or more accurately Plotinian. Kathleen Raine, discussing the tradition of ideal beauty in art and its philosophical sources, stresses Plotinus' role:

> Plotinus, more fully than Plato himself, has given expression to the traditional philosophy of art. A statue, he said, is not beautiful as stone; Phidias modelled his sculpture of Zeus not upon things of sense but by "apprehending what form Zeus must

11. William Guild Howard, *"Ut Pictura Poesis," PMLA,* o.s. XXIV, n.s. XVII (1909), 64. Although recognizing the Platonic aspects of Bellori's aesthetics, W. Rensselaer Lee believes Aristotelian and empirical concepts of ideal beauty are at least as significant in Bellori's theory, suggesting that he was primarily attempting to synthesize the conflicting elements—Platonic, Aristotelian, and Horatian—in the work of earlier theorists like Alberti, in the fifteenth century, and Dolce and Lomazzo, in the middle and later sixteenth century. See *"Ut Pictura Poesis:* The Humanistic Theory of Painting," *Art Bulletin,* XXII (1940), 197–269.

12. *Lives of Modern Painters, Sculptors and Architects* (Rome, 1672), in *A Documentary History of Art,* ed. Elizabeth G. Holt, 3 vols. (New York, 1958), II, 95.

take if he chose to become manifest to sight." . . . Plato, Plotinus and all who have followed their doctrine have known that to copy from a mental form, an idea, is to come nearer to perfection than to copy nature, which is itself only a reflection, image or imprint of an anterior pattern. The artist must look to the original, not to the copy.[13]

While it is necessary to indicate the various sources from which a theory of ideal beauty derives, it is no longer possible or even especially useful to attempt to separate the different strands at all precisely. Rensselaer Lee's point is well taken, that by the seventeenth century, when Bellori wrote his treatise, it was already difficult to differentiate among the classical philosophers and aestheticians who contributed to this theory.[14] Marcel Röthlisberger, focusing on the work of Claude Lorrain, asserts that ideal landscape ultimately means the same thing as classical landscape,[15] tacitly including in the word *classical* all that term implies: the various concepts and authorities cited, as well as other characteristics more potentially pictorial and less abstractly philosophical, like the necessity of proportion, symmetry, and unity. It is this return to classicism dominating the arts from the Renaissance to the end of the neoclassical period, except for the metaphysical or mannerist reactions against it, which characterizes the form and often dictates the content of ideal landscape. Such a concept could easily adjust itself to later idealist and rationalist philosophers; Louis Hourticq sees obvious similarities between the Cartesian theory of truth and the French academicians' inquiry into the beautiful and emphasis upon the doctrine of imitation, both of which pursue the same ideal.[16] Of the academicians, the one most influenced by Descartes was Charles LeBrun, and it is interesting to note here that H. W. Janson considers that Sir Joshua Reynolds' "views

13. *Defending Ancient Springs* (London, 1967), p. 165.
14. Lee, *"Ut Pictura Poesis:* The Humanistic Theory," p. 208.
15. *Claude Lorrain,* 2 vols. (New Haven, 1961), I, 18 n.
16. "La vraisemblance est la forme sous laquelle la vérité doit entrer dans l'art, parce qu'elle est la vérité raisonnable" *(De Poussin à Watteau* [Paris, 1921], p. 61).

were essentially those of LeBrun, tempered by British common sense" in the *Discourses*.[17]

In summary, the ideal landscape in painting expresses a prevailingly classical approach to art, even though it frequently enough reflected the mannerist and baroque tendencies so pervasive in the sixteenth and seventeenth centuries and included among its practitioners such proto-romantics as Salvator Rosa. Its dominance extended roughly from the early ideal landscapes of Giorgione, and later Annibale Carracci, to the romantic revolt, when the picturesque or more realistic concepts of external nature in a Constable became the preferred mode, and when the dramatic impressionism of a Turner overthrew the tyranny of line and developed a Claudian absorption with light to new heights of virtuosity.

The Sources and Background of Literary Ideal Landscapes

It is not surprising that the ideal landscape of the visual arts should have its roots in literature. Much of the effectiveness of the *ut pictura poesis* doctrine in Renaissance aesthetics can be attributed to attempts by painters to attain the prestige of poets and raise their positions from craftsmen to artists.[18] I have stressed the origins of ideal landscape in scriptural or mythological sources and its relationship to a highly literary art form, the history painting. The Vergilian *locus amoenus* and the biblical *hortus conclusus* provided two examples of this sort of borrowing; other types of heroic and ideal landscape with literary origins may be mentioned briefly.[19] The grove or "mixed forest" stimulates the classical poet to produce an epic catalogue of trees which are extravagantly varied; in Book X of

17. *History of Art*, p. 452.

18. Luigi Salerno, "Seventeenth-Century English Literature on Painting," *JWCI*, XIV (1951), 236.

19. E. R. Curtius discusses other types of ideal landscape, after meticulously tracing and cataloguing the *topoi* of the *locus amoenus*, in his *European Literature and the Latin Middle Ages* (New York, 1953), chap. 10, pp. 193–202.

Metamorphoses, Ovid presents the reader with twenty-six species in a single sixteen-line passage. Such groves are ideal, not real; the agricultural improbabilities inherent in juxtaposing palm and fir are not a consideration for either poet or painter. Another rather characteristic epic setting is the wild forest or wooded wilderness of Dante's *selva selvaggia* (in the *Inferno* a typical "landscape of symbols") and the poet of the Cid's forest of Corpes. Later in English poetry, during the vogue of the picturesque, it is common to combine the gentle "Claudian" landscape with features of the wild and sublime "Salvatorian" one. Milton's Eden, considered strikingly pictorial by both eighteenth-century poets and painters, is surrounded by this typical forest wilderness.

The visual arts owe a debt not only to poets but to classical rhetoricians as well, for isolating and fixing the conventions of ideal landscape. The branch of rhetoric Aristotle called epideictic dealt with topics to be praised or blamed, often describing, for instance, ideal man or ideal nature. Such a rhetorical classification was further elaborated by Quintilian who, however, preferred the term *panegyric* or *laudatory* rhetoric to the label *epideictic.*[20] Praises of natural beauty could serve several purposes—patriotic, moral, religious, or courtly. Ben Jonson's "To Penshurst" exemplifies the last type, as O. B. Hardison points out, by observing conventional procedures for celebrating a country estate and, in addition, gracefully complimenting its owner.[21] A similar purpose can be discerned in James Thomson's lines in praise of his friend Lyttelton's Hagley Park and in Alexander Pope's poem to Burlington, although in the latter a moral aim, the proper use of riches, predominates, and the poem's theme transcends conventional flattery. Andrew Marvell's "Upon Appleton House," like Pope's

20. *Institutio Oratoria,* 4 vols., trans. H. E. Butler, Loeb Classical Library (London, 1920–22) ; see Vol. I, Book III, iv. 395–97. The suiting of style to purpose in oratory is subsequently discussed by Quintilian in Vol. IV, Book XII, chap. X. He illustrates his passage with an elaborate and knowledgeable analogy to styles in painting.

21. *The Enduring Monument* (Chapel Hill, N.C., 1962) , p. 112.

poem, possesses larger thematic dimensions than simple compliment.

The hierarchy of forms was, of course, as much an issue in poetry as in painting, the epic occupying a pinnacle analogous to the position of history painting in the visual arts. Renaissance aestheticians conceded that poetic works in praise of nature could, under certain circumstances, display an epic quality, if such praise were directed toward lofty moral or religious ends. For example, when nature was dignified by being treated as the art of God and the reflection on earth of his presence, nature poetry took on added importance. According to Tommaso Campanella (*Opere,* I), men, after praising God, might hymn his works, "for they are the means to know him and praise him, it being impossible to please an artisan more than by looking on his works with admiration and declaring to others with what virtue and mastery they are made." [22] Certain painters of ideal landscape, most notably Nicolas Poussin, who was often called a history painter rather than a "mere" landscapist, communicated both the ethical and affective tones they wished to convey in a painting through their treatment of landscape. The expressions, poses, and gestures of figures in the scenes depicted only reinforced the dominant mood or intellectual attitude to be conveyed. Instead of being merely a decorative backcloth, landscape, no longer regarded as trivial, played the most important role in communicating the painting's moral and emotional impact. Poussin's two Phocion pictures of 1648 are good examples of this technique.[23] These masterpieces are entitled *Landscape with the Body of Phocion Carried Out of Athens* (alternatively titled *The Funeral of Phocion;* see plate 8 in chapter 3) and *Landscape with the Ashes of Phocion*

22. Cited in *ibid.,* pp. 85–86. Anthony Blunt notes similarities between Campanella's attitude toward nature and that of Nicolas Poussin, the *pictor philosophus* and master of the heroic landscape. See *Nicolas Poussin,* 2 vols. (New York, 1967), I, 327–31.

23. Anthony Blunt, "The Heroic and the Ideal Landscape in the Work of Nicolas Poussin," *JWCI,* VII (1944), 154–68. The Phocion pictures are both reproduced in Blunt, *Nicolas Poussin,* II, pls. 176, 177.

Collected by His Widow. In each a somber evening light shades much of the pastoral setting. The rigid vertical planes in the two backgrounds, depicting the unjust city of Athens, contrast with the sorrowful horizontal lines of the patriot Phocion's litter in one picture's foreground and the grieving figure of his stooping wife in the other, both further shadowed by overarching trees. These foreground figures in both cases are small, dominated by the pastoral landscape which contains them and which seems to enlarge their helpless human grief into a deep and dignified mourning all nature shares.

The Renaissance stress on the moral or religious function of poetry harmoniously coexisted with an aesthetics of ideal beauty. Scholars of the age echoed Aristotle's theory that ideal representations of reality, which revealed not what is but what might or ought to be, were, of necessity, noble as well as beautiful, and therefore indirectly served a moral end. The didactic element in art also gained impetus from Horace's dictum that it should instruct and delight. Rhetoric played a role in achieving both ends, by elucidating methods of persuasion which were designed to move both heart and mind. From Minturno's *De Poeta* to Dryden's *Essay of Dramatic Poesy,* critics and writers recognized the necessity of appealing to the passions of an audience in order to arouse them to admiration of the theme and sentiments expressed in the work of art.[24] In painting, a kind of visual rhetoric was articulated in the late seventeenth century by Charles LeBrun who popularized a method for delineating the different emotions suggested by figures in a history painting. Often illustrating from Nicolas Poussin's works such as *The Hebrews Receiving Manna in the Desert* and influenced by Descartes's *Traité des passions de l'âme,* LeBrun demonstrated the best way to depict sentiments like astonishment, anger, or despair.[25] His focus on figures rather than setting may be explained by his lack of interest in landscape; his concerns were characteristic of the history painter.

24. Joel Spingarn, *A History of Literary Criticism in the Renaissance,* 2d ed. (New York, 1924), pp. 52–53.

25. See LeBrun, *Méthode pour apprendre à dessiner les passions proposée dans une conférence sur l'expression générale et particulière,* 1698. In Holt, *Documentary History,* II, 159–63.

Besides the influence of rhetoric and of classical aesthetics, a few cultural developments, less important but still significant, may be cited briefly for helping to form and to popularize the conventions of ideal landscape in literature and art. One such influence was the new interest in gardens that were frankly created for purely aesthetic and recreational purposes. The estate gardens of the Renaissance were an ambitious attempt to blend landscape and villá into one harmonious setting. We have Vasari's authority for crediting Raphael and his pupil Giulio Romano with the design for the first such garden, that of the Villa Madama, begun in 1516 on a hillside outside Rome for Cardinal Giulio de' Medici.[26] Smaller gardens in the north of Italy (Ferrara and Tuscany), more transitional in style and still rather medieval in concept, antedated the Madama, however, just as northern landscape painters anticipated their Roman colleagues. One such medieval garden, which early found its way into English literature, provides the setting for the initial appearance of Emily in Chaucer's "Knightes Tale," adapted from Boccaccio. The garden remains more Tuscan than English and obviously exists for aesthetic rather than utilitarian purposes.

If the Renaissance man rejected the notion of creating his own earthly paradise all around him, he could, either actually or vicariously, join those who sought it at the edges of the then known world. The age of exploration and the resultant popularity of travel literature, maps, and all matters geographical renewed interest in remote lands as real or potential Arcadias. In England evidence of this interest in faraway and exotic countries is plentiful between the sixteenth and eighteenth centuries. Milton wrote a history of Russia and Marvell a poem on the Bermudas, while travel literature by Hakluyt, Purchas, and Sandys was extremely popular with seventeenth-century readers; Peter Heylyn's *Cosmographie,* for instance, was issued and reissued to keep up with public demand (1652,

26. Georgina Masson, *Italian Gardens* (London, 1961), p. 130. See also the chronological table which dates the initial emergence and later development of the Italian gardens in J. C. Shepherd and G. A. Jellicoe, *Italian Gardens of the Renaissance* (London, 1927), p. 22.

1657, 1660, 1665, 1666, 1670).[27] Travelers' fanciful tales, from
the sixteenth century on, employed markedly similar nature
images, often recalling the ancient Golden Age vividly and nostalgically.[28] Two movements, utopianism and primitivism, one
looking optimistically toward an Edenic future, the other sadly
celebrating a vanished perfection, came to reflect European
man's attitude toward these newly discovered lands and their
fictionalized counterparts.[29] Whichever of the two predomi-
nated in the writings of any given individual or group, both
attested to a dissatisfaction with the present and made "a
poetry of escape," as Remy Saisselin calls eighteenth-century
French literature's celebration of the Golden Age, a highly
popular genre.[30] Though the motive for creating ideal landscapes may differ in the literature of Renaissance Italy and that
of neoclassical France—for instance, whether such landscapes
are ultimately inspirational or recreational—their ingredients
change little if at all. The same may also be said whether the
burden of imitation rests primarily on the painters imitating
the poets, as in the Renaissance in Italy, or whether the imitation is more reciprocal, as it increasingly became in the later
seventeenth and eighteenth centuries when the conviction grew
among writers and aestheticians that "the pleasures of the
imagination" were primarily visual.

The increasing emphasis on the visual in poetry, combined
with earlier rhetorical and descriptive conventions, resulted in
the production of literary landscapes that were gradually more
pictorial, more numerous, and more important in the English
literature of the Renaissance and later than they had previously
been. Stimulants to this growing emphasis on the visual in-

27. Robert Ralston Cawley, *Milton and the Literature of Travel*
(Princeton, 1951), p. 88.

28. Henri Baudet, *Paradise on Earth: Some Thoughts on European Images of Non-European Man,* trans. Elizabeth Wentholt (New
Haven, 1965), p. 34.

29. Edward William Tayler interprets these two divergent views
of history as reflections of the perennial Nature versus Art conflict
in the Renaissance. See *Nature and Art in Renaissance Literature*
(New York, 1964), pp. 52–56.

30. *"Ut Pictura Poesis:* DuBos to Diderot," *JAAC,* XX (1961),
151.

Plate 2 N. Poussin, *Summer: Ruth and Boaz*

cluded emblem books, masque scenery, widely disseminated woodcuts and engravings, and even the great art collections that flourished in seventeenth-century England before 1640, though these were accessible to comparatively few. Henry and Margaret Ogden have traced tastes in landscape in painting, prints, masque scenery, and other visual media from the beginning of the seventeenth century in England; they have also studied contemporary art treatises, art collections, and preferences in subject and artist as the century progressed. Their findings document the increasing appreciation for the art of landscape and the growing connoisseurship it engendered among collectors. They conclude that "the great eighteenth-century vogues for landscape painting, for natural scenery, and for 'nature' poetry could not have developed as they did without the antecedent interest in landscape under the Stuarts." [31]

So far, in attempting to account for the genesis of ideal landscape in English poetry, it has seemed fitting to touch on influences as varied and disparate as the renewed interest in classically ordered gardens, the popularity of travel literature, and the somewhat belated response in England to landscape painting. One element remains which, while difficult to explicate clearly, is nonetheless significant. It is the baroque preoccupation with time—time personified in allegorical painting and emblem books [32] as well as time denied in the stasis achieved by some descriptive passages in pictorial poetry. Time can even be abolished in a linear, historical sense and replaced in art with a "time that is cosmic, cyclical, and infinite," one permitting man to indulge in his nostalgic dreams of an "eternal return" to a paradisal Golden Age. [33] If indeed time can have a stop, the

31. *English Taste in Landscape in the Seventeenth Century* (Ann Arbor, 1955), p. 164.

32. See Chew, *The Pilgrimage of Life;* Erwin Panofsky, *Studies in Iconology* (New York, 1962), chap. 3; Fritz Saxl, "Veritas Filia Temporis," in *Philosophy and History, Essays Presented to Ernst Cassirer*, ed. R. Klibansky and H. J. Paton (Oxford, 1936), pp. 197–222; and such emblem books as Geoffrey Whitney, *A Choice of Emblemes*, 1586 (New York, 1967), pp. 4, 167, 206, 230.

33. Mircea Eliade, *The Myth of the Eternal Return*, trans. Willard R. Trask (New York, 1954), pp. 153–54. Elsewhere Eliade suggests that a "return to Paradise" can only be won by "the overcoming

objections to the *ut pictura poesis* aesthetic in art and literature, first articulated by Lessing in *Laocoön,* can be challenged. Later critics have reiterated his argument that inevitably the temporal movement in literature produces a sequential effect fundamentally alien to the static and spatial effect of painting. The attempt by poets to deny time and achieve stasis in their art has been considered as foreign to the nature of the literary form as the comparable attempt by painters and sculptors to transcend the static and create a sense of movement in the visual arts.

As we know, this sort of striving to overcome the supposed limitations of an art form was especially characteristic of both poets and painters in the baroque period. The illusionistic ceiling paintings by artists like Cortona, Tiepolo, and Rubens display skillful virtuosity in suggesting movement through limitless space, and comparable experiments in the temporal sphere are markedly noticeable in the work of baroque poets—Italian, French, and English. Lowry Nelson, Jr., suggests that "the use of time as a significant structural device and, in more general terms, the poetic awareness of 'structural' time as contingent and manipulatable seem to be peculiar achievements of baroque poets." [34] An example of this sort of temporal preoccupation may be seen in Milton's *Paradise Lost.* Albert R. Cirillo has argued persuasively that Milton juxtaposed two dimensions, the temporal and the eternal, in his epic in order to deal effectively both with human truths, inherently "temporal and sequential," and with God's higher truth, which does not exclude such human truths but does transcend them. The result is that although Adam and Eve's drama is played out in a progressive, narrative form, it takes place against the backdrop of an eternal present so that "the temporal, in this view, is the

---

of Time and History (the 'fall') and the recovery of the primordial state of Man" (see "The Yearning for Paradise in Primitive Tradition," *Daedalus,* LXXXVIII [1959], 264–65) . In such a state historical time is displaced by mythical time, Eliade's *"in illo tempore,"* which Geoffrey Hartman believes might prove at least a partial answer to "the whole problem of temporality" in literature. (See *Northrop Frye in Modern Criticism,* ed. Murray Krieger [New York, 1966], p. 122.)

34. *Baroque Lyric Poetry* (New Haven, 1960) , p. 23.

19

metaphor for the eternal, and time in its dual aspect becomes a basis of structure." [35]

The recent revival of enthusiasm for baroque art and literature has led to a reevaluation of Lessing's criticism and, often, a repudiation of its premises. If certain subject matter—like ideal landscape—inevitably functions within an allegorical or mythical context, some suspension of the temporal sequence resulting in a sense of stasis is demanded, and it can be skillfully achieved. The necessity for dealing with the mythic [36] aspects of any Golden Age or earthly paradise landscape arises out of a deliberate attempt on the part of poet or painter to exclude the temporal and transient from such landscapes. The very knowledge that such an exclusion is impossible in human terms often provides a melancholy, even tragic, dimension to contrast with this world of eternal springtime, limpid streams, abundant verdure, perfumed breezes, and singing birds. Arcadia itself may be eternal but man is not, and the poet or painter deals with this hard fact moralistically, poignantly, stoically, or ironically as his own personality and beliefs dictate.[37] Consequently, although the ingredients of an ideal landscape have long since hardened into stereotyped convention and therefore can never be altered, both the purpose for using this convention and the method of presenting it may change significantly with the individual artist or writer.

35. "Noon-Midnight and the Temporal Structure of *Paradise Lost*," *ELH,* XXIX (1962), 372–73. Valerie Carnes has also pointed out the valuable insights to be derived from an analysis of *Paradise Lost* "from the vantage point of the various Renaissance traditions concerning time and history." See her recent article, "Time and Language in Milton's *Paradise Lost*," *ELH,* XXXVII (1970), 517–39.

36. The word *mythic* is employed here in the same sense that Jackson I. Cope uses it, as "man's practice of becoming the symbol of his own spiritual experience through projection of inner states into certain recurring narrative and scenic images" (see *The Metaphoric Structure of "Paradise Lost"* [Baltimore, 1962], p. 16).

37. Differing treatments of this theme of transience in paintings by Guercino, Poussin, Watteau, and others has been the subject of an iconographical study by Erwin Panofsky. See *"Et in Arcadia Ego,"* in *Philosophy and History, Essays Presented to Ernst Cassirer,* pp. 223–54.

Such flexibility in the form is undoubtedly attributable in large part to the universal appeal from age to age of the concept of an earthly paradise and its ability to combine with and absorb any number of variant forms, secular or biblical. This ability is strikingly evident in the "Christianizing" process that transformed the old classical pastoral into an adaptable literary vehicle which could be allegorized or mythicized as well as handled conventionally in the countless, highly forgettable literary exercises on a pastoral theme from the sixteenth to the eighteenth centuries. The pastoralism of the Old Testament was implicit, while the New Testament encouraged such exercises as the delineation of Christ as the Good Shepherd. He could also be portrayed in the guise of Orpheus or Pan, a familiar example of this last identification being that given in E. K.'s gloss on Spenser's May eclogue. Edward William Tayler asserts that prior to Spenser and Shakespeare the pastoral form had to "become 'allegorical,' an emblem or trope of the world at a particular moment in spiritual history: genre had to become metaphor." [38] The present revival of interest in the dimensions of pastoral, from the studies of Poggioli and Snell to those of Rosenmeyer and Cullen, provides ample evidence of the complexity and variety the genre provides.

The allegorical meanings and symbolic associations that gave fresh vitality to the imagery of the pastoral landscape in Renaissance poetry were also reinforced by the contemporary emphasis on the visual and the spatial referred to earlier in the chapter. When, in the later seventeenth century, English poets began to be aware of painted landscapes (Italian poets were much more precocious visually), the original debt which the pictorial art owed to the literary one was more than repaid. By the end of the eighteenth century poetic landscapes made it easy to surmise that traffic between the two arts had become almost a one-way movement and that the inspiration had now passed from the poets to the painters, the latter revitalizing the work of the former. Before seeing the work of Claude, Poussin, and other Italianate painters, English poets of classical persuasion committed to an aesthetics of ideal imitation found their task of

38. *Nature and Art in Renaissance Literature,* pp. 170–71.

exhibiting a view of external nature that was general and ideal a far from easy one. Like Renaissance painters, they could go to Vergil and Ovid, or even to their predecessors Homer and Hesiod, but only gradually did such poets acquire the practiced techniques of the verbal landscapist who could order and arrange the ingredients of his ideal landscape with a discriminating and sophisticated eye for the effectiveness of grounds and groupings and still avoid the sort of detailed particularity that was anathema to Imlac. Sometimes an emphasis on the general and an avoidance of limiting specifics may indeed seem to be not only nonpictorial but nonvisual as well; one may cite T. S. Eliot's criticism that Milton's imagery lacked a strong visual sense.[39] More recent scholarship, however, which has concentrated on a careful analysis of poetic images, cognizant of the sister arts tradition and its influence upon that imagery, is better equipped to perceive suggestive visual and pictorial nuances ignored in the earlier decades of our own age.[40] Even well into the nineteenth century, Leigh Hunt can still call upon the conventional eighteenth-century pantheon that included Raphael, Correggio, Titian, Michelangelo, and Guido Reni, all of whom are evoked for him by passages in Spenser's works.[41] Clearly, those living in visually imaginative times may be attuned to a whole gallery of pictorial subtleties all too easily missed by others less sensitized in a succeeding age.

The multiplicity of influences brought to bear upon literary ideal landscape engenders a number of thematic variations within it. In order to deal coherently with these differences, largely those of tone and purpose, it is necessary to resort to some method of schematizing or categorizing these landscapes

39. Eliot's statement has been challenged by several Milton scholars of the last two decades—Don Cameron Allen, Phyllis Mac-Kenzie, Isabel MacCaffrey, Arnold Stein, and Jackson Cope, to name only a few—who have insisted that Milton is often very visual indeed.

40. Examples of ostensibly nonvisual imagery which was considered highly pictorial to eighteenth-century readers abound in Jean H. Hagstrum's *The Sister Arts*. See esp. pp. 131, 146–47, 266–67.

41. "A Gallery of Pictures from Spenser," *Selections from the English Poets*, 3: "Imagination and Fancy," in *Works*, Vol. II (New York, 1859).

and defining the principal types. A brief examination of a few illustrative examples of such landscapes as they appear in Western literature of the classical, medieval, and Renaissance periods will make it possible to discriminate three main trends, to be labeled *decorative, sacramental,* and *emblematic* in this study. An analysis of the way they function in the later poetry of the seventeenth and eighteenth centuries will enable us to discern the different emphases and methods of presentation to which this type of landscape may be adapted for poetic purposes.

Types of Heroic and Ideal Landscape before 1650

The very terms *heroic* and *ideal* when used to modify landscape imply the exclusion from consideration in this study of any poetic setting which is only an incidental and atmospheric suggestion of a sense of place. A rural locale, however idyllic, sketchily presented and functioning only as backdrop is not, needless to say, an ideal landscape. To be so termed these landscapes must be important in themselves, apart from and regardless of the activities and emotions of the human beings involved therein. Consequently, though the first type of ideal landscape to be isolated and examined has been given the appellation *decorative,* there is meant to be in this label no implication of the extraneous or superficial. The term *decorative landscape* is not a pejorative designation but may be defined as a highly sophisticated, vividly delineated form of ideal landscape which has an aesthetic purpose primarily or exclusively and is not involved in thematically orchestrating any moral, religious, political, or intellectual leitmotiv in the poem. Since illustration may be more useful than further explanation in clarifying the characteristics of a decorative ideal landscape, let us examine Homer's well-known description of Alcinous' palace and orchard in Book VII of the *Odyssey.*[42]

Having been guided to the palace by a disguised Athena, Odysseus, we are told by Homer, "hesitated before setting foot

42. All quotations from this passage will be taken from the translation by E. V. Rieu made for the Penguin edition of the *Odyssey* (Harmondsworth, Middlesex, 1957), pp. 114–15.

23

on the bronze threshold." His hesitation suspends the poem's action while permitting the poet to draw in vivid pictorial detail a descriptive scene replete with that quality which, as we have seen, the Greeks called *enargeia*.[43] The first quality Homer stresses is the painterly ingredient of light: "For a kind of radiance, like that of the sun or moon, lit up the high-roofed halls of the great king." This light strikes with dazzling effect upon the metallic surfaces of the palace, the "walls of bronze," "golden doors," lintel and "posts of silver," "bronze threshold," and the "gold and silver dogs which Hephaestus had made with consummate skill." The overriding impression is one of wealth coupled with artifice; the sculpturesque figures of the dogs, wrought by an artist-god, are the culminating touch in the description of "Alcinous' splendid dwelling" which is itself a work of art.

Preceding the next section on the orchard and providing a transition to it is a short passage which stresses the industry and, even more important, the artistry of the Phaeacian maids:

> The house keeps fifty maids employed. Some grind the apple-golden corn in the handmill, some weave at the loom, or sit and twist the yarn, their hands fluttering like the tall poplar's leaves, while the soft olive-oil drips from the close-woven fabrics they have finished. For the Phaeacians' extraordinary skill in handling ships at sea is rivalled by the dexterity of their women-folk at the loom, so expert has Athene made them in the finer crafts, and so intelligent.

Besides sustaining the theme of art dominant in the description of the palace, the imagery of these transitional lines anticipates the landscape passage which follows it with the reference to "hands fluttering like the tall poplar's leaves." "The apple-golden corn" both looks back to all of the references to precious metals used in the palace and forward to the orchard section where there is a reference to "the apple [tree] with its glossy burden"; this glossy gold of nature inevitably recalls the metallic gold of the doors and of Hephaestus' dogs. Though there is

43. See my Introduction, n. 44.

24

movement in this passage, the effect is notably pictorial and stasis is not destroyed.

Next comes the orchard section itself.[44] We are now prepared to regard it both as a natural earthly paradise and as a work of art, in the sense that such natural perfection may constitute the art of the gods as easily as do the gold and silver statues of the dogs in Alcinous' palace. Further justification for this view is found in the concluding line: "Such were the beauties with which the gods had adorned Alcinous' home."

All of the Golden Age ingredients are present in the description of this ideal landscape: various fruit trees bear continually as the gentle "West Wind's breath" assists both bud and ripening fruit coexisting on the same bough; two springs (as in Dante's Earthly Paradise and Milton's Eden) water the garden-like enclosure; the sun shines on the "never-failing green" of vegetables and trees and on the unripe grapes showing "the first faint tinge of purple." This scene might well have beguiled the eye of a Roman painter given the task of beautifying the walls of an ancient villa with a frescoed landscape. Though Homer himself may not have been a painter (questionable tradition has made him blind), he has ordered his description pictorially,

44. Rieu's translation is as follows: "Outside the courtyard but stretching close up to the gates, and with a hedge running down on either side, lies a large orchard of four acres, where trees hang their greenery on high, the pear and the pomegranate, the apple with its glossy burden, the sweet fig and the luxuriant olive. Their fruit never fails nor runs short, winter and summer alike. It comes at all seasons of the year, and there is never a time when the West Wind's breath is not assisting, here the bud, and here the ripening fruit; so that pear after pear, apple after apple, cluster on cluster of grapes, and fig upon fig are always coming to perfection. In the same enclosure there is a fruitful vineyard, in one part of which is a warm patch of level ground, where some of the grapes are drying in the sun, while others are gathered or being trodden, and on the foremost rows hang unripe bunches that have just cast their blossom or show the first faint tinge of purple. Vegetable beds of various kinds are neatly laid out beyond the farthest row and make a smiling patch of never-failing green. The garden is served by two springs, one led in rills to all parts of the enclosure, while its fellow opposite, after providing a watering-place for the townsfolk, runs under the courtyard gate towards the great house itself. Such were the beauties with which the gods had adorned Alcinous' home."

moving from foreground (the orchard "stretching close up to the gates") to midground, where presumably the vineyard is located, since the vegetable beds "beyond the farthest row" of grapes make up the background. At the beginning of the description, a line of "hedge running down either side" of the area is noted; at the end, the two streams, also on opposite sides, return the viewer's attention to the left and right boundaries of this quite precisely defined landscape.

The reader who has not adverted to the realization that Homer was suspending the action to paint a scene—or rather two companion pieces, palace and orchard—may be taken aback by the next section which begins, "Stalwart Odysseus stood before the house and eyed the scene. When he had enjoyed all its beauty, he stepped briskly over the threshold and entered the palace." Stasis has ended; the narrative resumes. But if Odysseus all this time has remained motionless on the threshold, through whose eyes did we see the palace halls, the industrious maidens, and the four acres of orchard? Obviously through the poet's who could not resist suspending his tale and even his hero's foot on Alcinous' threshold while he painted these scenes for his audience. Here then is an ideal landscape which has an aesthetic *raison d'être;* it is "decorative" in the sense defined above. It reflects the Greek hero's healthy materialism, his taste for opulence, and it suggests an idealized society, productive and beautiful, where art and nature blend into a perfect whole.[45]

A second example of decorative landscape, this time from Ovid, may be cited. Another earthly paradise, this is a description of the world during the first Golden Age, at the dawn of creation:

> And Earth, untroubled,
> Unharried by hoe or plowshare, brought forth all
> That men had need for, and those men were happy,
> Gathering berries from the mountain sides.
> Cherries, or blackcaps, and the edible acorns,
> Spring was forever, with a west wind blowing

45. John Ruskin notes the Greek fondness for the pleasant and useful while discussing instances of ideal landscape in the Alcinous section. See *Modern Painters,* 5 vols. (New York, 1897), III, 235.

Softly across the flowers no man had planted,
And Earth, unplowed, brought forth rich grain; the fields
Unfallowed, whitened with wheat, and there were rivers
Of milk, and rivers of honey, and golden nectar
Dripped from the dark-green oak trees.[46]

[I.101-11]

While less pictorially ordered than the longer passage from the *Odyssey*, these lines nonetheless suggest vivid colors: the multi-hued flowers, the red of berries and cherries, the whitened wheat and milky river, the gold of nectar and river of honey, and the green trees. It is easy enough to appreciate Ovid's appeal to Renaissance and baroque painters. By the time he re-creates poetically this ideal landscape of the Golden Age, its ingredients are well established; the picture paints itself with the minimum of poetic cues. Although there is implied in the lines cited a degenerative view of history and a reminder that men are no longer free from strife, toil, and want, the primary impression is still an aesthetic one. Later "moralized Ovids" of the Renaissance will stress these graver implications; Ovid himself touches on them only lightly.

Another decorative Ovidian landscape in *Metamorphoses*, alluded to by Milton in Book IV of *Paradise Lost*, is "that fair field of Enna" where Proserpine was seized by Pluto:

There is a pool called Pergus, whose deep water
Hears the swans singing, even more than Cayster.
A wood surrounds the pool, and the green leaves
Keep off the sunlight, and the ground is cool,
And the ground is moist, with lovely flowers growing,
And the season is always spring; and in this grove
Proserpina was playing, gathering flowers,
Violets, or white lilies, and so many
The basket would not hold them all. . . .

[V.384-92]

This shaded pool with only its singing swans to break the silence, the cool green wood, the moist earth carpeted with flowers, and the graceful girl all combine for memorable pic-

---

46. All quotations from *Metamorphoses* will be taken from the translation by Rolfe Humphries (Bloomington, 1955).

torial effect. Ovid here handles his story in much the same structural fashion Homer used in the Alcinous section of the *Odyssey;* that is, he presents the scenes in a sequential order. First we are given a picture of perfect tranquility: in a Golden Age landscape a girl gathers flowers; hers is the only movement in an otherwise static passage. Abruptly the transition comes with the arrival of Pluto's chariot:

> So, in one moment,
> Or almost one, she was seen, and loved and taken
> In Pluto's rush of love. She called her mother,
> Her comrades, but more often for her mother.
> Where he had torn the garment from her shoulder,
> The loosened flowers fell, and she, poor darling,
> In simple innocence, grieved as much for them
> As for her other loss.
>
> [ll. 394–401]

Dramatically, stasis is replaced by sudden movement; the stillness and tranquillity are shattered by agitation and violence. Proserpine is objectified in the falling flowers—appropriately the violet and lily with their traditional connotations of gentle retirement and virginal innocence. The furious movement passes and another landscape scene follows: in sharp contrast with the first idyllic one, this is a somber, turbulent terrain.

> Her ravager
> Drove the car fiercely on, shook up the horses,
> Calling each one by name, the reins, dark-dyed,
> Sawing the necks and manes. Through the deep lakes,
> Through the Palician pools, that reeked with sulphur,
> That boiled where earth was cracked, beyond the city
> Corinthian men once built between two harbors,
> One large, one small, they rode.
>
> [ll. 401–8]

The motif of deep pool and lake remains, but here no singing swans float amid the reeking sulphurous fumes that suggest Hades. As the swans themselves, like the flowers, resembled Proserpine, so the dark, plunging horses and the volcanic land of boiling waters and cracked earth exemplify Pluto. Although we know the horses are moving swiftly, the pictorial, static effect of the scene is never destroyed.

This passage from Ovid has inspired a number of paintings, the best-known treatment being that by Rubens which anticipates Shaftesbury's recommendation in *Second Characters* to seize the time of greatest dramatic suspense, the moment of crisis.[47] Choosing what may be designated as the central panel in Ovid's triptych, the moment of abduction itself, Rubens has tried to capture the shock and suddenness of Ovid's narrative and has perfectly caught the furious but frozen movement of the lines cited above (394–401). Concentrating on the figures, however, he has practically ignored the possibilities inherent in the two landscapes—Proserpine's idyllic one and Pluto's, terrible and "sublime"—which are a triumph of ecphrastic poetry. The setting in this case has been transformed by the poet into a pictorial objectification of the dramatic action. The resultant landscape has the important function of directing the reader's aesthetic and emotional response to Ovid's scene; indeed, it helps both to elicit it initially and to strengthen its total impact.

Another journey through the portals of dark Dis to Pluto's realm, this time in the company of Vergil's epic hero Aeneas, will exemplify a different kind of ideal landscape in classical literature. This second type will be called *sacramental*, indicating that the landscape functions as a sign or symbol of a mystical dimension that the poet wishes to convey in his work. Perhaps an equally appropriate term would be *anagogical*, since this type of symbolic landscape is invested with an essentially spiritual or sacred meaning beyond the literal, allegorical, or moral levels that may also be present.[48] In Book VI, prior to his descent into the underworld, Aeneas, following the Sibyl's bidding, holds funeral rites for Misenus and searches out the golden bough in a gloomy wood. Both the wood, ancient and seem-

47. Shaftesbury debates which of four "orders of time" should be chosen to exploit most fully the suspense and dramatic potential of a subject suitable for a history painting (in this case, the Judgment of Hercules). *Second Characters,* ed. Benjamin Rand (Cambridge, Mass., 1914), pp. 34–38.

48. On the concept of "sacramental pictorialism," see Hagstrum, *The Sister Arts,* pp. 44–47.

ingly endless in its depths, and the bough shining on a dark oak tree near "the jaws of dank Avernus" provide richly symbolic revelations. Poets as notable as Dante and Spenser have seized upon the landscape of the dark wood for its suggestive objectification of their epic heroes' mental and spiritual states; the golden bough itself has been recognized, since Sir James Frazer, as a symbol of complex Protean form and multiple interpretations.

It is this highly symbolic aspect of Vergil's landscapes that makes it necessary to regard them as intrinsically different from the almost purely aesthetic and decorative Homeric and Ovidian landscapes. Modern Vergil scholars interpret the section of Book VI which deals with Aeneas' quest in the wood as "an initiation or mystery with both sacrificial justification and the offsetting of mortality by a magic life-giving talisman." [49] This kind of language is characteristic of commentators on Vergil since early Christian times; he has often been regarded with a kind of religious veneration that is extra-literary and conceives of him as a prophet or seer, even as a magician. Domenico Comparetti illustrates a discussion of Vergil's prestige in the Middle Ages by referring to the *sortes Virgilianae* and noting that, except for the Bible, few books have received such quaintly superstitious respect as that accorded the works of Vergil.[50] Although part of this veneration derives from the stature of the so-called Messianic Fourth *Eclogue,* supposedly a prophetic revelation of the birth of Christ, the imagery of the *Aeneid* has mystical or religious overtones as well, of which the landscape of Book VI provides a vivid pictorial example.

Aeneas has prayed to Venus for aid in finding the golden bough, hidden somewhere in the forest's vastness. Responding, she sends two doves to guide him:

> The birds flew on a little, just ahead
> Of the pursuing vision; when they came
> To the jaws of dank Avernus, evil-smelling,
> They rose aloft, then swooped down the bright air,

49. Brooks Otis, *Virgil, A Study in Civilized Poetry* (Oxford, 1963), p. 288.

50. *Vergil in the Middle Ages,* trans. E. F. M. Benecke (reprinted from the 2d ed., London, 1908; Hamden, Conn., 1966), p. 48.

Perched on the double tree, where the off-color
Of gold was gleaming golden through the branches.
As mistletoe, in the cold winter, blossoms
With its strange foliage on an alien tree,
The yellow berry gilding the smooth branches,
Such was the vision of the gold in leaf
On the dark holm-oak, so the foil was rustling,
Rattling, almost, the bract in the soft wind
Stirring like metal.[51]

[pp. 150–51]

Aeneas' journey through the somber wood has brought him to
the mouth of Avernus, "a cavern, yawning wide and deep,/
Jagged, below the darkness of the trees,/ Beside the darkness
of the lake." Armed with the bough he must enter this portal
to the land of the dead and, his mission fulfilled, rise again
from his self-sought entombment. Robert A. Brooks has noted
that the spatial structure of Book VI is developed "in the pene-
tration of one recess after another" (temple, cave, grove, underworld), and that Aeneas' progress "is cast into the rhythmic
structure of ritual." [52]

This landscape of symbols foreshadows in its descriptive details all the perils of the epic hero's quest—in its reiterated
darkness, in the fearful jagged aperture of Avernus, in the
wintry simile of the mistletoe, and in the golden gleam of the
bough itself, metallic and dead yet grafted on the living oak.
The juxtaposition of the bough and the tree suggests the intimate association of the living and the dead that is inherent in
Aeneas' journey to the underworld.

Other Vergilian passages, especially those picturing a paradisal or Golden Age realm, may also be categorized as instances
of sacramental landscape. Elysium, in *Aeneid*, VI, and the new
Arcadia of the Fourth *Eclogue* are well-known examples of
Vergil's tendency to enlarge setting into myth, making its function essentially symbolic. Bruno Snell has singled out the
Eclogues as "the first serious attempt in literature to mould the

51. The translation used is that of Rolfe Humphries (New York,
1951).
52. "*Discolor Aura:* Reflections on the Golden Bough," in *Virgil*,
ed. Steele Commager (Englewood Cliffs, N.J., 1966), p. 144.

Plate 3 N. Poussin, *Autumn: The Grapes of the Promised Land*

Greek motifs into self-contained forms of beauty whose reality lies within themselves. Thus art became 'symbol.' " [53] As symbol, Vergil's landscapes translated themselves into Christian literature in other than aesthetic and decorative terms. They were portents, visible signs *in themselves* of a spiritual, intangible, and invisible reality. They communicated themselves with such forceful, vivid authenticity that up to the time of the Renaissance Vergil was often depicted in religious art in the company of Isaiah, whose prophecies of the birth of a Messiah are strikingly echoed in Vergil's own, and of David, the pastoral psalmist and shepherd-king. Much of Vergil's impact upon Christian poets derives, as has been noted, from the Fourth *Eclogue* and from the belief that the poet had been inspired by God to prophesy the coming of the Messiah, a belief held from the time of Constantine to well into the eighteenth century.[54] Statius' speech to Vergil in *Purgatorio,* xxii, indicates that Dante certainly viewed the latter's poem in this light.

> Then he: "Thou first didst guide me when I trod
>   Parnassus' caves to drink the waters bright,
>   And thou wast first to lamp me up to God.
>
> Thou wast as one who, travelling, bears by night
>   A lantern at his back, which cannot leaven
>   His darkness, yet he gives his followers light.
>
> 'To us,' thou saidst, 'a new-born world is given,
>   Justice returns, and the first age of man,
>   And a new progeny descends from Heaven.'
>
> Poet through thee, through thee a Christian—
>   That's my bare sketch; but now I'll take to limning,
>   And make a clearer page for thee to scan. . . ." [55]

[ll. 64–75]

53. *The Discovery of the Mind: The Greek Origins of European Thought* (Cambridge, Mass., 1953), p. 308.
54. Joseph B. Mayor, W. Warde Fowler, and R. S. Conway, *Virgil's Messianic Eclogue: Its Meaning, Occasion, and Sources* (London, 1907), pp. 11–12.
55. Trans. Dorothy Sayers, Penguin edition (Baltimore, 1955). All subsequent quotations from *The Divine Comedy* will be taken from this edition.

That this "first age of man" had made an equal impact on Dante the poet and Dante the epic hero, we learn from the conclusion and culmination of the *Purgatorio,* when the Christian poets, Statius and Dante, are led by Vergil to the top of the purgatorial mount, the location of the Earthly Paradise. Awaiting them and the reader there is a poetic re-creation and reinterpretation of the classical *locus amoenus* that is a complex of symbols elegantly contrived and elaborately portrayed; in its scope, intensity, and pictorial detail, this is certainly the supreme example of a sacramental ideal landscape in literature.

An indication of the importance of this climactic section to the poet is the careful preparation he employs in presenting it to the reader. In Canto xxvii, having surmounted the last Cornice (of the lustful) and braved the cleansing wall of fire, Dante and his companions prepare to rest for the night. Dante composes himself for sleep, likening his situation, in an appropriately anticipatory though homely pastoral simile, to a goat (Purgatory's terrain being steep and mountainous) being watched over by vigilant herdsmen, Vergil and Statius (ll. 76–87). When he falls asleep, his dream is a visionary preview of the Earthly Paradise in which a young and beautiful girl gathers flowers, weaves them into garlands, and identifies herself, through her song, with Leah, traditionally a type of the active life, just as her sister Rachel represented the contemplative ideal. We are thus prepared in the succeeding cantos to assign these roles to Matelda and Beatrice.

In Canto xxviii Dante's dream becomes reality as he describes being in a "sacred wood, whose thick and leafy tent,/ Spread in my sight, tempered the new sun's rays" (ll. 2–3). This "ancient wood" recalls, of course, the dark wood of the *Inferno,*[56] providing an image both reiterating and antithetical, and helping to bind the first two canticles together structurally in a way that sets them off from the *Paradiso,* the journey's end. This sacred

56. Renato Poggioli, "Dante Poco Tempo Silvano: Or a 'Pastoral Oasis' in the Commedia," *Dante Society Papers,* LXXX (1962), 11. Poggioli calls the *selva antica* a "transfiguration" of the *selva oscura,* an indication of the sort of supernatural flavor which characterizes the vocabulary of those who attempt to define the quality this landscape possesses.

34

and ancient wood also suggests the wood of the golden bough in *Aeneid,* VI, especially with Vergil present to remind us of that other epic journey to the world of the dead. There too both the great age of the wood and its supernatural aura were stressed. There the bough, rich with symbolic implications, was to be a passport of safe conduct and a gift to Proserpine, queen of the underworld. Here another Proserpine figure, Matelda, will conduct Dante safely to Beatrice and, in doing so, will function allegorically as prelapsarian human perfection or on another, pre-Christian level, as Astraea, the personification of Justice, who fled the earth at the end of the Golden Age.[57]

All of the Golden Age ingredients are here; curiously enough the landscape often seems more Ovidian and Vergilian than biblical. For example, the first appearance of Matelda is modeled upon that of Proserpine in *Metamorphoses;* Dante himself confesses it. He sees

> A lady all alone, who wandered there
> Singing and plucking flower on floweret gay,
> With which her path was painted everywhere.
>
> [ll. 40–42]

He addresses her:

> O thou dost put me to remembering
> Of who and what were lost, that day her mother
> Lost Proserpine, and she the flowers of spring.
>
> [ll. 49–51]

The lady's meadow is in a wood where gentle breezes and singing birds abound. The setting recalls Proserpine's, although a river (Lethe) instead of a pool is in this scene and Matelda's flowers are gay red and yellow blossoms, not the sober purple and white of Proserpine's violets and lilies. Additional evidence that this landscape is a classical *locus amoenus* as well as the biblical Eden can be deduced from the reference to Venus,

57. Charles S. Singleton, *Journey to Beatrice,* Dante Studies, Vol. II (Cambridge, Mass., 1958), p. 218.

whose eyes are compared to Matelda's (ll. 64–66) ,[58] and from
the emphasis upon the fullness and variety of the flowers and
fruit, growing abundantly from a fecund earth that "teems with
seeds of everything,/ And in its womb breeds fruits ne'er
plucked of men" (ll. 119–20). Matelda's recital of this paradise's resources stresses the two qualities, variety and abundance,
that especially characterized both Eden and the world of the
Golden Age. To insure that we understand that this is the
Earthly Paradise of classical as well as Christian myth, Matelda,
at the end of Canto xxviii, specifically states that this is so,
causing Vergil and Statius to smile in pleased recognition and
assent:

> Those men of yore who sang the golden time
> And all its happy state—maybe indeed
> They on Parnassus dreamed of this fair clime.
>
> Here was the innocent root of all man's seed;
> Here spring is endless, here all fruits are, here
> The nectar is, which runs in all their rede.
>
> [ll. 139–44]

Since the previous canto had ended with Dante's prophetic
dream which was a vision of a supernatural reality, the "dreams"
of ancient poets of an idyllic natural paradise may also have
been authentic though partial glimpses of a world which once
was truly innocent and filled with every earthly perfection. So
Dante makes use of the "scripture of the pagans" as a "con-
cordance and confirmation of Christian truths," a habitual
practice for him.[59]

58. Both Singleton and Thomas G. Bergin (*Dante* [Boston,
1965]) agree that this episode is a *pastorela*, a Provençal form which
presents a dialogue between a courtly troubadour and a rustic shepherdess, usually ending with the girl's surrender to her wooer's
amorous entreaties. The sensuality of the *pastorela* would seem to
make it an inappropriate choice in this context, but if Matelda is
interpreted allegorically as Justice or Human Perfection, Dante's
desire to possess her becomes not only understandable but laudable.
See Singleton, *Journey to Beatrice*, pp. 211–18.

59. Singleton, *Journey to Beatrice*, p. 189. Renato Poggioli has also
pointed out that the pastoral form "has been one of the main ob-

There is some indication in this canto of a tableau and text arrangement reminiscent of the famous *Tablet* of Cebes.[60] This method (first painting a scene through verbal description in literature or visual representation in art, then commenting upon it and explaining its meaning) operates most effectively in an allegorical form like that of Dante's Earthly Paradise. In dealing with the poets' perplexity about their surroundings and their significance, Matelda first suggests that the psalm *Delectasti* may offer "light/ To illuminate your clouded intellect." The psalm cited is a praise of God's handiwork in nature which was thought to be especially applicable to Eden before man's fall. Matelda also goes on to state that she has come "to answer questions and content thee quite," following this avowal with a lecture to her audience that is a succinct and even sprightly disquisition on the peculiarities of the landscape (waters not fed by rain, plants growing without apparent seed) and the wonderful powers of the twin streams, Lethe and Eunoë.

In Canto xxix and those that follow, Dante abandons his usual realism to present two elaborate masques or pageants in which the same tableau-text, description-explanation arrangement still governs to some extent the narrative structure. Now, however, the focus is on the allegorical and emblematic figures —the gryphon, the four cardinal and the three theological virtues, not to mention Beatrice herself—and the landscape is reduced to mere background setting, only occasionally recalling its vivid and prominent effectiveness in Canto xxviii. Nature seems to have been replaced by art, an art that is dazzling but often hardly natural or even remotely realistic. The poets see "seven golden trees" in the luminous air which reveal themselves to be candlesticks; the water flashes "like a mirror," and the candle flames make the air look

> as it had been painted on;
> They looked like pictured pennants, as it were,

---

jects or tools in the repeated attempt to reconcile the 'two antiquities,' the classical and the biblical, in new syncretic forms." See "The Oaten Flute," *Harvard Library Bulletin*, XI (1957), 161.

60. For a discussion of the *Tablet,* see Hagstrum, *The Sister Arts,* pp. 33–34.

> Whose seven great bands of colour lodged and shone,
>   Till the sky stood with all those hues engrossed
>   That streak the Sun's bright bow and Delia's zone.
>
> [ll. 74–78]

This sort of substitution of the unnatural or supernatural for the natural, of the extraordinary for the ordinary, continues, for the most part, to the end of the *Purgatorio*. Only occasionally, as in the metamorphosis of the barren Tree of Knowledge, does a feature of the landscape again bear the burden of the poetic utterance and pictorially objectify the epic's theme. It is, however, with lines that repeat the tree's rebirth on a more natural level and identify it with Dante's own spiritual regeneration that the poet ends the *Purgatorio,* reinforcing once again for the reader the imagery of the pastoral freshness characteristic of the Earthly Paradise.

> From those most holy waters, born anew
>   I came, like trees by a change of calendars
>   Renewed with new-sprung foliage through and through
>
> Pure and prepared to leap up to the stars.
>
> [ll. 142–45]

A summary reiterating the salient characteristics of this second type of landscape will supplement the illustrations chosen from Vergil and Dante. This symbolic sacramental landscape, like the decorative type exemplified in the passages from Homer and Ovid, is an ideal one: elevated, naturalistic but not realistic, usually general rather than particularized, but highly pictorial, composed to present an ordered and static scenic arrangement using certain staple landscape ingredients hallowed by convention and long use and deriving originally from both classical and biblical literature. This ordered arrangement may not, in terms of compositional organization, betray any very highly developed understanding of the techniques of visual art, but it is nonetheless addressed to the eye and reflects an *ut pictura poesis* orientation or tradition. Where aesthetic and symbolic landscapes differ is in their purpose rather than in

their style and component parts.[61] The symbolic ideal landscape, besides contributing to aesthetic effects, functions sacramentally as an outward, visible sign of a mystical, religious, or
supernatural dimension in the poem, and it objectifies in itself
that unseen reality.

A third and final type of ideal landscape, to be designated
emblematic in this study, next requires definition. Such a landscape, possessing all the familiar ingredients of types one and
two, makes use of its imagery to focus upon a predominantly
moral and ethical or, more rarely, philosophical emphasis in a
poem or poetic passage. The effect of an emblematic landscape
in poetry approximates, in its pictorial method of presentation
coupled with its moral intent, the visual-didactic style of the
emblem book.[62] Its impact is neither primarily aesthetic, like
decorative landscape, nor religious and mystical, like sacramental landscape. Many Renaissance poetic texts may be culled for
illustrations of this third type, although the point should be
made that a poem's chronology does not necessarily determine
its type. The other-worldly preoccupations of medieval man
made his literature and art especially susceptible to the in-
corporation of mystical religious symbolism; Renaissance man's
concerns, however, were more usually ethical and moralistic.
Exceptions, of course, abound. The greatest poet of English
medieval literature, Geoffrey Chaucer, is much more likely to
employ the decorative Ovidian ideal landscape in his poetry
than to use the sacramental kind so often favored by his nearer

61. Relevant in this context is Rosemond Tuve's point that "we
cannot decide about the decorativeness of images by noting their
pretty content; we must look to the demands made by the poem's
subject" (see *Elizabethan and Metaphysical Imagery* [Chicago, 1947],
p. 65).
62. Elizabeth K. Hill has rightly objected to the confusion created
by "the widespread modern practice of using the term *emblem* to
indicate both a rhetorical trope and a genre," while noting that even
in the sixteenth and seventeenth centuries the word referred both
to symbol and genre. In the Renaissance, however, "when the term
meant symbol, it meant a moral sign and not a poetic figure." My
use of the term is designed to indicate my adherence to this traditional and primary moral signification. See "What Is an Emblem?,"
JAAC, XXIX (1970), 261.

contemporary Dante, even though his knowledge of Italian literature was vast and his borrowings from it extensive. The humanistic tenor of much Renaissance literature and art often found expression in an interest in matters of ethical or social significance; the form most clearly reflecting this concern, and combining art and literature, was the emblem book. It enjoyed great popularity during the Renaissance and was widely disseminated among all classes of men, enriching poetic imagery with new, visually striking motifs and, in turn, taking from contemporary literature (Spenser's *Faerie Queene* was a favorite source) new material congenial to emblematic treatment.[63]

The use of the Earthly Paradise landscape to show emblematically the moral dangers inherent in luxury and sensuality finds copious illustration in the Renaissance epic. The bowers of Alcina, Armida, and Acrasia rendered with lavish pictorial detail by Ariosto, Tasso, and Spenser all share the same theme and point an identical moral: that the apparent perfections of the Earthly Paradise are designed to lull and deceive those who succumb to its beauty and, thereby, risk moral corruption. "It is the garden where insidious luxury and sensual love overcome duty and true devotion." [64] The woman in the garden is no longer an innocent Eve before the Fall or a virginal Proserpine terrified by her abductor or the bride of the Song of Songs seeking her beloved—she is an evil temptress, a Circe figure, alluringly fair without and invariably foul within. Occasionally she may be treated less severely by a poet like Marino who eschews moral allegory in his *L'Adone* to stress the delights rather than the dangers of erotic pleasure. His Venus is still, however, the sexually aggressive pursuer who initiates her inexperienced partner, the warrior-hunter, into the joys of love, causing him to abandon, at least temporarily, the masculine obligations of battle or the hunt for dalliance in a paradise garden. The theme can, of course, assume a larger significance and become a dramatic objectification of man's archetypal struggle between flesh and spirit, love and duty, virtue and vice—all of

63. See Rosemary Freeman, *English Emblem Books* (London, 1948).

64. A. Bartlett Giamatti, *The Earthly Paradise and the Renaissance Epic* (Princeton, 1966), p. 126.

the implications which made Hercules at the crossroads such a perennial favorite of the Renaissance and baroque artists who elaborated the iconography and often chose to express much of the thematic significance of the subject through the landscape setting.[65]

To a Renaissance reader the ideal landscape of pastoral poetry suggested prelapsarian Eden, "the moment in scriptural history when Nature operated without impediment and had no need of Art to attain perfection." [66] For that reason the intrusion of art or artifice into the bower or garden was frequently an indication that it was a spurious Eden, a counterfeit of that original made by nature and God. So it is with Spenser's Bower of Bliss (*The Faerie Queene,* Book II, canto xii) which exemplifies in a quite typical fashion this pernicious aping of nature by art. Phrases like "the painted flowres" and "the christall running by" (stanza lviii) anticipate the statement, in the lines that follow (stanza lix), that art and nature have been so cunningly conjoined that each is concealed in the other.[67] The deception implicit here has obvious pejorative implications. Other moral implications in the imagery are less obvious to the nonscholarly eye; for instance, the fact that ivy (stanza lxi) in Renaissance poetry signified wantonness and was often associated with lewdness and drunkenness has been pointed out by Don Cameron Allen.[68] Such an interpretation coming right after Guyon has dashed a proffered wine cup from Acrasia's hand and broken it on the ground reinforces the negative connotations of the ivy's being gilded and hence false. The fountain in the

65. See Erwin Panofsky, *Hercules am Scheidwege un andere antike bildstoffe in der neueren kunst* (Berlin, 1930). Panofsky stresses the importance of Annibale Carracci's version in establishing the iconographical conventions of this subject. Most relevant to the present study are Carracci's landscapes (pl. XLIV): that forming the background to the figure of Virtue (Athena) is rocky, bare, and mountainous, while that associated with Vice or Voluptuousness (Venus) is lush, green, and gardenlike. The two divide equally the left and right halves of the picture.

66. Tayler, *Nature and Art,* p. 112.

67. All references are taken from *The Complete Poetical Works of Spenser,* Cambridge edition (Boston, 1936).

68. *Image and Meaning* (Baltimore, 1960), p. 18.

previous stanza, with its "silver flood," is "overwrought" with
carved images of naked boys; they suggest nothing as much as
a swarm of mischievous amoral cupids. The fountain itself is
another perversion, like the painted flowers, of an image which
ordinarily suggested to Renaissance minds a positive good, like
renewal, purification, baptism, or life itself.[69] Examples could
be multiplied, but they would only reemphasize the point that
this is a highly pictorialized moral landscape. It exists to objectify allegorically the outwardly good and beautiful and the
inwardly evil and ugly Acrasia with just about the same point
for point fidelity as the landscape of *Pilgrim's Progress* signifies
Christian's journey to eternity. It is, in short, a landscape of
moral emblems.[70] A stanza (II.xii.lv) depicting a vine with
golden grapes concealing themselves amid the real ones "lurking
from the vew of covetous guest" needs only a text beneath the
picture to utter the obvious aphoristic sentiment about deceit
and greed. Sometimes a tableau comes already endowed with
text, the two woven together as in this passage:

> Thus being entred, they behold arownd
> A large and spacious plaine, on every side
> Strowed with pleasauns, whose fayre grassy grownd
> Mantled with greene, and goodly beautifide
> With all the ornaments of Floraes pride,
> Wherewith her mother Art, as halfe in scorne
> Of niggard Nature, like a pompous bride
> Did decke her, and too lavishly adorne,
> When forth from virgin bowre she comes in th' early morne.
>
> [II.xii.1]

69. Gerhart B. Ladner, "Vegetation Symbolism and the Concept
of Renaissance," in *Essays in Honor of Erwin Panofsky,* ed. Millard
Meiss, 2 vols. (New York, 1961), I, 320.

70. The function of allegory is more restricted than that of symbol. The sacramental landscapes in this study are symbolic; they
"stand for" a wide range of ideas and intuitions, some too nebulous
or mystical for direct expression. Emblematic landscapes, while often
subtle in a poet of complexity, are not intended to possess unlimited
reverberations for the reader. Rather they set up certain specific correspondences to indicate a moral meaning.

Pernicious luxury and a decadent superfluity are pictorialized in an emblem of a personified Flora decoratively overembellished by her mother Art.

Of course, not all of Spenser's ideal landscapes are negative inversions of positive motifs; they all, however, tend to be emblematic and allegorical, signifying and representing the moral, occasionally philosophical dimensions in the poem. Rudolf Gottfried's objections to labeling Spenser pictorial rest largely on just this point: "In general . . . Spenser subordinates the pictorial element to moral allegory" and even when "conspicuous," as in the Bower of Bliss, it fulfills the function of "a kind of commentary on that essential text." [71] Lyle Glazier agrees that when faced with the necessity of being "pictorially grotesque" in order to be "symbolically true" Spenser does not hesitate; [72] he is faithful to the allegorical tenor rather than to the pictorial vehicle. A valid point has been raised, but this order of priorities does not make Spenser less pictorial; though his purpose goes beyond wanting simply to paint a picture, his imagination is ever "alert to visual detail" and "tenacious and exact in his memory of it." [73] The vivid scene of the Graces dancing on Mount Acidale in Book VI, the pastoral interlude of Calidore and Pastorella in the same book, and the Garden of Adonis, a true paradise of nature in Book III, are examples of this emblematic use of landscape. Perhaps the most interesting is the last, in which Spenser deals with the concept of time and mutability, referred to earlier in this chapter. He wrestles with the philosophical implications of the presence of "wicked Tyme" (temporal progression) in this paradise of "continuall spring, and harvest . . ./ Continuall, both meeting at one tyme" (an eternal present), and, like Poussin in *Et in Arcadia Ego*, he combines a gentle melancholy with resignation, finding in the figure of Adonis a paradoxical image of the "eterne in mutabilitie" (see III.vi.xxix–xlvii).

71. "The Pictorial Element in Spenser's Poetry," *ELH,* XIX (1952), 210, 212.
72. "The Nature of Spenser's Imagery," *MLQ,* XVI (1955), 303.
73. Rosemond Tuve, "Spenser and Some Pictorial Conventions," *SP,* XXXVII (1940), 175.

Turning from Spenser to his contemporary William Shakespeare, one is struck initially with the sparseness and brevity of pictorial passages that are natural to the epic and congenial to the more rhetorical style of French plays. Shakespeare seems to have lavished little attention on pictorial landscape detail, even in nondramatic works like *Venus and Adonis*. This early composition (tentatively dated 1592–93) is ornately descriptive and derives quite obviously from an Ovidian source—*Metamorphoses*—either directly or through some of the contemporary imitations of Ovid which were frequent in Renaissance poetry. Almost all of Shakespeare's painterly passages in this lengthy poem, however, are concerned with the persons of the lovers themselves: sullen or sparkling eyes, blushing or pale cheeks— the endless though virtuoso variations on such repetitive, hackneyed themes are finally wearying. Painting and statuary are not only suggested in these lavishly decorative descriptive passages but are evoked directly, by specific reference to the visual arts. Venus addresses the reluctant Adonis thus:

> Fie, lifeless picture, cold and senseless stone,
> Well-painted idol, image dull and dead,
> Statue contenting but the eye alone,
> Thing like a man, but of no woman bred! [74]

[ll. 211–14]

When, rarely, the primary emphasis is placed on nature itself, the ingredients of the *locus amoenus* landscape, inevitably associated with Shakespeare's subject, are quite often personified by the poet until very little feeling of a natural landscape remains.

> Lo, here the gentle lark, weary of rest,
> From his moist cabinet, mounts up on high
> And wakes the morning, from whose silver breast
> The sun ariseth in his majesty;

74. *The Complete Plays and Poems of William Shakespeare,* ed. Neilson and Hill (Cambridge, Mass., 1942). All subsequent references will be to this edition.

Who doth the world so gloriously behold
That cedar-tops and hills seem burnish'd gold.

[ll. 853–58]

It is as though the poet-dramatist instinctively prefers to focus on actors, not setting, on people and only incidentally on places, even going to the extent of personifying natural phenomena when he dwells at any length upon them. Sonnet XXXIII provides this example:

Full many a glorious morning have I seen
Flatter the mountain tops with sovereign eye,
Kissing with golden face the meadows green,
Gilding pale streams with heavenly alchemy;
Anon permit the basest clouds to ride
With ugly rack on his celestial face,
And from the forlorn world his visage hide,
Stealing unseen to west with this disgrace:

Another passage from *The Winter's Tale* further illustrates the poet's tendency to invoke the pathetic fallacy. It is Perdita's famous catalogue of flowers in Act IV, scene iv:

O Proserpina,
For the flowers now, that frighted thou let'st fall
From Dis's waggon! daffodils,
That come before the swallow dares, and take
The winds of March with beauty; violets dim,
But sweeter than the lids of Juno's eyes
Or Cytherea's breath; pale primroses,
That die unmarried, ere they can behold
Bright Phoebus in his strength—

Shakespeare's plays seem at first to be replete with pastoral landscapes. *Cymbeline, As You Like It,* and *The Tempest,* like *The Winter's Tale,* employ the theme of the remote or bucolic refuge from the corruption or falsity of the court. These wild and pastoral locales, however, are charming stage sets—landscapes of fantasy like Marie Antoinette's elegant dairy farm, filled usually with displaced aristocrats (and a few rustic clowns

45

for comic effect), all of whom overpopulate forests of Arden, mountaintops in Wales, or seacoasts in Bohemia until injustices at home can be rectified, returning them to their proper settings and their accustomed roles. The artificiality of these settings is not the point at issue, since all ideal landscape employs artifice. What must be emphasized is the consistency and frequency with which Shakespeare uses his landscape settings as social or moral metaphors of his characters' plights. One gets the impression that Shakespeare's mind, like Spenser's, is often not on the terrain itself but on the meaning to be derived from it. He employs this useful technique to show the deficiencies of one type of society by contrasting it with another, one in many ways more ideal though undeniably more primitive. When it is rendered pictorially, such landscape can be categorized as emblematic in the same sense already applied in this chapter to Spenser's poetic landscapes. An interesting example of this use of landscape occurs in *Cymbeline* (Act III, scene iii) where Belarius discourses to the younger Guiderius and Arviragus on the moral lessons to be derived from climbing to the top of their mountain retreat:

> Now for our mountain sport. Up to yond hill!
> Your legs are young; I'll tread these flats. Consider,
> When you above perceive me like a crow,
> That it is place which lessens and sets off;
> And you may then revolve what tales I have told you
> Of courts of princes, of the tricks in war;

The soaring bird provides one kind of moral as well as visual perspective; the struggling climber will suggest another:

> Did you but know the city's usuries,
> And felt them knowingly; the art o' th' court,
> As hard to leave as keep, whose top to climb
> Is certain falling, or so slipp'ry that
> The fear's as bad as falling;

This second passage is especially easy to visualize in an emblematic form, pictorially representing the slippery and precipitate heights and the desperate men who attempt the precarious task

46

Plate 4 N. Poussin, *Winter: The Flood*

of scaling them. Such an emblematic landscape has the didactic purpose of imaging allegorically an ethical situation or conflict. Here, of course, the hazards of mountain climbing provide a visual representation for the equivalent perils of social climbing at court. In both cases death may await the unskillful.

Shakespeare and Spenser both use the mythic connotations of ideal landscape. The Earthly Paradise can become in their poetry an extended metaphor for England. That "Eden fayre" which Redcrosse (or St. George) defends in Book I of *The Faerie Queene* resembles the "other Eden, demi-Paradise" that John of Gaunt movingly celebrates in his dying speech in *Richard II*. These two passages assume larger implications than mere coincidence when Northrop Frye reminds us that this tendency to identify England with Eden or with the legendary Islands of the Blest or with a sylvan Arcadia "runs through English literature at least from the end of Greene's *Friar Bacon* to Blake's 'Jerusalem' hymn." [75] Few poets have taken Samuel Johnson's strictures about patriotism seriously when writing about the rural beauty of their homeland, and it may be this propensity for idealizing the landscape which lies all about them that makes Englishmen create literary Edens which are astonishingly vivid, various, and meaningful.

When nature poetry in England began to be significantly affected by the growing awareness of landscape painting in the seventeenth century, the tendency toward ideal representation, already characteristic of much of it, was strengthened, and poetic landscapes that had always been visual, even pictorial in a relatively unsophisticated sense of the word, became much more ecphrastic. That is, they grew to be virtuoso exercises in verbal landscape form, so that by the mid-eighteenth century a Thomson could posthumously inspire a Turner, poet and painter complementing each other's work until the English landscape rivaled the Roman campagna's ability to generate works of art incomparably more lovely than the original that stimulated them. The artist's vision of ideal landscape ends by remaking reality, until we are persuaded to see through his eyes, by means

75. *Anatomy of Criticism* (Princeton, 1957), p. 194.

of his painting or his poem, an imperishable world of art. We behold at last "nature transformed by poetry and painting" into "the legendary Eden whose reflected beauty we discern, which is the environment imagination inhabits." [76]

76. Raine, *Defending Ancient Springs,* p. 130.

Plate 5 Bosch, *The Garden of Earthly Delights*   Mas—Art Reference Bureau

⟶ 2 ⟵

Marvell:

The Emblematic Landscape

Though they cannot be dated precisely, most of Marvell's lyric poems were written in the early 1650s while the poet was at Appleton House acting as tutor to Mary, the daughter of Lord Fairfax. The number of landscape poems in this rather small collection testifies to the impact of Marvell's surroundings upon his work and even more to the primary importance he placed upon themes and images dealing with nature, that green world he depicted with such an original sensibility.

Marvell's poetic landscapes reveal that he often uses nature emblematically; his ideal landscapes exhibit, therefore, the characteristics of the third category described in the previous chapter. His emblematic imagery becomes pictorial allegory in brief, designed to objectify a private moral vision.[1] Allegory may be considered a long emblem; conversely, the emblem is a

1. As Geoffrey Hartman says, "Marvell's poems . . . are autonomous emblems in verse, approaching the compactness of pictorial form and even implying, at times, a scripture text for motto" ("Marvell, St. Paul, and the Body of Hope," *Andrew Marvell, A Collection of Critical Essays,* ed. George deF. Lord [Englewood Cliffs, N.J., 1968], p. 112).

short allegory. Both emblem and allegory establish certain correspondences between an object or action and a secondary level
of meaning; the purpose of this correspondence is ultimately
didactic. This relationship between emblem and allegory permits Marvell to enrich his landscape settings by providing them
with an important ethical dimension through imagery impreg-
nated with subtle and extensive implications taken from both
classical and Christian traditions. Emblems, being pictorial,
tend to have a single effect, while allegory, used most often in a
narrative structure, has greater range for development but still
operates within clearly defined limits.[2] "There is in one sense
only one allegorical theme—loss and salvation."[3] If that generalized assertion is not interpreted too narrowly, its validity
holds for Marvell's particular emblematic landscapes. Joseph H.
Summers believes that "in Marvell's poetry the man-made garden and the 'natural' meadows are significant not intrinsically
but instrumentally."[4] Though the significance of these settings
usually seems both intrinsic emblematically and functional
instrumentally, one must agree with Summers that much of
Marvell's landscape poetry is "ultimately concerned with lost
perfection."[5] Even when vanished Eden is recaptured in these
poems, the temporary and precarious nature of its possession is
obliquely suggested.

The emblematic character of Marvell's imagery has been the
subject of much scholarly attention.[6] Writing at the end of a

2. Ann Berthoff suggests that when the narrative element intrinsic
to allegory is checked, the resultant "static moments . . . are emblematic in character." Berthoff's discussion of Marvell's poetry is
founded upon her judgment that his manner is fundamentally allegorical. See *The Resolved Soul* (Princeton, 1970), p. 24.

3. Rosemond Tuve, *Allegorical Imagery* (Princeton, 1966), p. 28 n.

4. "Marvell's Nature," *ELH*, XX (1953), 125.

5. Summers further reinforces Miss Tuve's point above by his remark that "Marvell's image of the lost garden is as much an occasion for the recognition of man's alienation from nature as it is
for remembered ecstasy" (*ibid.*).

6. See especially Ruth Wallerstein, *Studies in Seventeenth-Century
Poetic* (Madison, 1965), chap. 7. Stanley Stewart, in *The Enclosed
Garden* (Madison, 1966), relates the imagery of "The Garden" to
the iconography of the *hortus conclusus* in seventeenth-century emblem books. M. C. Bradbrook and M. G. Lloyd Thomas view "The

long and vital tradition, Marvell made use of a recognized technique that permitted him to employ simultaneously and to maximum effect his highly pictorial imagination, his intellectual and ironic wit, and his strong moral sense. The emblematic nature of Marvell's ideal landscape reveals itself more or less openly through an examination of the individual poems. Some of these revelations are quite cryptic; indeed Marvell's metaphysical subtleties often recall the enigmatic character of the *impresa* (a private, esoteric device adopted by Renaissance noblemen) more than they do the comparatively clear emblem, as the number and diversity of interpretations of a poem like "The Garden" demonstrate.

Only very occasionally does Marvell attempt the kinds of ideal landscapes labeled decorative and sacramental in the previous chapter. In stanzas vi and vii of "The Garden" he comes closest to achieving the latter but in the last analysis does not, for reasons that will be discussed subsequently. The decorative landscape, however, is effectively exemplified in "Bermudas." Before focusing, therefore, in the rest of the chapter upon the emblematic method Marvell almost invariably employs, we will briefly examine "Bermudas." Such an examination will also help indirectly to define and isolate further the contrasting and dominant emblematic.

The Golden Age setting in "Bermudas" is exotic and opulent; it glitters with artifice.

> He hangs in shades the Orange bright,
> Like golden Lamps in a green Night.
> And does in the Pomgranates close,
> Jewels more rich than *Ormus* show's.
>
> [ll. 17–20]

Marvell was aware of the tradition which described the New World as an earthly paradise, even though scholars agree that

---

Garden" and "The Unfortunate Lover" as poems "composed of a series of emblematic pictures" (*Andrew Marvell* [Cambridge, 1940], p. 29). Kitty W. Scoular analyzes many emblematic elements in the treatment of nature in "Upon Appleton House" (*Natural Magic* [Oxford, 1965], chap. 3).

he must have received firsthand knowledge of the Bermudas from John Oxenbridge, with whom he lived in 1653. He seems to have preferred less literal sources, however, drawing upon Edmund Waller's *Battle of the Summer Islands* and Captain John Smith's *The Generall Historie of Virginia, New-England and the Summer Isles,* 1624; the latter, H. M. Margoliouth suggests, was a source Waller too may have used.[7]

Long before the seventeenth century, of course, the legend of an earthly paradise persisted. As a place untouched by the effects of the Fall, it combined features reflecting both pagan and Christian tradition. Like the Bermudas, it was most often an island (the Fortunate Islands, the Islands of the Blest), to be reached only after a long and perilous sea voyage. A ninth- or tenth-century tale of a sixth-century Irish monk, St. Brendan, recounts how he found the Earthly Paradise somewhere in the Western Ocean. "By the Grace of our Lord Jesus Christ," the saint's boat was carried along for forty days until it reached the paradisal shore.[8] The beauty and fertility of the land, its unchangingly perfect climate, and its abundant fruits are all standard details in such accounts. George Boas notes that the twelfth century was the period in which legendary journeys to earthly paradises flourished most abundantly; these were succeeded by satirical treatments, such as "the Land of Cocaigne," most familiarly depicted in the painting of that title by Brueghel the Elder.[9] Marvell need not have depended on contemporary, or nearly contemporary, sources for his earthly paradise; indeed, his pious pilgrims depending on the Lord to bring them safely to their destination may have essentially more in common with St. Brendan's mythical account than with Waller's mock heroic one, despite the small details (orange trees, ambergris) which link it to the latter. Pinning down exact sources in a tradition whose staples are so constantly and almost un-

7. *The Poems and Letters of Andrew Marvell,* textual notes, I, 220.

8. A long excerpt from this legend, translated from Latin into English, can be found in George Boas, "Earthly Paradises," *Essays on Primitivism and Related Ideas in the Middle Ages* (Baltimore, 1948), pp. 158–59.

9. *Ibid.,* pp. 160, 167–68.

varyingly reiterated is, however, an unrewarding task. It is sufficient to refer to the durability of this myth of a lost paradise on an island remotely and vaguely located somewhere in the vastness of the Western Ocean, forever beckoning to the eager, credulous explorer who sought a mountain of gold or the fountain of youth.

No such frivolities attract Marvell's voyagers to these shores. They are there to share "the Gospels Pearl" of great price and to praise God in the natural temple formed by the rocks in the island's harbor. Though their purpose is austerely spiritual, the central and longest part of the poem (ll. 5–32) is a gorgeous and sensuously rich celebration of the beauties of this fabled land.[10] It is as though Marvell's visual inspiration came this time not from any spare emblematic drawing but from a Renaissance painting glowing with color, lush and Venetian, "which there enamells every thing." This central section contrasts curiously with the moral "text" appended to it at the poem's conclusion (ll. 33–40). Marvell's method here is emblematic; his pictorialization is not, except perhaps for the opening section of the poem. The description of the small boat "unespy'd" in the ocean's vastness, the anthropomorphic "list'ning Winds," and the suggestion of "huge Sea-Monsters . . ./ That lift the Deep upon their Backs" recall the numerous emblems allegorically depicting the voyage of the human soul through life's perilous, shipwreck-strewn waters to an eternal paradise, "Heavens Vault."

When the island itself is reached, however, the pictorial impression changes, shifting to a richer canvas where exotic figs, melons, and magnificent apples—delicacies almost as plentiful and amorous as those in "The Garden"—flourish, along with the sacred cedars, chosen by God's own hand from among those in Lebanon (ll. 25–26). The superb lines, quoted at the beginning of this section, which describe the orange trees, create

10. It is interesting to note in the accounts of the Jesuit explorers and missioners an increasing emphasis on parallels between Vergillian and biblical idealizations of man's beginnings and the primitive societies they encountered. See Henri Baudet, *Paradise on Earth: Some Thoughts on European Images of Non-European Man,* trans. Elizabeth Wentholt (New Haven, 1965), pp. 36 ff.

a blend of colors—orange, gold, and green—and of contrasted light and shadow. The "golden Lamps" are not really light at all, but fruit, and the "green Night" cannot be wholly dark because it still remains green. Though metaphysical paradox may operate in these lines, the exactness of the poet's visual perception also suggests the subtle effects sought by Renaissance painters of ideal landscapes.[11] The stress on the aesthetic rather than the moral in this poem results in a curiously uneven tonal effect. Instead of being edified, as expected, by a straightforward and pious celebration of an intrepid group of Puritan saints, the reader is diverted into enjoying the sophisticated depiction of their new Eden. Clearly the poet's central focus is upon the ideal landscape itself, not the figures therein. Here Marvell resembles those sixteenth- and seventeenth-century painters who chose a subject like St. George or The Flight into Egypt primarily for its outdoor setting, subordinating the often tiny figures to the extensive, detailed landscapes.

Figures in a landscape achieve a more equal balance with the setting in certain of Marvell's most characteristically emblematic poems. Landscape itself becomes emblem, often embodying in its details certain qualities possessed by those poetically sketched within the framework of their accustomed setting. In poems like "Upon the Hill and Grove at Bill-borow" and "The Picture of little T. C.," a central figure is defined by the landscape he or she inhabits. In a second kind of poem ("Upon Appleton House" and "The Garden"), larger philosophical and moral issues, not always specifically related to the individuals in the poem, are adroitly objectified through the landscape medium which changes and shifts to accommodate the increased complexity of its thematic burden. Finally, another group of poems, those dealing with the figure of the Mower, uses an emblematic ideal landscape ironically and contrapuntally to dramatize the extent of a central figure's alienation

11. See, for example, Correggio's *Madonna and Child With St. John,* 1515 (The Art Institute, Chicago). A landscape background is at right; at left in midground is placed a stylized panel painted with golden lemons or oranges shining out among the surrounding dark leaves.

from his pastoral world. In the rest of this chapter each of these ways of using the landscape as an emblem is discussed in turn.

The Emblematic Portrait in a Landscape

"Upon the Hill and Grove at Bill-borow" looks superficially like a fairly typical example of what Dr. Johnson called "local poetry" (and what has also been called topographical or loco-descriptive poetry), that is, "some particular landscape to be poetically described, with the addition of such embellishments as may be supplied by historical retrospection or incidental meditation." [12] Though Johnson credits Sir John Denham with the invention of the form, the inclusion of the convention of praising a great man—directly or indirectly—by viewing his estate as an emblematic objectification of its owner's excellences is an aspect of local poetry that goes back to Ben Jonson's "To Penshurst" in English poetry and ultimately to classical ante-cedents, notably to the lines in the Odyssey on Alcinous, his house, and his garden.[13] In *Cooper's Hill* (1642), Denham, be-sides striving for that sense of a particular locale that topo-graphical poetry tries to impart, also anticipates Marvell's emblematic landscape in "Bill-borow" by embellishing his poem with a passage which treats Windsor as a moral emblem.[14]

12. "Sir John Denham," in *Lives of the English Poets*, ed. George Birkbeck Hill, 3 vols. (Hildesheim, 1968), I, 77.
13. See Don Cameron Allen, *Image and Meaning* (Baltimore, 1960), pp. 119–20.
14. See Scoular, *Natural Magic*, pp. 157–59, for a discussion of Denham's emblematic nature and his choice, in making poetic use of the gentle hill at Windsor, of "a middle place in the debate be-tween mountain and valley" that was traditional in sixteenth- and seventeenth-century poetry. This debate found its way into the visual arts too, of course. One may instance Titian's *Sacred and Profane Love* (Borghese Gallery, Rome), whose iconography has been analyzed by Edgar Wind (*Pagan Mysteries in the Renaissance,* rev. enl. ed. [New York, 1968]). The landscape background for the nude female figure who represents sacred love is a gentle valley, while profane love, attired in opulent silks, is posed against a landscape background which includes a castle situated commandingly on a mountaintop.

> *Windsor* the next (where *Mars* with *Venus* dwells,
> Beauty with strength) above the Valley swells
> Into my eye, and doth it self present
> With such an easie and unforc't ascent,
> That no stupendious precipice denies
> Access, no horror turns away our eyes:
> But such a Rise, as doth at once invite
> A pleasure, and a reverence from the sight.
> Thy mighty Masters Embleme, in whose face
> Sate meekness, heightened with Majestick Grace
> Such seems thy gentle height, made only proud
> To be the basis of that pompous load,
> Than which, a nobler weight no Mountain bears,
> But *Atlas* only that supports the Sphears [15]

[ll. 39–52]

Here Windsor emblematically represents the British monarch's qualities much as we shall see Bill-borow representing those of Lord Fairfax.[16] But Denham's didacticism is more conventional and less witty than Marvell's, however similar their initial response to the poetic task of praising the great man through a celebration of his estate. Marvell's more complex wit, his sensitive treatment of the retirement theme, and the sturdiness of his moral commitment should cause us to look ahead to Pope's Epistles to Bathurst and Burlington as well as backward to the metaphysical style of Donne. Marvell is a transitional figure, a poet who "was not willing, at least in the lyrics to abandon entirely the old emblematic universe with its multi-leveled correspondences for a rational deistic universe." [17]

15. *The Poetical Works of Sir John Denham,* ed. Theodore Howard Banks, Jr. (New Haven and London, 1928). On p. 64 of this edition, a variant text (MS. Harley 837 in the British Museum) provides a slightly expanded version of the above passage; both texts, however, bear the same similarity to Marvell's poem.

16. Earl R. Wasserman, discussing poetic procedure in *Cooper's Hill,* stresses Denham's use of Windsor as an " 'Embleme' of the King" combining majesty and meekness to achieve an "ideal *concordia discors.*" See *The Subtler Language* (Baltimore, 1968), p. 59. Marvell's emblematic equation of Fairfax and Bill-borow attempts the same sort of harmony of seemingly discordant aspects—recluse and general—in Lord Fairfax's person.

17. Harold Toliver, *Marvell's Ironic Vision* (New Haven, 1965), p. 4. J. B. Leishman also notes Marvell's transitional quality. While

That emblematic universe served him well, providing him with a type of expandable and richly suggestive metaphor that could be dwelt upon and lavishly elaborated in a poem like "Upon the Hill and Grove at Bill-borow."

The poem's opening stanza celebrates Bill-borow's hill in strikingly pictorialist terms.

> See how the arched earth does here
> Rise in a perfect Hemisphere!
> The stiffest Compass could not strike
> A Line more circular and like;
> Nor softest Pensel draw a Brow
> So equal as this Hill does bow.
> It seems as for a Model laid,
> And that the World by it was made.
>
> [i.1–8]

That this emblematic microcosm drawn with such perfect proportions should provide the model for the macrocosm rather than be a reflection of it is a witty Marvellian inversion employed to instruct even more than to divert. The regular outline and moderate height of Bill-borow's hill exemplify the *discordia concors* and make manifest a moral lesson which the harsher, higher mountains around Lord Fairfax's domain must recognize and to which they, though greater in size and impressiveness, must defer.[18]

> Here learn ye Mountains more unjust,
> Which to abrupter greatness thrust,

---

granting his similarities to earlier seventeenth-century poets, Leishman suggests that "Marvell's wit had decided affinities with that of Pope and Prior." See *The Art of Marvell's Poetry* (London, 1966), p. 10.

18. The well-established aversion to mountains in much seventeenth-century poetry is only peripherally an issue here. The transformation of taste from "mountain gloom" to "mountain glory" has been thoroughly studied, most significantly by Marjorie Nicolson. The incidence and popularity of mountain scenes in seventeenth-century painting collections have been recorded by Henry and Margaret Ogden in *English Taste in Landscape in the Seventeenth-Century* (Ann Arbor, 1955).

That do with your hook-shoulder'd height
The Earth deform and Heaven fright.
For whose excrescence ill design'd,
Nature must a new Center find,
Learn here those humble steps to tread,
Which to a securer Glory lead.

[ii.9–16]

As the poem proceeds it becomes clear to the reader that the poet views Bill-borow hill not only as an emblematic representation of virtuous abstractions like modesty, propriety, and regularity, but also as an equivalent for Lord Fairfax and his life of retirement and contemplation, his renunciation of martial glory and worldly fame, and his consequent paradoxical attainment of a higher, nobler way of life, even though he has ostensibly chosen a more humble path than destiny seemed originally to have marked out for him. "Bill-borow" contains none of the doubts and regrets about retirement that are apparent in "Upon Appleton House."

After having, in imagination, climbed to the top of the gently rising hill (stanza iii) and responded to the prospect from that vantage point (stanza iv), the poet turns his attention to the grove of trees which adorns the summit.

Upon its crest this Mountain grave
A Plump of aged Trees does wave.
No hostile hand durst ere invade
With impious Steel the sacred Shade.
For something alwaies did appear
Of the *great Masters* terrour there:
And Men could hear his Armour still
Ratling through all the Grove and Hill.

[v.33–40]

H. M. Margoliouth's textual notes suggest a possible reading of "Plume" for "Plump" in line two,[19] furthering the image of a giant helmet with its stiff crest of trees thrusting vertically upward like the horsehair crests on the helmets of the warrior-

19. Kitty Scoular also recommends this reading. See *Natural Magic*, p. 161.

heroes of classical epics. The metaphysical wit of the double
sense of "crest" underscores the gigantic dimensions (essentially spiritual, though metaphorically physical) of that *"great
Master"* whose ghostly presence in this "sacred" wood is now
and then betrayed by the rattling of his armor. Fairfax, the
"genius" of the place, is like a hidden god; his retirement has
not diminished his power but merely transmuted it into a
moral force rather than a military one. His warfare has become spiritual, waged against the powers of darkness.

> Much other Groves, say they, then these
> And other Hills him once did please
> Through Groves of Pikes he thunder'd then,
> And Mountains rais'd of dying Men.
> For all the *Civick Garlands* due
> To him our Branches are but few.
> Nor are our Trunks enow to bear
> The *Trophees* of one fertile year.
>
> [ix.65–72]

Maren-Sofie Røstvig's remark that loco-descriptive poetry involves as part of its technique the animation of the landscape [20]
is well illustrated in this passage in which men and mountains,
groves of pikes and groves of trees are mingled together in
images that are simultaneously natural and allegorical, literal
and moral. The "Mountains rais'd of dying Men" recall the
"Mountains more unjust/ Which to abrupter greatness thrust"
of stanza ii. Implicit in these lines is a contrast between Fairfax's soldierly image which is closer to St. Paul's Christian
hero or to the already cited classical warrior of the epics than
it is to the fearful and excessive harshness of the "hook-
shoulder'd" symbol of unchecked aggression—the neighboring
mountain.[21]

The "humble steps" the ex-general treads in retirement at
Bill-borow paradoxically lead to a "securer Glory" and a more

20. *The Happy Man,* Vol. I, rev. ed. (Oslo, 1962), p. 193.
21. It is interesting to note that Marvell later used the phrase
"hook-shouldered" to describe the despised Sir Henry Wood who
represented Hythe from 1661 to 1671 in Parliament. See "Last Instructions to a Painter," l. 163 in the Margoliouth edition of the
poems, and the editor's note on p. 275.

lasting peace than the proud and bloody exploits of his earlier life. His brightness now is interior and intrinsic; it does not depend upon the luster of worldly renown:

> Therefore to your obscurer Seats
> From his own Brightness he retreats:
> Nor he the Hills without the Groves,
> Nor height but with Retirement loves.
>
> [x.77–80]

The qualities of this higher, contemplative life are, throughout the poem, made manifest through the medium of the landscape, especially in the gentler aspects of Bill-borow hill with its symmetrical configuration, "soft access," "courteous" ascent, trees, "sacred Shade," "flutt'ring Breez," and even (stanza vi) a resident nymph—Vera, who is Lord Fairfax's wife Anne Vere. In contrast to this *locus amoenus,* equated with a life of retirement and restful ease, stand the "unjust" mountains deforming earth and frightening heaven, representing the cruel, oppressive seekers after power and wielders of force who flourish in the world beyond the boundaries of Lord Fairfax's estate. This is a world where the bubble reputation and a haughty pride of place can effect crippling character changes upon men less endowed than Fairfax with the necessary combination of Christian meekness and spiritual fortitude. What Marvell may be trying to express obliquely and metaphorically in his landscape imagery is a sentiment similar to that set forth by the neo-Platonist Pico della Mirandola in his oration *On the Dignity of Man* as described by Edgar Wind:

> Man's glory is derived from his mutability. The fact that his orbit of action is not fixed, like that of angels or of animals, gives him the power to transform himself into whatever he chooses and become a mirror of the universe. He can vegetate like a plant, rage like a brute, dance like a star, reason like an angel, and surpass them all by withdrawing into the hidden centre of his own spirit where he may encounter the solitary darkness of God.[22]

22. *Pagan Mysteries,* p. 191.

Another portrait in its emblematic landscape, "The Picture of little T. C. in a Prospect of Flowers" resembles "Upon the Hill and Grove at Bill-borow" in important ways. Though its subject is a little girl (probably Theophila Cornewall), not an ex-general, she is, like Lord Fairfax, surrounded by images whose significant associations invest her with a quasi divinity. Like Fairfax she rules over a domain which, in its turn, emblematically defines her, while enlarging her importance beyond the personal to touch upon universal concerns. Marvell's ability to make poetic use of natural imagery that evokes reverberations of both classical and Christian tradition gives greater complexity and a denser texture to the apparent simplicity of his poem. "Little T. C." is radically transformed from a playful variation on a pastoral theme to a serious, even weighty, moral statement in which the lightness of tone contributes an ironic distancing and prevents the poet from lapsing into sententiousness.

Helping Marvell to fuse the seemingly disparate elements of his imagery in "Little T. C." is the whole tradition of the Christianized *locus amoenus*. The Vergilian Golden Age landscape in seventeenth-century poetry inevitably carried echoes of Genesis or The Song of Solomon or the parable of the Good Shepherd. Indeed, a poet of that period would have had to make a conscious and sustained effort to "paganize" his nature imagery if he wished to divest it of Judaeo-Christian associations. The emblem books had played a significant part in this Christianizing process. They had reinforced a similar tendency in baroque art to perceive an allegorical significance in classical imagery until a subject ostensibly treating an event in Greek mythology might actually exhibit a complicated, esoteric Christian iconography to noble patrons of art, especially churchmen, who had moral qualms about decorating their salon walls and ceilings with purely pagan mythologies. Both of these visual art forms, emblem books and allegorical mythologies, seem reflected in Marvell's poetic procedure in "Little T. C."

The very title of the poem attests to the poet's debt to pictorial sources. It is a "Picture" of a young girl in a "Prospect of Flowers." The fact that Marvell conceives of his poem as a portrait puts it at once into a recognizable genre, but one al-

legorized into a representation of mythic significance. Little
T. C., besides being indisputably herself, is also a nymph who
is the "Darling of the Gods," "Whom Nature courts," who is
endowed with powers that can "Reform the errours of the
Spring," thus making a lovely but natural landscape into one
in which the Golden Age is restored. The youthful goddess is
"painted" by Marvell in the kind of landscape setting that
reminds the reader of Ovid's Proserpine and Pomona,[23] giving
her the qualities of virginal innocence, youthful freshness, and
springtime hope associated with these deities. Such qualities
are also a reverse echo of other lovely and powerful ladies, like
Alcina, Armida, and Acrasia, who inhabit paradise gardens in
Christian epics.

Little T. C. has, however, a moral function as well as a
decorative one. Marvell's poetic text directs our response to his
portrait in much the same way as an emblematic text appended
to the design calls attention to and explicates certain features
of that design. In the opening verse the reader is invited to
observe the unassuming "simplicity" of this young nymph who
exercises her considerable powers over the natural landscape
with a charmingly offhand insouciance.

> See with what simplicity
> This Nimph begins her golden daies!
> In the green Grass she loves to lie,
> And there with her fair Aspect tames
> The Wilder flow'rs, and gives them names:
> But only with the Roses playes;
> And them does tell
> What Colour best becomes them, and what Smell.
>
> [i.1–8]

Hers is a civilizing power; she "tames/The Wilder flow'rs,"
reminding us of the similar tasks given to Adam and Eve in
Milton's Eden. They too are charged with the responsibility for
curbing the Garden's overluxuriant floral growth; they too, at
least in Adam's case, assume the task of naming the flora and
fauna in the Earthly Paradise. Marvell has, all at once, made

23. Leishman, *Art of Marvell's Poetry*, pp. 182–83.

us aware simultaneously of a little girl playing games in a garden and a goddess or a prelapsarian Eve exercising her dominion over Nature. We will see something of the same double effect in the depiction of Mary Fairfax in "Upon Appleton House."

The child's preference for the rose is a significant one. The rose is traditionally preeminent among flowers just as T. C. is preeminent among ordinary little girls. The rose is an important image in The Song of Songs; in the whole *hortus conclusus* tradition it assumes a prominent role, representing the Virgin. Henry Hawkins' emblematic "character" of the rose stresses its dominant position: "The Rose is the Imperial Queene of Flowers, which al doe homage to, as to their Princesse, she being the glorie and delight of that Monarchie. . . . It is the Darling of the Garden-Nimphs, and the cause sometimes perhaps of much debate between them, while each one strives to have it proper to herself, being made for al, and is verily enough for al." [24] In Milton's Eden the rose symbolized both chaste love (the nuptial bower) and innocence (the garland Adam wove for Eve which withered and dropped its petals at the recital of her Fall). T. C.'s preference for the rose tells us much about her moral and allegorical meaning.[25]

All the suggestions of virginal chastity in the imagery of the opening stanza are reinforced and made explicit in stanzas ii and iii:

> Who can fortel for what high cause
> This Darling of the Gods was born!
> Yet this is She whose chaster Laws
> The wanton Love shall one day fear,
> And, under her command severe,

24. *Parthenia Sacra* (Rouen, 1633), pp. 17–18. This book of twenty-four emblems honors the Virgin Mary, using as a framework the concept of the *hortus conclusus*.

25. Don Cameron Allen, *Image and Meaning*, devotes a chapter to George Herbert's "The Rose," and in that chapter discusses both classical and Christian rose symbolism in some detail. Also see George Ferguson, *Signs and Symbols in Christian Art* (New York, 1966), pp. 37–38.

See his Bow broke and Ensigns torn.
> Happy, who can
Appease this virtuous Enemy of Man!

O then let me in time compound,
And parly with those conquering Eyes;
Ere they have try'd their force to wound,
Ere, with their glancing wheels, they drive
In Triumph over Hearts that strive,
And them that yield but more despise.
> Let me be laid,
Where I may see thy Glories from some shade.

[ll. 9–24]

Significantly, in stanza ii, the poet anticipates T. C.'s subjection of Cupid, "wanton Love." She is a "virtuous Enemy of Man" whose male counterpart is to be found in the poetic protagonist of "The Garden." Although Eros was associated with the rose in classical mythology,[26] T. C. is identified clearly with Christian symbolism that rejects the amorous connotations possessed by the rose, or rather sublimates them and makes them mystical, religious, and decidedly non-fleshly. The spiritual overcomes the carnal in Marvell's poetic emblem; Cupid's defeat is rendered in a conventionally emblematic fashion by his broken bow and torn ensigns. The imagery of conquest is developed in stanza iii, in which a triumphant T. C. rides her war chariot over the hearts of those who have tried vainly to win her. The painterly effect of this stanza recalls depictions of Diana, the huntress "chaste and fair," and of the Amazonian Camillá in Vergil's *Aeneid*.

After having gone forward in time to depict the future conquests of the mature T. C., Marvell, in stanza iv, returns to the present time and to the little girl-goddess in her flowery prospect. The word *prospect* may be used here in a double punning sense: to suggest the future, what is the prospect before T. C., as well as to convey the more obvious sense of view or vista. T. C. is reforming "the errours of the Spring." By

26. See Ernst and Johanna Lehner, *Folklore and Symbolism of Flowers, Plants and Trees* (New York, 1960), p. 78.

doing so, she is strongly identified with the figure of the Virgin, the *hortus conclusus*. Her salvific role as the new Eve postulates the eventual possession of a new Eden. T. C. is creating that new Eden and renewing the Golden Age; the poet bids her

> Make that the Tulips may have share
> Of sweetness, seeing they are fair;
> And Roses of their thorns disarm:
> > But most procure
> That Violets may a longer Age endure.[27]
>
> > > [ll. 28–32]

Why the wistful prayer for the violets' longer duration? Again, the emblem book, *Parthenia Sacra,* provides a clue. Commonly the violet represented humility; it also, however, represented the springtime of promise and awakening. A religious application is made on this ground by Henry Hawkins: "The Spirit of Grace so appearing, and opening the breast, after so tedious a Winter overpast, of horrid Sinne and frozen Infidelitie, our MARIE the *Violet,* or the *Violet-Marie* rather, is put forth, as a joyful present to glad the time withal." [28]

The cautionary advice tendered by the poetic persona in the last stanza appears as something of an afterthought. T. C. is told to be careful not to antagonize Flora by cutting the buds as well as the full-blown flowers, lest, in doing so, she incur that goddess' wrath and herself be untimely plucked, to "Nip in the blossome all our hopes and Thee." It is curious that T. C., whom "Nature courts" and the gods love, should be warned to fear Flora, even though the precariousness of man's position is a familiar theme in Marvell. We will see it in the Mower poems where Damon, before Juliana's coming, lords it over his landscape with as much confidence as T. C. exhibits here. We can only surmise that the poet is suddenly aware, at

27. According to tradition, roses in Eden had no thorns. Hawkins, in *Parthenia Sacra,* hailing Mary, the mystical rose, as the new Eve says, "She sprang likewise from the thornie Eva; but yet tooke not after her nature" (p. 23). Also, *"The Virgin spring even from the barren earth,/ A pure white Rose was in her happie birth,/* Conceav'd without a thorne . . ." (p. 25).

28. *Ibid.,* pp. 42–43.

the end of the poem, of the little girl before him, the real T. C., not the moralized and allegorical figure in his poetic emblem. Though the emblematic T. C. is immortalized in art, the real child is human and vulnerable. Marvell cannot discard his frame of imagery, but within it he can utter his poignant warning to that real child, unaware of the dangers of maturity as she plays in her seventeenth-century garden.

Larger Themes in Emblematic Landscape

The sort of portrait-emblem that provided theme and dictated structure in poems like "Bill-borow" and "Little T. C." may also be found in Marvell's more lengthy, elaborate estate poem, "Upon Appleton House," also dedicated to Lord Fairfax. Here, however, as in "The Garden," Marvell has enlarged his scope and varied his method in order to touch more easily on miscellaneous, disparate, sometimes abstruse matters of both ethical and philosophical import. These thematic strands are woven into a unified whole through landscape imagery.[29] To a series of emblematic landscapes—lovely or grotesque, clear or cryptic —the poet adds, as he confronts them, his subtle cautionary text. "Upon Appleton House" (unlike "The Garden") contains no single landscape to whose overriding significance all others defer; rather it reveals successive views which together constitute a putative earthly paradise, a *locus amoenus* beset from within and besieged from without, threatened but maintaining somehow its precarious integrity.

The opening stanzas of "Upon Appleton House" employ architectural imagery to suggest the notion that a man's dwelling to a degree defines him, becoming an emblem of his own nature, though it can never fully contain him or hedge him about as can the nests and dens of lower species. Indeed,

29. See a recent article by David Evett, " 'Paradice's Only Map': The *Topos* of the *Locus Amoenus* and the Structure of *Upon Appleton House*," *PMLA*, LXXXV (1970), 504–13. In its discussion of the role of the *locus amoenus* in Marvell's poem, the article has anticipated certain points made in this chapter, one being that the poem's various themes achieve unity by means of the consistent use of landscape imagery, specifically that of the *locus amoenus*.

more often, man's dwellings err in the opposite direction, being ostentatiously grandiose and "superfluously spread." Marvell asks, "Why should of all things Man unrul'd/ Such unproportion'd dwellings build?" Appleton House is an exception to this self-aggrandizing propensity of man, being "composed . . . Like Nature" to more modest dimensions suitably reflecting Lord Fairfax's humility. Just as Appleton House's comparatively unpretentious size reflects its great master's humility and condescension, so are his other noble qualities revealed through details even more specific and allegorical:

> A Stately *Frontispice of Poor*
> Adorns without the open Door:
> Nor less the Rooms within commends
> Daily new *Furniture of Friends.*
>
> > [ix.65–68]

Significantly this house, the very emblem of its master, is, like Bill-borow, set within an ideal landscape, an unfallen Eden, ruled by Nature not by Art.

> But Nature here hath been so free
> As if she said leave this to me.
> Art would more neatly have defac'd
> What she had laid so sweetly wast;
> In fragrant Gardens, shaddy Woods,
> Deep Meadows, and transparent Floods.
>
> > [x.75–80]

Art is implicitly equated with the more worldly sort of pretensions Marvell has been decrying earlier in the poem—the "Marble Crust" of many a "hollow Palace." Here at Appleton rigid order and uniformity seem too coldly sophisticated and artificial; a qualified delight in disorder stressing variety and contrast reveals an aesthetic still responding to the Nature versus Art antithesis of the earlier Renaissance, with the attendant moral implications of that antithesis. Milton's Eden landscape in *Paradise Lost,* Book IV, is, of course, another instance of the triumph of Nature over Art or of Nature as the

Art of God. A more exaggerated treatment of the Nature versus Art theme occurs in Marvell's "The Mower Against Gardens." The Appleton estate also demonstrates affinities with the art of landscape painting as it was then understood and practiced. Kitty W. Scoular has pointed out that "the qualities which Marvell has discovered in his patron's estate are those valued by seventeenth-century [landscape art] theorists, 'sudden, quicke, and flickering light,' 'an orderly and pleasant confusion,' and 'a strange stealth of change.' " [30] The play of light and shadow, of meadow and stream, of hill and hollow reflect these principles, blending naturalness and diversity with an underlying order which is easy, subtle, but never stiff. The best example of this idyllic, only semi-serious notion of order occurs in the lengthy section (stanza xxxvi ff.) which describes the flower gardens as forts and treats the flowers themselves as "sweet *Militia*."

> When in the *East* the Morning Ray
> Hangs out the Colours of the Day,
> The Bee through these known Allies hums,
> Beating the *Dian* with its *Drumms*.
> Then Flow'rs their drowsie Eylids raise,
> Their Silken Ensigns each displayes,
> And dries its Pan yet dank with Dew,
> And fills its Flask with Odours new.

> These, as their *Governour* goes by,
> In fragrant Vollyes they let fly;
> And to salute their *Governess*
> Again as great a charge they press:
> None for the *Virgin Nymph;* for She

30. The passage quoted is taken from Franciscus Junius, *The Painting of the Ancients* (1638) ; Junius himself is citing Zeuxis. Miss Scoular has also pointed out and illustrated the similarities between Marvell's Appleton landscape with its illusory visual effects and the painter's notion of landscape being "nothing but Deceptive visions, a kind of cousning or cheating your owne Eyes, by your owne consent and assistance," quoting here from Edward Norgate's *Miniatura*. See *Natural Magic,* p. 188.

Seems with the Flow'rs a Flow'r to be.
And think so still! though not compare
With Breath so sweet, or Cheek so faire.

Well shot ye Firemen! Oh how sweet,
And round your equal Fires do meet;
Whose shrill report no Ear can tell,
But Ecchoes to the Eye and smell.
See how the Flow'rs, as a *Parade,*
Under their *Colours* stand displaid:
Each *Regiment* in order grows,
That of the Tulip Pinke and Rose.

[xxxvii–xxxix]

This passage strikes the reader as quintessentially Marvellian in its fanciful elaborations on a theme appropriately chosen to be a light but fitting tribute to Fairfax, the ex-general. The-garden-as-fort conceit, however, is not original with Marvell; he may have borrowed the basic idea and some details of its treatment from Henry Hawkins' *Parthenia Sacra.* The first emblem in this collection of twenty-four depicts a walled garden with flower beds (roses, violets, tulips, lilies, and many others—all of emblematic significance), trees (palm and olive), and a central fountain. The emblem is followed by an "essay" which consistently uses the kind of martial imagery that Marvell employs in the passage cited above and elsewhere in this section of "Upon Appleton House." Hawkins' presiding spirit in this essay is the rose (as we have seen, a traditional symbol of the Virgin, the "mystical rose" in religious emblem books); he mentions the "Garrison of thornes, that serves for a Corps-de-guard to that Queene of flowers." [31] Marvell's *"Virgin Nymph"* is "Maria," Fairfax's daughter, who is presented in the lines cited above as a flower among flowers, not saluted by their "fragrant Vollyes" only because she seems herself to be one of them. The warlike images in *Parthenia Sacra* are echoed in the stanzas quoted. These can be compared with the following passage:

31. *Parthenia Sacra,* p. 9.

71

I will not take upon me to tel al; for so of a Garden of flowers, should I make a labyrinth of discourse, and should never be able to get forth. Cast but your eyes a little on those goodlie Allies, as sowed al over with sands of gold, drawne-forth so streight by a line. Those cros-bowes there (be not affrayed of them) they are but cros-bowes made of Bayes; and the Harque-busiers, wrought in Rosmarie, shoot but flowers, and dart forth musk. . . . Al those armed Men with greenish weapons . . . are but of Prim, Isop, and Tyme, all hearbs very apt to historify withal. I wil quite passe over those little Groves, Thickets, and Arbours, and speake nothing of those Pety-canons there. . . . Behold there the Lillies of ten forts. . . .[32]

Hawkins calls his garden a "Paradice of flowers" and employs several characteristics of the *locus amoenus,* long since Christianized. Birds "descant" here, flowers have "enameled" the bushes, and the "ayre" is filled with their perfume. Marvell, too, wants the reader to realize the paradisal quality of Fairfax's garden, and here his moral flavors his wit. Only in this little Eden do flowery sentinels suffice; the rest of England is a fallen world:

> Oh Thou, that dear and happy Isle
> The Garden of the World ere while,
> Thou *Paradise* of four Seas,
> Which *Heaven* planted us to please,
> But, to exclude the World, did guard
> With watry if not flaming Sword;
> What luckless Apple did we tast,
> To make us Mortal, and The Wast?
>
> [xli.321–28]

Even in this Arcadian paradise Marvell cannot forget the political realities of mid-seventeenth-century England. Like the nuns who formerly dwelled in their cloister at Appleton, the poet and his patron may pretend that "these Walls restrain the World without," only to find that world intruding unbidden into their thoughts and symbolically, if temporarily, blighting their landscape's pastoral perfection.

32. *Ibid.,* pp. 8–9.

This intrusion is signaled, in the next section of the poem, by a series of muted but clearly hostile and ultimately destructive acts, beginning with the mocking cries of the giant grasshoppers who from their high perch exult over the shrunken men passing beneath them. These human beings are pictured now as diminished to grasshopper size through another Marvellian inversion:

> And now to the Abbyss I pass
> Of that unfathomable Grass,
> Where Men like Grashoppers appear,
> But Grashoppers are Gyants there:
> They, in there squeking Laugh, contemn
> Us as we walk more low then them:
> And, from the Precipices tall
> Of the green spir's, to us do call.
>
> [xlvii.369–76]

The grassy meadow has become an unfathomable abyss; from its depths insectlike men creep on their way. Their lowly state contrasts with the positions assumed by the plague of giant locusts who from the "Precipices tall" of the grass spears, "in there squeking Laugh, contemn" the men beneath. The negative impression of this image upon the reader is toned down by its wit and the bizarre extravagance of its caricature, but "Precipice" suggests again the "hook-shoulder'd height" of the "unjust" mountains near Bill-borow. The theme of deformity coupled with unseemly elevation is repeated in these lines. The grasshoppers themselves resemble the outsize, predatory insects of Bosch and Brueghel who prey on human victims in paintings like *Hell, The Last Judgment,* and *The Fall of the Magician.* Like Marvell's grasshoppers, these creatures are simultaneously comic and terrifying, and they suggest an imaginative affinity between the poet and these Lowland painters who, a hundred years or more before Marvell, looked out upon the world before them with a moral vision as ironic and eccentric as his own.[33] They too felt drawn to biblical imagery,

33. Ogden and Ogden comment on the extent to which Brueghel's work was known in England before 1660; see *English Taste in*

to iconographic echoes of scriptural disasters—Fall, Flood, Damnation, and Death—made newly powerful by being set forth in a contemporary landscape often, like Appleton, ideal. Like Bosch and Brueghel, Marvell is capable of achieving dramatic impact by using a kind of contrapuntal effect: Flood (lix-lx) or Crucifixion (lxxvii) imagery is placed in disturbing juxtaposition to sunlit meadows and shady groves.

The next destructive force that invades the meadows seems, at first, after the giant grasshoppers, disarmingly ordinary and human. The "tawny mowers" part the sea of grass that surrounds them like "Israalites" passing through the Red Sea—another neat biblical echo that ties the mowers to the grasshoppers two stanzas earlier and to the flood ten stanzas later. The uneasy effect upon the reader, evoked by this association, is heightened by the death not only of the grass but of the birds who nest therein.

> With whistling Sithe, and Elbow strong,
> These Massacre the Grass along:
> While one, unknowing, carves the *Rail*,
> Whose yet unfeather'd Quils her fail.
> The Edge all bloody from its Brest
> He draws, and does his stroke detest;
> Fearing the Flesh untimely mow'd
> To him a Fate as black forebode.
>
> [l.393–400]

A mock war ensues, and the "Death-Trumpets" sound for more slaughtered birds. The *memento mori* connotations of the last two lines of stanza 1 would inevitably have reminded contemporary readers of the many treatments of the "all flesh is grass" theme in emblem books. In these emblems the presence of mowers, bound sheaves or single stalks of grain, and skulls, hourglasses, or a funeral procession are common. Wither

---

Landscape, pp. 13, 32. Ann Berthoff also points out suggestive parallels in Marvell to Brueghel's work (see *The Resolved Soul*, pp. 147, 173). We have reacted similarly though independently, since this chapter was completed before I read her fine recent study of Marvell's major poems.

(Book IV, No. 19) has one emblem which shows an infant with a truss of hay in the foreground and mowers at work in a field in the background. The motto states, *"All* Flesh, *is like the wither'd Hay,/ And, so it springs, and fades away."*

> The Mower now commands the Field;
> In whose new Traverse seemeth wrought
> A Camp of Battail newly fought:
> Where, as the Meads with Hay, the Plain
> Lyes quilted ore with Bodies slain:
> The Women that with forks it fling
> Do represent the Pillaging.

[liii.418–24]

Though the use of the mower figure to represent death is common in emblem books, it is rare in seventeenth-century poetry; indeed, only Marvell uses it more than once in the poetry of the mid-century period. Pierre Legouis, crediting Marvell with the introduction of the mower figure into English verse, regards this contribution as an original and powerful poetic device.[34] The mower has also been given mythic stature by others, most notably William Empson.[35] Into the heretofore highly wrought artifice of his pastoral scene, Marvell has introduced the brutish forcefulness of his peasants. A curious effect is gained by the placement of these lumpish yet vital figures upon the considerably less realistically rendered rural landscape. The reader is reminded that even into the idyllic world of Nun Appleton reality intrudes, a reality that may be healthy but is also gross, one that may both contribute to the agricultural prosperity of Lord Fairfax's estate and underscore the realization that toil and sweat are intrinsic parts of country life in an age of iron, not gold. The presence of death in the mowers' mock war suggests the theme of *Et in Arcadia Ego,* insistently, almost obsessively reiterated in seventeenth-century painting (Guer-

34. *Andrew Marvell, Poet, Puritan, Patriot* (Oxford, 1965), p. 50. Legouis does call attention (p. 90 n.) to Maren-Sofie Røstvig's article (*HLQ,* 1954), crediting Benlowes rather than Marvell with the first use of the mower character in poetry (*Theophilia,* XIII.ii), but Benlowes' mower is a single and incidental figure in his pastoral landscape, not a significant emblematic presence.

35. *Some Versions of Pastoral* (New York, 1960), pp. 122–23.

cino, Poussin, G. B. Castiglione). In pictures on this subject, a tomb, testifying to death's reality even amid Arcadian perfection, could elicit from the rustics who discovered it attitudes varying from incomprehension to resignation or even morbid attraction.

Yet the mower stanzas are one small part of the whole landscape of Appleton and must not be too much emphasized. A parallel to Marvell's kind of inclusiveness occurs in the visual arts, where Ambrogio Lorenzetti's *Good Government in the Country* fuses a number of disparate elements into a thematically and artistically unified whole. While mowers appear in the left foreground and right midground of the painting, they do not dominate the scene but are well integrated into a rural vista. The viewer's eye is initially attracted to the troop of aristocrats on horseback descending the hill, also in left foreground. This picture, perhaps the first in the landscape genre, has interesting iconographic similarities to Marvell's poems on Fairfax's estates at Bill-borow and Nun Appleton. The Sienese painting, done in 1338 or 1339, depicts an idealized but detailed pastoral scene where lord and peasant, hill and valley, field and village are all harmoniously blended into a perfect whole. The small cosmos depicted is a perfect rendition of the *discordia concors.* Whether or not Marvell saw the picture on his Italian sojourn, and it is not unlikely that he did, the spirit of good government and rural harmony that he poetically depicts Fairfax as presiding over is very similar in mood and illustrative detail to Lorenzetti's painting.

The mower figures themselves suggest another visual analogue, again to Peter Brueghel. In his Seasons series *The Harvesters* (see plate 6) is a mowing scene where, in the foreground, two powerful scythe-wielders have, like their poetic counterparts, divided the "Grassy Deeps" of the sea of grain to form "a Lane to either Side." The grass already cut resembles "*Pyramids* of Hay" after being "pil'd in Cocks." In the foreground, some of the mowers, resting after their exertions, eat and drink. Their powerful bodies, somewhat distorted by foreshortening, contrast oddly with the more delicately rendered landscape. One is reminded of Empson's apt phrase, "the Clown as Death," applied to Damon, another mower figure in

Plate 6 Brueghel, *The Harvesters*   The Metropolitan Museum of Art, Rogers Fund, 1919

Marvell's poetry.[36] The stolidity of the mowers is as emphasized as their power, used to "Massacre the Grass along." The range of meanings conjured up by the mowers in this context is richly eschatological, recalling not only death but judgment and a harvest of both rewards and retribution. It is not surprising that Marvell found the mowers in their landscape an effective image and chose to return to deal with it at more length in the so-called mower poems.

The rest of "Upon Appleton House" which treats of the poet's withdrawal into the depths of the woods and his meditation among the trees translates, in terms of changing, kaleidoscopic landscapes, the poet's own chaotic thoughts. Gradually these resolve themselves into a peaceful order, "mirroured" (an image repetitively and suggestively used in the poem) in the regenerated and tranquil order of the *locus amoenus* landscape.

> For now the Waves are fal'n and dry'd,
> And now the Meadows fresher dy'd;
> Whose Grass, with moister colour dasht.
> Seems as green Silks but newly washt.

[lxxix.625–28]

Predictably enough, into this new Eden enters a new Eve, the Latinized "Maria" recalling the ancient Christian tradition, still common in art and emblem books, of considering Mary as the second Eve. Lord Fairfax's daughter resembles that other Mary, represented so often through the image of the *hortus conclusus* or simply painted in a garden setting by countless medieval and Renaissance artists. She bestows beauty on the garden; in turn it offers back to her in tribute the reflected image of her own beauty.

> 'Tis *She* that to these Gardens gaye
> That wondrous Beauty which they have;
> *She* streightness on the Woods bestows;
> To *Her* the Meadow sweetness owes;
> Nothing could make the River be
> So Chrystal-pure but only *She*;

36. *Ibid.*, p. 123.

She yet more Pure, Sweet, Streight, and Fair,
Then Gardens, Woods, Meads, Rivers are.

Therefore what first *She* on them spent,
They gratefully again present.
The Meadow Carpets where to tread;
The Garden Flow'rs to Crown *Her* Head;
And for a Glass the limpid Brook,
Where *She* may all *her* Beautyes look;
But, since *She* would not have them seen,
The Wood about *her* draws a Skreen.

[lxxxvii–lxxxviii]

The "genius" of Appleton turns out to be not Fairfax, as it was in "Upon the Hill and Grove at Bill-borow," but instead his daughter Mary. The landscape, appropriately, is one more suited to Proserpine than to Mars. Even Mars retired kept some vestiges of his former state in the emblematic setting of Bill-borow—the helmet of trees at the top of the hill and the ghostly sound of his armor rattling. Maria's flowery garlands and garden setting are less visually striking than Lord Fairfax's sylvan helmet, perhaps because the former are more conventional, less dramatic and original. At any rate they perform the same emblematic function for her that Fairfax's trees at Bill-borow do for him; they represent certain of her qualities that Marvell wishes to emphasize: her youth, beauty, and innocence are suggested by the flowery landscape, and its subordination to her underscores her "divine" attributes and destiny. She is a nymph, but she is also Eve unfallen and Mary through whom salvation will come. A certain measure of this is playful and hyperbolic but by no means all of it.

At the end of "Upon Appleton House," we remember chiefly the great landscape scenes not so much because of any extraordinary pictorial vividness alone, though that is often there, but because of the heavy freight of meaning with which they have been loaded. Marvell's technique, like the emblem books, combines text and picture; the text is often witty and ingenious while the picture, or basic poetic image, is conventional, even stale. It is the allegorical associations and moral connotations investing the visual image that are of crucial import. The design itself may be commonplace, even crude—a few details to suggest a personified abstraction (Occasion's forelock, Time's scythe) or even the unadorned object itself. So it is with Marvell's landscape imagery. He presents a meadow, a garden, a grove, and then expatiates poetically on the intellectual, ethical, and aesthetic implications of that image, until it is imbued with thematic significance. He does not often elaborate in the manner of Spenser or of Marino, piling up sensuous details around a central image to achieve a lush, pictorial effect. Instead, employing the method of the emblematists, he provides an image economically sketched in a few words, an image which may vary from the eccentric or exotic (like those providing the basic concept for the metaphysical conceit in poetry or the cryptic *impresa* in art) to the conventional *topoi* of the pastoral *locus amoenus*—the trite crystal streams and flowery meadows of the stanzas just quoted from "Upon Appleton House." The image, like the emblem, then becomes the departure point for Marvell's "text," poetic commentary that enlarges the image's associations until it ends by objectifying the ideas Marvell is concerned with in the poem.

Although the themes engaging the poet's attention in "The Garden" are as numerous and heterogeneous as those in "Upon Appleton House," a single emblematic landscape accommodates them all. The attributes and associations with which the image of the garden has been invested are flexibly adapted to Marvell's poetic purpose. The garden is an enclosure; it offers "delicious Solitude," shutting out the world. It is "a Place so pure, and sweet," filled with "sacred plants," an Eden wherein man and nature are perfectly attuned. Though possessing a floral sundial, the garden is essentially timeless; its perfections are unchanging, and man, within this earthly paradise, shares its immutability and self-sufficiency.

The poetic canvas of "The Garden" is so uncommonly allusive that it resists any attempt to label it simply as Hermetic or *libertin,* to see it only as an endorsement of soft primitivism or as a rejection of the courtly love tradition. Its imagery is both classical and Christian, its significance both allegorical and literal. The central theme is a praise of solitude and contemplation; it reveals none of the reservations about retirement implicit in "Upon Appleton House." In "The Garden" public life is dismissed as a vain pursuit of empty honors; "uncessant Labours" can win for men leafy crowns of palm, oak, and bay, but they might more profitably and certainly more delightfully possess the trees themselves by reposing in their shade. By doing so, the poetic narrator has exchanged the "busie companies of men" for the more congenial companionship of "Fair Quiet" and her "Sister dear" Innocence. These allegorical female figures are placed in a garden setting, and the green hue that predominates there is hailed as more beautiful and even more "am'rous" than love's traditional colors of "white and red." The first four stanzas and perhaps the fifth make use of the *topoi* of the *locus amoenus* and recall classical traditions like Epicurean retirement. In stanza vii and those following, the fountain, the bird, and the reference to Eden clearly shift the visual frame of reference to the *hortus conclusus*. Thus biblical imagery is again combined with that deriving ultimately from pagan sources.

The erotic motif, which reaches its height in the controversial fifth stanza, at first appears inconsistent with an explicit repudiation of carnal pleasures in stanzas iii and iv. "Fond lovers, cruel as their Flame," are chided for carving their mistresses' names in these trees whose vegetative beauty far exceeds mere woman's human charms. Only those who, all passion spent, have transferred their affections from girls to groves can find repose here. Marvell's wit plays briefly with the notion that Apollo and Pan pursued Daphne and Syrinx with increased ardor when these maidens became respectively the laurel and the reed. The poet's meditative musings upon the varieties of libidinous expression culminate in the hyperbolic outburst of stanza v:

> What wond'rous Life in this I lead!
> Ripe Apples drop about my head;
> The Lucious Clusters of the Vine
> Upon my Mouth do crush their Wine;
> The Nectaren, and curious Peach,

81

Into my hands themselves do reach;
Stumbling on Melons, as I pass,
Insnar'd with Flow'rs, I fall on Grass.

[ll. 33-40]

Ruth Wallerstein and, more recently and elaborately, Stanley Stewart have insisted upon the importance of the *hortus conclusus* tradition in interpreting this complex poem. To those familiar with emblematic literature, the affinity between Marvell's erotic imagery and that of the Song of Songs is clearly present. Marvell's poetic debts are many, however, and placing his poem within the *hortus conclusus* tradition and the earlier one of the pastoral *locus amoenus* does not exhaust them. Certain similarities exist between the lush exaggeration and pictorial vividness in Marvell's poem and the work of the French *libertin* poets. Especially provocative is a comparison of "The Garden" and Saint-Amant's "Le Melon." Both poets combine sensuous imagery and extravagant wit.[37] We know that Lord Fairfax and his brother-in-law Mildmay Fane translated Saint-Amant's poetry, and Marvell may have come to know "Le Melon" and "La Solitude" through his patron's interest in their author. Another interpretation of the lyric as a Hermetic poem notes that the literary Lord Fairfax was also occupied in translating the Hermetic books while Marvell was at Appleton House.[38] All of these readings stimulate us anew to reexamine the text from a different perspective, and few critics appear willing to respond to Frank Kermode's plea for a moratorium on adding further complications to the analysis of Marvell's work.[39]

Certainly interesting in the context of this poem and its crucial fifth stanza is Ficino's Neoplatonism which Edgar Wind

37. Imbrie Buffum provides a lengthy commentary on the poem with extensive quotations from it. See *Studies in the Baroque From Montaigne to Rotrou* (New Haven, 1957), chap. 4. Ruth Wallerstein has commented on its relevance to Marvell. See *Studies in Seventeenth-Century Poetic,* p. 326.

38. See Maren-Sofie Røstvig, "Andrew Marvell's 'The Garden,' A Hermetic Poem," *ES,* XL (1959), 71.

39. "Marvell Transposed," *Encounter,* XXVII (1966), 77-84.

sees as "marked by a curiously anti-ascetic strain" that considers *voluptas* a noble passion.[40] The sensuous ecstasy of stanza v leads to the contemplative experience of stanza vi in which all forms of created existence are transcended and finally annihilated "To a green thought in a green Shade." [41] Stanley Stewart has demonstrated that this "erotic imagery functions to suggest the innocent fulfillments of the spiritual life" [42] and is perfectly consonant with a tradition quite accustomed to interpreting the Song of Songs allegorically as a yearning of the soul for Christ. H. R. Swardson agrees that the sensual delight in "The Garden" aids rather than destroys the contemplative mind's perceptions.[43]

The sixth and seventh stanzas of "The Garden" come closer than any of Marvell's poetic passages to using the ideal landscape in the sacramental sense that we shall find in certain sections of Milton, like the "Hail Holy Light" opening of Book III. The poet-speaker has divested himself not only of his "Bodies Vest" but of his "otherness," the awareness of his separate human state, and has merged his consciousness with an intuitive, nonrational apprehension of the forms of nature all about him.

> Here at the Fountains sliding foot,
> Or at some Fruit-trees mossy root,
> Casting the Bodies Vest aside,
> My Soul into the boughs does glide:
> There like a Bird it sits, and sings,
> Then whets, and combs its silver Wings;
> And, till prepar'd for longer flight,
> Waves in its Plumes the various Light.

[ll. 49–56]

40. *Pagan Mysteries in the Renaissance,* p. 69.
41. Ruth Wallerstein perceives another similarity to Ficino in stanza vi. The notion of the mind as an ocean which re-creates and transcends forms is, she says, "an emblem for the mind's possession of the forms of all things, forms through which it turns to their essence" (*Studies in Seventeenth-Century Poetic,* p. 328).
42. *The Enclosed Garden,* p. 183.
43. *Poetry and the Fountain of Light* (Columbia, Mo., 1962), p. 100.

One is reminded of Yeats's Byzantine bird "Of hammered gold and gold enameling," but with a difference. Marvell, unlike Yeats, would not say, "Once out of nature I shall never take/ My bodily form from any natural thing"; it is the forms of nature precisely that possess for Marvell the highest significance, and that significance is ultimately moral, not mystical. Marvell does not, in the final analysis, even identify wholly with the singing bird on the fruit tree's bough; he says his soul is "like a Bird." The preference for simile over metaphor here is important. Marvell is still using his landscape and its furnishings emblematically.[44] The bird is content in the landscape of the garden; it "whets, and combs its silver Wings" while preparing "for longer flight." That longer flight is in the indefinite future, however. At present the bird is completely satisfied to maintain a perch in the sunlit garden, to preen its plumes, and to admire their silvery reflection of the garden's "various Light." The soaring, celestial flight toward pure light and ultimate oneness with its source which transfigured the poetic vision in *Paradise Lost* and the *Paradiso* is not congenial to Marvell's kind of insight.

In the last two stanzas of the "The Garden," the poet returns to his praise of solitude, his half-humorous antifemale bias reasserted in the observation that man was better off in that original "happy Garden-state" when he "there walk'd without a Mate." The poem concludes with a reference to the garden's sundial, an image of great emblematic significance [45] usually carrying with it an implicit exhortation to make good use of one's time on earth in order to win heavenly bliss, emulating "th'industrious Bee," another common emblematic figure. In this context, however, their impact is less homely and straight-

44. Rosalie Colie has reproduced an emblem by Camerarius of a preening bird on a bough which provides a striking visual analogue for Marvell's poetic image. See *"My Ecchoing Song": Andrew Marvell's Poetry of Criticism* (Princeton, 1970), fig. 18.

45. For a discussion of the sundial in seventeenth-century gardens, as an emblem for Time's swift passage toward eternity, see Stewart, *Enclosed Garden,* pp. 99–104. A more controversial interpretation of Marvell's sundial as a metaphor of the garden itself may be found in Berthoff, *The Resolved Soul,* pp. 158–61.

forward. Marvell appears to be suggesting a paradoxical moral: he who would use his time well should lose himself in timeless contemplation, in seeming indolence and retirement amid the "herbs and flow'rs" of an unchanging earthly paradise. The poem looks back at one unspoiled garden, that of Eden, and forward to a future paradisal state in which that Eden will be restored. In the meantime, the poet suggests that we on earth can gain intermittently some measure of the bliss which we have lost and, it is hoped, will gain again in moments of solitude and reflection in an ideal landscape representing perfect fulfillment and repose.

The Inverted Pastoral World

Such rapport between man and nature as existed in "The Garden" is not a constant in Marvell's poetry. The dissociation that can occur between the two and between man and woman forms the twin themes of the three poems next to be discussed: "Damon the Mower," "The Mower to the Glo-Worms," and "The Mower's Song." A fourth poem in the mower group, "The Mower Against Gardens," is less interesting because it is not as complex as the other three. It focuses wittily on a variation of the nature versus art theme and castigates man for seducing "plain and pure" Nature until a despoiled and artificial landscape emblematically mirrors forth man's own vices— luxury, vanity, even idolatry and perverted sexuality.[46] The other three poems present a pastoral world still unspoiled but inhabited by a swain who can no longer live in harmony with it; rejected love has dissipated his habitual felicity, and he finds himself, in the course of the poems, progressively more alienated, not only from his beloved but from his pastoral *locus amoenus*, ironically indifferent to his state. Nature's

46. Edward William Tayler points out the not infrequent Renaissance tendency to regard the art of gardening with suspicion, contrasting it with an unspoiled nature "associated with Eden and the Golden Age." Viewed thus, gardens underscore the alienation which has come to exist between man and nature; they serve as a reminder, even a reenactment, of the Fall. See *Nature and Art in Renaissance Literature* (New York, 1964), pp. 16–19, 37.

wholeness and self-sufficiency cannot be communicated to man
—at least until, as in "The Garden," he rejects woman.

Marvell's emblematic method in the mower poems is especially effective. Like Spenser he can adapt selections from the
emblem books to his own purposes as well as create his own
emblems (though usually from natural phenomena rather than
from abstractions or qualities). His own method is so close to
that of the emblem books, it is hard to separate the "borrowed"
emblems from Marvellian inventions. Especially striking similarities exist between Marvell's style and chosen images and
those of George Wither whose *Collection of Emblemes, ancient
and moderne* appeared in 1634 and 1635 (the later edition
containing his four previous books in one volume).[47] Marvell
appears to "quote" Wither's emblems rather frequently. While
they may both be deriving their iconography from a common
source antedating their own work (Wither openly admitted
borrowing his emblems, though he created his own text), it is
not unreasonable to assume that Marvell knew Wither's emblem books and even Wither himself; certainly they had in
common the employment of their talents for the Puritan cause
in the period of the interregnum. Marvell's affinity for Wither's
emblems can be best shown in an examination of the mower
poems which contain some of the poet's most effective emblematic imagery.

In the first of the three mower poems named above, "Damon
the Mower," the poetic protagonist looks back regretfully to
happier days before Juliana's entrance into his Edenic environment sundered those bonds which he had shared with
idyllic nature (specifically objectified in the meadows).
Formerly he had been the lord of this particular corner of creation, exercising the power of life and death over his fields,
growing rich "in hay," finding himself the companion to fairies
and leading them "in their danses soft." This last is a passage
which provides echoes of the fellowship (though not of the
mysticism) granted by the Graces to the shepherd Colin on

47. I have consulted a copy of the 1635 edition in the Newberry
Library collection, and all citations from Wither that follow refer
to this edition.

Spenser's Mount Acidale. Naïvely self-important, this rustic Adam can still boast retrospectively of his central position in his small universe:

> I am the Mower *Damon,* known
> Through all the Meadows I have mown.
> On me the Morn her dew distills
> Before her darling Daffadills.
> And, if at Noon my toil me heat,
> The Sun himself licks off my Sweat.
> While, going home, the Ev'ning sweet
> In cowslip-water bathes my feet.
>
> [vi.41–48]

The coming of Juliana into Damon's earthly paradise is like the entrance of the serpent into Eden. However in a reversal both clever and paradoxical, the serpent is a sacrificial victim offered to the cruel Juliana in hopes of propitiation:

> How long wilt Thou, fair Shepheardess,
> Esteem me, and my Presents less?
> To Thee the harmless Snake I bring,
> Disarmed of its teeth and sting.
>
> [v.33–36]

The snake assumes a greater significance in the poem when the reader recalls its unique position in stanza ii. The terrible summer heat which has seared the meadow and scattered the insects and animals has not affected the snake.

> Oh what unusual Heats are here,
> Which thus our Sun-burn'd Meadows sear!
> The Grass-hopper its pipe gives ore;
> And hamstring'd Frogs can dance no more.
> But in the brook the green Frog wades;
> And Grass-hoppers seek out the shades.
> Only the Snake, that kept within,
> Now glitters in its second skin.
>
> [ii.9–16]

The "unusual Heats" clearly derive from a source that is more emotional than climatic. They are, in stanza i, "scorching like his am'rous Care." This is, furthermore, a "heat the Sun could never raise"; at length we are told directly, in stanza iii, that it emanates from "an higher Beauty," that it is not *"July"* which causes this extreme heat, "But *Juliana's* scorching beams." While this is a conventional enough observation for a lovesick swain to make in a lyric poem of the sixteenth or seventeenth century, Marvell's treatment is characteristically original. The heat which is an amorous fire, a symbol of the mower's "hot desires," has its source in a goddess who must be propitiated by gifts, though she spurns them and the giver. The snake is such a gift—and a puzzling one. Though it would be easy enough to interpret this passage of the poem in Freudian terms, such an interpretation, while superficially plausible, would be misleading. The clue to the snake's meaning lies not in Freud but in Wither, where in no less than five emblems the snake represents prudence.[48] If such an emblematic significance is given to the snake in this poem, not only does its escape from *"Juliana's* scorching beams"* becomes perfectly comprehensible, but its reappearance in stanza v *sans* teeth and sting, as a sacrificial offering to Juliana, obliquely suggests the Mower's willful, even suicidal (see the self-inflicted scythe wound later in the poem) delivering up of both his prudence *and* his manhood to this despoiler of his Eden. The offering of a chameleon is emblematically significant as well. It is associated with the lover's willingness to assume the attitudes, feelings, and desires of the beloved, submerging his own identity in the process.[49]

The Mower sacrifices the sovereignty of his little kingdom and even of himself to his cruel lady. The destruction of the Mower's Eden (signified by the hamstrung frogs, the sunburned vegetation, the scythed grass, as well as by the wounds

48. Book I, No. 5; Book II, Nos. 12 and 47; Book III, No. 17; Book IV, No. 12, *Collection of Emblemes.* In Wither and other emblematists the serpent can also represent wisdom (Book III, No. 8), and frequently, when forming a ring with its tail in its mouth, eternity or infinity (Book I, No. 45; Book II, No. 40; Book III, No. 23). These meanings may have secondary relevance in the iconology of Marvell's poem.

49. See Arthur Henkel and Albrecht Schöne, *Emblemata* (Stuttgart, 1967), p. 666. This emblem shows a chameleon in Cupid's hand with the motto *"Omnis Amatorem Decuit Color."*

of the snake and the Mower) carries weightier reverberations than simply the objectification in pastoral images of Marvell's supposed misogyny. Damon's ingenuous view of himself as the center of the cosmos suggests only a charming temerity to the reader at first. If, however, all nature comes to share in and reflect Damon's own defeat, as in this poem it evidently does, one must translate this seemingly trivial rejection of a lover as perhaps containing a larger symbolic significance than it would have in the conventional Renaissance love lyric of Petrarchan tradition. Damon's world is destroyed by man's (and woman's) weakness and cruelty. Juliana in the fallen world of the Mower's lost earthly paradise provides a portrait that is exactly opposite to Mary Fairfax in her emblematic Eden (the flower-filled garden which reflects the order and harmony with which she invests her world) in "Upon Appleton House." The Mower's field has been sown with thistles by a personified "Love" whose very name is a bitter irony. This Love has a henchman Death who is "a Mower too," ready with his scythe to cut down "those that dye by Loves despight." At the end of the poem, the Mower can only survey his destroyed world and muse on the fatal effects Juliana has had upon it and upon him, an Adam unparadised, no longer the companion of "the deathless Fairyes" and no longer inhabiting a timeless, perfect universe. Bleeding from wounds both physical and psychical, Damon's realization of his vulnerable mortality anticipates a similar discovery by the youth in Dylan Thomas' "Fern Hill": "Time held me green and dying. . . ."

Marvell's next mower poem, "The Mower to the Glo-Worms," presents a brief, four-stanza picture of Damon, voicing his lament while wandering lost through a pastoral landscape, this time given an evening setting, with emblematic flora and fauna. The Mower-lover, a distracted insomniac, addresses his plaint to the Glo-Worms, apostrophizing them as "Ye living Lamps" and "Ye Country Comets" who light the way home for "wandring Mowers"; these "in the Night have lost their aim,/ And after foolish Fires do stray." The nature of these "foolish Fires" is implied rather than stated; they appear to be the fires of love which figured so heavily in the imagery of the previous poem with its references to *"Juliana's* scorching beams" and "the Fires/ Of the hot day, or hot desires." The theme of love in the poem is obliquely introduced as early as line two.

> Ye living Lamps, by whose dear light
> The Nightingale does sit so late,
> And studying all the Summer-night,
> Her matchless Songs does meditate;

The nightingale, in literary as well as emblematic tradition, is associated with a tragic and fatal love, and her "matchless Songs" may be, like the Mower's own, plaintive love songs. The implications of the imagery in this poem are larger and less explicit than is the case in "Damon the Mower," but the tone of the poem throughout makes it clear that love, at least for the Mower, is still neither a source of fulfillment nor a state of bliss.

In stanza ii the allusions to war and the death of princes, though seemingly rejected by the poet as soon as they are uttered, reinforce the somber responses evoked by the Mower's grassy fields, about to be cut down.

> Ye Country Comets, that portend
> No War, nor Princes funeral,
> Shining unto no higher end
> Then to presage the Grasses fall;

Just as the previous poem ended with a reference to death coming after lines devoted to love, so here too the note of mortality is sounded. The anticipated fall of the grass must be associated with the equally imminent fall of the Mower. The popularity of the "all flesh is grass" theme in emblem books has already been noted, and we have learned by now that the Mower and his meadow are to be closely associated, even identified with each other. This identification is explicitly made in the opening lines of the next poem, "The Mower's Song":

> My Mind was once the true survey
> Of all these Medows fresh and gay;
> And in the greenness of the Grass
> Did see its Hopes as in a Glass;

When *Juliana* came, and She
What I do to the Grass, does to my Thoughts and Me.

[i.1–6]

The "greenness" of the grass belongs, of course, to time past, to a hopeful, youthful spring rather than to summer's maturity which looks toward the harvest-death of autumn. The fields are called the Mower's "Glass"; they mirror not his physical form but his soul, once full of hope (represented by the color green), now despairing and lost.

It is this dislocation from his environment that receives the strongest stress in "The Mower to the Glo-Worms"; along with a sense of impending doom, the Mower is conscious of a feeling of alienation. Once again, the reader is reminded of the Fall and the expulsion from Paradise. The Mower's nocturnal wanderings take on larger dimensions than they appeared to have at the beginning of the poem. The darkness of the night matches the darkness of his mind as, in stanza iv, he knows himself forever isolated, excluded from his former earthly paradise: [50]

Your courteous Lights in vain you wast,

Since *Juliana* here is come,
For She my Mind hath so displac'd
That I shall never find my home.

The sentiments expressed in this poem bear a strong resemblance to lines appended by George Wither to his emblem forty in Book I of *Collection of Emblemes*. The emblem itself, titled "cosi vivo piacer conduce a morte," depicts a fly attracted to the light of a burning candle. The latter is imposed upon a landscape background in which, at left, lovers dally in a wood and, at right, two men (rivals for a lady?) duel on a seashore. The first twelve lines of the verse paragraph warn the curious fly to avoid the perils of the flame which is pre-

---

50. As Donald M. Friedman suggests, "Juliana can stand for whatever it is that lures man's mind away from its true communion with nature, and from the moral ends proper to a rational being" (see *Marvell's Pastoral Art* [Berkeley and Los Angeles, 1970], p. 136).

dictably enough associated with woman and the scorching fires of love. These lines more closely recall the imagery of the previous Marvell poem, "Damon the Mower," but the rest of the passage from Wither (quoted below) exhibits striking similarities to "The Mower to the Glo-Worms." It echoes the phrase "foolish Fires" and the notion of "unwary *Travellers*" being led astray in the night by *"Wandring-Fires,"* until "they have altogether lost their way."

> Remember, then, this *Emblem;* and, beware
> You be not playing at such harmefull Games:
> Consider, if there sit no *Female,* there,
> That overwarmes you, with her *Beauties Flames.*
> Take heed, you doe not overdally so
> As to inflame the Tinder of *Desire;*
> But, shun the Mischiefe, e're too late it grow,
> Lest you be scorched in that *Foolish-Fire.*
>   For, as those *Wandring-Fires* which in the Night,
> Doe leade unwary *Travellers* astray,
> Alluring them, by their deceiving *Sight,*
> Till they have altogether lost their way:
> Right so, fantasticke *Beauty* doth amaze
> The Lust-full *Eye,* allures the *Heart* aside,
> Captives the *Senses* (by a sudden blaze)
> And, leaves the *Judgement* wholly stupify'd.
> Nay, if Men play too long about those *Torches,*
> Such is the Nature of their wanton *Flame,*
> That, from their Bodies (unawares) it scorches
> Those *Wings* and *Feet,* on which they thither came.
> It wastesth (ev'n to nothing) all their *Wealth,*
> Consumes their precious *Time,* destroyes their *Strength,*
> Bespots their *Honest-Fame,* impaires their *Health,*
> And (when their Fatall Thread is at the length)
>   That thing, on which their Hope of *Life* is plac't,
>   Shall bring them to *Destruction,* at the last.

It is possible to see the destruction, alluded to above, as a spiritual as well as a psychological threat. The moralist might well suspect that the "home" which the Mower will now never find may refer to a heavenly rather than an earthly dwelling. Some knowledge of emblematic imagery helps to clarify many of the graver moral implications that underlie the light tone and often noncommital vocabulary of the poem. The bucolic landscape of the Mower poems continually illustrates the concept of Renaissance pastoral as "one distinct mode of allegory, of the order, if not the gravity, of the tragic." [51]

Whether or not the poet meant it to be so, a kind of climax of despair is reached in the last of the mower poems, "The Mower's Song." Again Marvell's deliberately nonidealized rustic, disappointed in love, is placed incongruously in an ideal landscape, where he recalls his former happy state and contrasts it with his present wretchedness. [52] As his thoughts become progressively more suicidal, his bitterness is increasingly directed against nature with which he enjoyed, before the coming of Juliana, a harmonious self-identification. When, therefore, the Mower decides, at the end of the poem, to employ his scythe against the green and flowery meadows in order both to gain revenge for their lack of "Compassion" and to obtain flowers to deck his tomb, Marvell succeeds in using the pastoral elegy tradition against itself in an inversion both fresh and powerful. In "The Mower's Song" the meadows, fresh, green, and progressively more luxuriant throughout the poem, quickly achieve a prominence almost equal to the Mower's own. They, not Juliana, are called "unthankful" for rejecting "a fellowship so true" with the Mower and for continuing their "gawdy May-games," while he, in a paradoxical reversal, lies "trodden under feet." The two, Mower and meadows, simultaneously occupy the world of the poem, producing an ironic, purposely disharmonious counterpoint instead of the conventional pastoral lament in which nature reflects the mood of the dejected swain. The long last line of each stanza functions as a kind of metrical underscoring that intensifies the impression of the Mower as out of tune with his idyllic pastoral environment. The abrupt change of rhythm is almost comic and effectively

51. Richard Cody, *The Landscape of the Mind* (Oxford, 1969), p. 3.
52. As Harold Toliver says, "The Mower's Song" is "a song of experience in which innocence is all but destroyed" ("Pastoral Form and Idea in Some Poems of Marvell," *Texas Studies in Literature and Language,* V [1963], 96).

distances the reader from the Mower's woe, by seeming to
mock it. The Mower, then, suffers in isolation, while an un-
feeling nature and an unresponsive Juliana both flourish.

> But these, while I with Sorrow pine,
> Grew more luxuriant still and fine;
> That not one Blade of Grass you spy'd
> But had a Flower on either side;
> When *Juliana* came, and She
> What I do to the Grass, does to my Thoughts and Me.
>
> [ii.7–12]

A correspondence between Marvell's poem and a similar
approach to man in nature can again, as in the mower section
of "Upon Appleton House," be perceived in the visual arts in
the work of Peter Brueghel the Elder. W. H. Auden's poem,
"Musée des Beaux Arts," is a memorable tribute to Brueghel's
theme of the isolated sufferer in an indifferent universe. Over
and over in Brueghel, too, appear the clownish rustics in an
ideal landscape who, suffering, rejoicing, or toiling, seem a
clumsy intrusion on the rural scene—realistic Flemish peasants
out of harmony with their Vergilian surroundings. There is
pathos rather than tragedy in Damon's act of destruction; there
is even an undercurrent of mockery in the pretension inherent
in the Mower's designation of the meadow flowers as "the
Heraldry . . ./ With which I shall adorn my Tomb." These
lines recall the naïve self-importance of the Mower before
Juliana's entrance into his life ("I am the Mower *Damon,*
known/ Through all the Meadows I have mown"). Marvell's
denial of heroic stature to his rustic sufferer maintains the
lyric's requisite witty tone; it does not, however, lessen the impact of its moral force.

The identification of the Mower with his meadow in the
mower poems permits, as we have seen, the fate of the meadow
(from green and flourishing to withered and destroyed) to represent allegorically the life of the Mower. The same point is
elaborately made in another of Wither's emblems (Book I,
No. 44) which depicts two large bound sheaves in the foreground against a background scene in which mowers labor to

harvest the grain. The opening lines of the appended verse present the meadows in their springtime freshness:

> When, in the sweet and pleasant Month of *May,*
> We see both Leaves and Blossomes on the Tree,
> And view the *Meadowes* in their best array,
> We hopefull are a *Joyfull-Spring* to see;

This picture is succeeded by one showing the destruction of the grass, now bereft of *"Sweetnesse"* and *"Beautie,"* with the observation, "Such is the state of ev'ry mortall Wight." The obvious lesson is explicated in the lines that follow:

> But, let us learne to *heed,* as well as *know,*
> That, *Spring* doth passe; that, *Summer* steales away;
> And, that the *Flow'r* which makes the fairest show,
> E're many Weekes, must wither and decay.

Marvell's verse stops short of Wither's optimistic conclusion, which implies that in losing this life we shall be reborn into a better one. The grain of wheat that must fall into the earth before it can bring forth fruit is the comforting coda to most sobering meditations on the theme of "all flesh is grass." Marvell omits it; a "happy ending" would blunt his ironic effect as well as point too explicit a moral. He may take an idea from Wither or another emblematic source, but he uses it imaginatively and selectively. J. B. Leishman's assessment of these poems pays tribute to their author's unique ability to blend "the conceptual and the pictorial," while calling the mower poems "perhaps the most wholly characteristic of Marvell's pastorals." [53]

Bosch and Brueghel: Pictorial Parallels to Marvell's Ideal Landscapes

The stress upon Marvell's emblematic method in this chapter should not be allowed to leave the impression that emblem

---

53. *The Art of Marvell's Poetry* (London, 1966), p. 130.

books provide the only context within which to study Marvell's poetic pictorializations. While the emblematic style combining picture and text and allegorically revealing its attendant moral connotations is congenial to the poet, he also exhibits an affinity with another visual genre—certain landscape paintings by the Dutch Hieronymus Bosch (1450–1516) and the Flemish Peter Brueghel (1520–69). Both painters share with Marvell an ironic eye, a deliberately ambiguous tone, and a strong moral viewpoint. All three make satiric use of the grotesque and fantastic—like Marvell's giant grasshoppers in "Upon Appleton House." Brueghel, like Marvell, often effectively combines an idyllic pastoral landscape with relentlessly realistic, often suffering figures—like the Mower.

An especially striking parallel to Marvell's "The Garden" exists in Bosch's *The Garden of Earthly Delights* (see plate 5). As a conclusion to this chapter, a brief discussion of this parallel may provide a perspective for viewing Marvell's garden imagery (and some of his larger landscapes as well), since painter and poet share both themes and iconography.

The Garden of Earthly Delights, acknowledged as Bosch's masterpiece, was painted about 1500. A triptych, it was displayed first in the Escorial and is now in the Prado. It is a work that makes use of a landscape of symbols that are enigmatic, even eccentric. Probably Marvell saw it while in Spain; certainly he would have remembered it. At the left, a narrow panel depicts the creation of Eve in a pastoral setting of dreamlike fantasy. Adam, newly wakened, gazes upon her with a certain tentative, wary pleasure; her downcast gaze is as much withdrawn as demure. Compared to Michelangelo's more famous Adam, that of Bosch appears vulnerable, even frail. At right a matching panel depicts Hell in grotesque, nightmare images. The center portion of the triptych, twice as large as the other two, portrays The Garden of Delights, a crowded canvas of nudes, both male and female, of giant fruits, birds, and fish, of strange surrealistic forms both animate and inanimate. All inhabit a *locus amoenus* landscape where sun and shade, meadow, grove, and stream are pleasingly if fantastically portrayed. The many interpretations of this central panel rival in number and variety the interpretations of Marvell's "Garden."[54] Two suggestive parallels with Marvell's poem are worthy of note. One is the use of fruit—gorgeous, huge, brilliantly colored strawberries, grapes, and cherries—in an obviously sexual sense, in repeated and intimate juxtaposition with the nude human forms in various attitudes all over the panel. The effect is lush but disquieting. What at first may appear to be the kind of innocent eroticism of Marvell's paradisal garden is, upon closer inspection, the symbolic depiction of a fallen, perverted Eden.[55] Teeming humanity, dwarfed by grotesque, outsized animal forms and bizarre architectural structures, fills this central panel. The contrast with the panel at left, the creation of Eve, is dramatic: the "Fair quiet," "Innocence," and "delicious Solitude" seen in Bosch's Eden as well as in Marvell's garden are forever fled. Bosch also appears to share Marvell's negative view of human sexuality in "The Garden," offering a visual equivalent of the poet's judgment:

> Such was that happy Garden-state,
> While Man there walk'd without a Mate:
>
> [viii]

The "delights" in Bosch's garden are spurious; they lead to damnation not contemplation, if one accepts a progression from left (Eden) to right (Hell) while viewing the triptych. Marvell's condemnation of *voluptas* is more ambiguous and less inclusive in "The Garden," but this difference between painter and poet is not of major importance. In neither, of course, is the sexual motif meant to be narrowly interpreted but must be

54. A number of colored plates and a selection of often contradictory critical commentary, from the mid sixteenth century to contemporary times, can be found in Hieronymus Bosch, *The Garden of Delights*, ed. Wolfgang Hirsch (London, 1954).

55. The earliest commentator on Bosch's painting, Fray José Siguenza, writing in 1560, praises the vigor and power with which Bosch portrays his moral universe. Fray José points up the apparently well-known use of the strawberry as a symbol for the alluring but transitory pleasures of this life (*ibid.*, p. 16).

97

understood in a wider, metaphoric sense which includes man's creative, generative urge and his perversion of it.

Of great significance is the similar concept of man in nature that Bosch and Marvell share. The garden, whether an enclosure or a pastoral *locus amoenus,* is a reminder of man's original innocence. It can be perverted, until nature itself is as fallen as the humanity which inhabits it. It can also be regenerative, even when its original power has been lost and can be recalled only through retrospective meditation. It can finally be a refuge, an unspoiled enclave like Nun Appleton, shutting out, if only for a time, the world's corruption. Poet and painter alike make flexible and suggestive use of the iconography of Eden and Arcadia.

In seeking out visual analogues for Marvell's pictorial landscapes, one returns again and again to Bosch and to Brueghel in order to supplement what the emblem books reveal about the poet's painterly imagination and experience of the visual arts. Marvell shares with these other artists a strong affection for earthly beauty, especially as revealed in landscape, an intense though often ironic moral sense, and an individualistic tendency to blend the bizarre—and even the grotesque—with the ideal and idyllic. The effect is witty in the highest sense, an attempt to reconcile profoundly antithetical aspects of man's existence which the artist perceives intuitively to be somehow complementary. Though Marvell's purpose is ultimately to instruct, his poetic landscapes are primarily visions of delight—emblems of the world as Earthly Paradise, lost now but poetically reconstructed.

Plate 7 Sacchi, *The Divine Wisdom*   Gabinetto Fotografico Nazionale, Rome

⚞ 3 ⚟

Milton's Epic Landscapes:
Responses to the
Classical Baroque

Milton's spatial sense is reflected in two ways in the landscape passages of the poet's great epics. At times baroque movement, intensity of light and darkness, and a feeling of vast,
limitless space combine to produce effective "cosmic" landscapes. These coexist, within the framework of the poem, with
more classically ordered, static, and self-contained settings. Both
can be highly visual though they are less often pictorial in the
strict sense (i.e., like a picture), owing not so much to the poet's
lack of sight as to his evident lack of sophistication in the visual
arts. Generality need not be a barrier to pictorial passages, as
we shall discover when analyzing Dryden's landscapes, but Milton's descriptions are sometimes vague as well as nonparticularized. His order is almost invariably miscellaneous; the
ingredients of a Miltonic landscape are offered in what appears
to the reader a haphazard sequence, ungoverned by certain
painterly conventions which operate in Augustan poetry of natural description. These conventions include isolating and emphasizing the focal points of a scene; they also require working
in an orderly progression from foreground to distant view, or,
not as frequently, moving from less carefully delineated back-

ground elements to details prominent in the foreground of a landscape setting.

Despite these relatively technical limitations on his pictorialism, Milton possesses a strong visual sense, as Don Cameron Allen has asserted, questioning T. S. Eliot's allegation that Milton responded more to aural than to visual stimuli. While acknowledging that imagery designed to appeal to the eye requires "words suggesting color, shape, and motion," Allen adds that much depends as well upon "the imaginative faculty of the reader."[1] A visually sensitive reader, most especially an artist, as we have seen in Milton's case, is more likely to perceive subtle visual nuances in poetry than one less endowed. It is particularly in Milton's epic landscapes, both terrestrial and cosmic, that a classical baroque ideality is coupled with a strongly visual sense to produce a literary pictorialism which is both uniquely Miltonic and, at the same time, highly reminiscent of the Italianate ideal landscapes of the sixteenth and seventeenth centuries. Another English poet, touring Italy almost exactly two hundred years later, appears to have recognized to what extent Milton's epic landscapes were an expression of his poetic spirit:

> for his Spirit is here;
> In the cloud-piercing rocks doth her grandeur abide,
> In the pines pointing heavenward her beauty austere;
> In the flower-besprent meadows his genius we trace
> Turned to humbler delights, in which youth might confide,
> That would yield him fit help while prefiguring that Place
> Where, if Sin had not entered, Love never had died.[2]

The Landscape of Epic

Cromwell's chaplain, Peter Sterry, Puritan, Platonist, and Milton's associate, once wrote a catechism which contained this entry:

1. *The Harmonious Vision, Studies in Milton's Poetry* (Baltimore, 1954), p. 96.
2. William Wordsworth, "At Vallombrosa," *Memorials of a Tour in Italy, 1837, The Complete Poetical Works*, Cambridge ed. (Cambridge, Mass., 1932), p. 754.

Q. What was Paradise?
A. Paradise was the Similitude and Presence of God in the whole Creation. The creation was a Garden: All the Creatures were Divine Flowers in this Garden, animated with a Divine Life, cloth'd with a Divine Beauty, breathing a Divine Sweetness. Every one did bear the Figure of, and answer to a Glory in the Face of God: The Face of God was as a Sun, shining with all its Glories upon these Flowers, distilling its own Influence upon them, attracting their Sweetnesses to itself; descending into them, drawing them up into itself. This was the Divine Similitude, and the Divine Presence in the Creation, the Earthly Paradise; In the midst of Man stood this Paradise; In the midst of this Paradise Man walk'd.[3]

These lines help to reveal another facet of Milton's mind which balanced the baroque and Italianate forces influential in his epic poems. Like Peter Sterry, Milton was a Puritan and an Englishman. Though his Platonism was not appreciably different from Tasso's, for instance, the religious orientation which accompanied it certainly was. A moralistic emphasis was characteristic of both Protestant and Catholic art and aesthetics during the Renaissance, but the mystical or visionary element in religious art and literature found its expression in rather different ways. To generalize is risky; yet it is possible to recognize in Northern art and literature with a religious theme a fidelity to the things of earth and a ready acceptance of what was concrete and everyday. These qualities were coupled with an instinct for analogy that encouraged poets and painters to discern what was unseen in what was seen and to transcend the ordinary by using it to help express the inexpressible. If Bernini's St. Teresa seems in her ecstasy to have repudiated earth and to be poised only momentarily in her flight heavenward, Bunyan's Christian, on the other hand, plods along a very terrestrial highway en route to the same heavenly kingdom. Though these are extreme examples, they serve the purpose of illustration and aid us in realizing that Milton's art is much more elusive than either Bernini's or Bunyan's and much less easily categorized.

3. Cited in Louis Martz, *The Paradise Within* (New Haven and London, 1961), p. 33.

Like so many writers on religious themes, Milton uses landscape in a way that is obviously symbolic. Life as a journey,
Eden as God's garden—these are archetypal symbols, ancient,
pre-Christian, and endlessly reinterpreted, the kinds of symbols, in short, congenial both to Milton and to his two Puritan
contemporaries, however widely they differ stylistically. Jackson Cope suggests the way such symbols function when he says
that in *Paradise Lost* "scene continually acts as mimesis of argument."[4] Somewhat the same point of view lies at the heart of
Northrop Frye's discussion of the theory of symbols. Using
Aristotle's terms, Frye identifies the *mimesis praxeos,* or imitation of an action, with the *mythos,* or narrative. Attempting to
relate this narrative element to a poem's meaning or *dianoia,*
he asserts that each should complement and include the other;
this is true especially in classically ordered literature. The result is that "the *mythos* is the *dianoia* in movement; the *dianoia*
is the *mythos* in stasis."[5]

It is in such a way that Milton's ideal landscapes function in
Paradise Lost and, to a lesser extent, in *Paradise Regained.* They
symbolically represent or objectify the poems' thematic content;
the poet's argument is obliquely set forth in the iconography of
his landscapes. At this point the baroque, Italianate, and even,
to a degree, the Counter-Reformational elements mix and
mingle with those aspects of Milton's mind and art which are
characteristically English and Puritan. These "foreign" qualities contribute to the various kinds of pictorialism that the
imagery of his landscapes suggests. Analyses of selected passages
are necessary to demonstrate this point. Prior to presenting such
analyses, however, it would be useful to indicate two general
categories into which most of Milton's epic landscapes fall.
First, though he does not do so invariably, Milton has a tendency to embody the meaning of the Eden landscape in emblematic pictorial forms which emphasize the moral, philosophical,
or ethical element in his epic scheme; his treatment of the landscapes of *Paradise Regained* stems from a similar objective.

4. *The Metaphoric Structure of Paradise Lost* (Baltimore, 1962),
p. 76.
5. *Anatomy of Criticism* (Princeton, 1957), p. 83.

Here he is perhaps most like Spenser and, to some extent, like Marvell, revealing an imagination that is traditionally English and at times highly didactic, showing the influence of wide learning, both classical and continental. Second, the cosmic and panoramic landscapes of the epics, alternatively (especially *Paradise Lost*), seem closer in their visual qualities to the baroque, largely Italian art of the seventeenth century. These poetic landscapes are more likely to be of the symbolic kind labeled "sacramental" in chapter 1—grand, mystical, and apocalyptic. Milton's heavens are usually designed to "show forth the glory of God"; his earth is a metaphor of man's sinless state, lost at the Fall. Each kind of ideal landscape has been precisely structured in order to endow it with that visual quality which will best communicate poetic subtleties in an indirect yet meaningful way. Jackson Cope has asserted that the very form of *Paradise Lost* has been "composed in the manner of a painting," until "metaphoric tenor and vehicle merge, an inevitable process in painting, where the artist must visually express a theme which cannot be discursively appropriated to the form, but a distinctively rare achievement in longer literary works."[6] Somewhat analogous is Serge Eisenstein's remark that "the structure of *Paradise Lost* was conceived . . . cinematographically," in a succession of scenes.[7]

Since Milton's pictorial landscapes contribute intrinsically to both theme and structure in the epics, their importance is fundamental. Their stylistic mode determines the nature of their impact; therefore, at the conclusion of this section the characteristics of a baroque heroic landscape are enumerated and then illustrated by referring to visual parallels in the sister art of painting.

Milton's cosmic landscapes exhibit an affinity with the illusionistic ceiling paintings so characteristic of baroque art. Like Andrea Sacchi (1599–1661) and Pietro da Cortona (1596–1669), whose work he saw at the Barberini Palace, he often uses allegorical personifications (Sin, Death) to populate the vastness of his planetary space; natural personifications (Night, the

6. *The Metaphoric Structure of Paradise Lost,* pp. 75–76.
7. Cited in John Arthos, *Dante, Michelangelo and Milton* (London, 1963), p. 106.

Moon) abound as well. Such repetitive, almost invariable use of personification is typical of heroic landscape. Another quality Milton shares with the two aforementioned artists is an instinctive appreciation for the contribution of chiaroscuro effects to such cosmic landscapes: deepening the sense of mystery, heightening the dramatic impact, and intensifying thematic polarities like good and evil, salvation and damnation, wisdom and ignorance. Much scholarly attention has been paid, and rightly so, to Milton's preoccupation with light and darkness. In his most sacramental landscapes both light and darkness possess a mystical force equal to that exhibited in Michelangelo's apocalyptic visions of Creation and Judgment painted on the ceiling of the Sistine Chapel. In addition to the use of various types of pictorial personification and the extensive employment of chiaroscuro, Milton resembles baroque painters in the frequency with which he incorporates movement into his scenes. This movement is invariably vertical; it is also highly dramatic— soaring or plunging angels test the boundaries of a limitless universe.

As a visual analogy to Milton's sacramental landscapes, we may instance the ceiling frescoes of Cortona and Sacchi in the two largest salons of the Barberini Palace. The movement of the figures, even in the corner structures; the floating forms, dramatic and monumental; the use of mythological illustrations with an allegorical significance—all of these characteristics of Cortona's work in the Great Salon have affinities with *Paradise Lost*. Even more provocative as a possible part of Milton's *musée imaginaire* is Sacchi's painted ceiling in the second-largest room of the Palace (see plate 7). The design is grandly intellectual in concept, depicting Divine Wisdom presiding over "The rising world of waters dark and deep,/ Won from the void and formless infinite" (*Paradise Lost*, III.11–12). The central figure, crowned, queenly, surrounded by a sunburst of radiant light, perfectly evokes Milton's Urania, the invocation to whose mysterious powers begins Book III of *Paradise Lost*. Cortona's theme is Divine Providence, Sacchi's Divine Wisdom; both of Milton's epic poems reflect these two themes, highly congenial in their cosmic scope to baroque art attempting to express infinitude.

Even on earth a sense of vastness persists in the epics; only the space of the Edenic *locus amoenus* in *Paradise Lost* is circumscribed. Milton's consistently panoramic vistas are another baroque manifestation, adding a solemn grandeur to certain significant passages. Although a century after Milton's death, it was quite unremarkable for a poet to begin a poem

> Let observation, with extensive view,
> Survey mankind, from China to Peru;

no such offhand calling up of the prospect view was natural to Milton. In *Paradise Lost,* Book II, his prospect has a strangeness and solemnity attested to by Adam's reaction to the panorama Michael discloses from the Paradisal mount: he closes his eyes and sinks to the ground, "all his Spirits . . . intranst."

> It was a Hill
> Of Paradise the highest, from whose top
> The Hemisphere of Earth in clearest Ken
> Strecht out to the amplest reach of prospect lay.[8]
>
> [XI.377–80]

The passage continues with explicit but nonpictorial references to ancient empires, again from China (*"Cambalu,* seat of *Cathaian Can"*) to Peru ("the richer seat/ Of *Atabalipa"*). Inevitably a moment of stasis in the epic action is created as Michael and Adam observe the series of scenes constituting mankind's history from the Fall to the Flood. Parenthetically, it is interesting to note the decline in poetic vividness and in emotional power which occurs in Book XII when Adam's "mortal sight" finally fails and Michael must relate rather than show the events from the Flood to the founding of the Church.

Milton's Eden is notably less baroque than either his earthly prospects or celestial expanses tend to be. Intensities of light and shadow are more muted; movement is less frequent and theatrical; and a sense of vast, boundless space gives way to the intimate serenity of a pastoral setting. Certain classicizing tend-

---

8. All references to *Paradise Lost* will be to the edition prepared by Merritt Y. Hughes (New York, 1962).

encies become apparent. Stasis suspends the action while figures are carefully posed in a garden. Eve resembles a Venus by Titian; ideal form is delineated in an ideal landscape, while Adam possesses the sculpturesque dignity and grace of Poussin's *Bacchus-Apollo,* presiding over a sylvan paradise. But now and then a feeling of baroque opulence disturbs Milton's classical moments. At such times he may recall Rubens, in a painting like *The Judgment of Paris,* lingering almost too long over a goddess' elaborately curled hair or the crimson sheen of her brocaded robe. This sort of vacillation between two styles was typical of both verbal and visual arts during the restless seventeenth century. Milton's pictorialism may often enough lack technical refinements, but his instinct for the most effective style to use in a given landscape never fails him. He is rarely decorative, though Henri Glaesner perceives Ovidian touches (Philemon and Baucis in *Metamorphoses*) in Adam and Eve's entertainment of Raphael.[9] He is also rarely emblematic in the way of Marvell; rather he tends to expand the fairly specific moral correspondences characteristic of the emblematic style until they take on a larger symbolic meaning.

Most characteristic of Milton is the sacramental landscape which is congenial to his prevailingly baroque style and consonant with his epical ambition to "justify the ways of God to men."

Paradise Lost

While it is a relatively simple matter to find and examine brief passages which contain different kinds of highly effective visual imagery, it would be misleading to conclude from these instances that Miltonic landscapes in *Paradise Lost* were usually painted in such miniatures and vignettes. It is far more characteristic for the poet to create his visual effects cumulatively, building them up gradually in sizable segments of certain books, notably Books IV (Eden) and VII (Creation). To some extent

9. "Le Voyage de Milton en Italie, Prélude au *Paradis perdu,*" *Revue de littérature comparée,* XVI (1936), 309–10.

this style is also characteristic, on a less sustained level, of the vision given to Adam in Book XI.

The analysis of these larger ideal landscapes is hampered by their unwieldy length and by their relative dearth of quotable short segments. Milton's epic generality does not lend itself to the scholarly equivalent of an excision and examination of a microscopic slice of tissue that can reveal a whole organism's qualities. There are a few exceptions—one is the first description of Eden surrounded by that Salvatorian "steep savage Hill" which offers the kind of contrast between the wildly sublime and the delicately beautiful that beguiled eighteenth-century eyes.

> So on he fares, and to the border comes
> Of *Eden,* where delicious Paradise,
> Now nearer, Crowns with her enclosure green,
> As with a rural mound the champaign head
> Of a steep wilderness, whose hairy sides
> With thicket overgrown, grotesque and wild,
> Access deni'd; and over head up grew
> Insuperable highth of loftiest shade,
> Cedar, and Pine, and Fir, and branching Palm,
> A Silvan Scene, and as the ranks ascend
> Shade above shade, a woody Theatre
> Of stateliest view. Yet higher than thir tops
> The verdurous wall of Paradise up sprung:
> Which to our general Sire gave prospect large
> Into his nether Empire neighboring round.
> And higher than that Wall a circling row
> Of goodliest Trees loaden with fairest Fruit,
> Blossoms and Fruits at once of golden hue
> Appear'd, with gay enamell'd colors mixt:
> On which the Sun more glad impress'd his beams
> Than in fair Evening Cloud, or humid Bow,
> When God hath show'r'd the earth; so lovely seem'd
> That Lantskip:
>
> [IV.131–53]

Although in twenty-three lines Milton manages more specific details than usual, even here, especially once the general prospect view succeeds the rugged wilderness of the foreground, more is suggested than delineated.[10] The scene develops vertically; Satan, its observer, is flying up toward the summit of a mountain where Paradise is situated. The traditional ingredients of classical ideal landscapes are duly struck off: the catalogue of trees or mixed forest (l. 139), the requisite shade (l. 141), the fruits and blossoms existing at once (ll. 147–48). Within the next hundred lines or so, Milton adds the traditional perfumed breezes, water from river and fountain, green lawns, and singing birds. But the description remains largely general, and visual detail is not abundant.

Adam and Eve make their entrance on this carefully prepared stage in l. 288. The *locus amoenus* setting has been designed to mirror their own perfections; they themselves are described in terms reminiscent of the many paintings of gods and goddesses which were exercises in the depiction of ideal form from the time of the High Renaissance. It is in this section that the distance which divides Milton's technique from James Thomson's is most apparent. Thomson, the minor poet, could have shown the greater Milton how to arrange the ingredients of his ideal landscape with a precise and painterly eye for the manipulation of masses, exact color tones, and nuances of shading and light. And yet some of the effects of the grand style with its generality, sweep, and vastness seem to depend upon Milton's sensitive, though at times ponderous, gestures toward creating his epic landscape. The result of his efforts is a setting which is a visual metaphor of his theme in its richness and variety. Like Pous-

---

10. The ideality and preference for the general over the particular inherent in Milton's description of Eden have helped to emphasize the deliberately unreal quality of that landscape's impression on the reader. To Theodore Banks, the idealized elements combine to "suggest an artistic composition rather than the open country" of England or any other specific locale (*Milton's Imagery* [New York, 1950], p. 103). To M. M. Mahood, Eden is transformed by its generality into a kind of mythic "dream world" (*Poetry and Humanism* [London, 1950], p. 181). Arnold Stein also emphasizes the mythic element, viewing Eden as "an archetypal state that can be known only through the metaphorical creation of an image . . . a symbolic image in a dramatic situation" (*Answerable Style* [Minneapolis, 1953], p. 62).

sin's paintings,[11] Milton's landscapes are strongly intellectualized and amazingly diverse. In two or three lines he can move from a description that is all art,

> if Art could tell,
> How from that Sapphire Fount the crisped Brooks,
> Rolling on Orient Pearl and sands of Gold,
>
> [IV.236–38]

to one that is disarmingly artless:

> Flow'rs worthy of Paradise which not nice Art
> In Beds and curious Knots, but Nature boon
> Pour'd forth profuse on Hill and Dale and Plain,
> Both where the morning Sun first warmly smote
> The open field, and where the unpierc't shade
> Imbrown'd the noontide Bow'rs: thus was this place
> A happy rural seat of various view: [12]
>
> [IV.241–47]

Some of Milton's pictorial effects come from his ability to manipulate language and image to gain an impression of immobility. Even when his descriptions lack visual particularity, Milton can often achieve a sense of arrested motion that is like a painting.

11. Several scholars have perceived parallels between Milton's visual imagery and the baroque classicism of Nicolas Poussin. See D. S. Bland, "Poussin and English Literature," *Cambridge Journal,* VI (1952), 108, and Mario Praz, "Milton and Poussin," *Seventeenth-Century Studies Presented to Sir Herbert Grierson* (Oxford, 1938), pp. 192–210. If one agrees that a Stoic orientation is apparent in both poet and painter, it is interesting to reread the passages leading up to the expulsion in *Paradise Lost* in conjunction with the analyses of Poussin's *Et in Arcadia Ego* by Erwin Panofsky and Anthony Blunt.

12. Mario Praz has traced the taste for "neglectful simplicity" and "comely negligence" back to Tasso's description of Armida's garden. Milton's position as the father of the eighteenth-century English garden may owe a debt to Tasso's poetic landscape. See "Armida's Garden," *Comparative Literature Studies,* V (1968), 14.

> airs, vernal airs,
> Breathing the smell of field and grove, attune
> The trembling leaves, while Universal *Pan*
> Knit with the *Graces* and the *Hours* in dance
> Led on th' Eternal Spring.
>
> [IV.264–68]

To Hilda M. Hulme the "ever-circling movement" of the dancers in this passage "is changed into a pictorial impression of the single moment" which becomes finally "a scene of static beauty" until disturbed again by other activity.[13] One is struck by the resemblance between the lines above and Botticelli's *Primavera* which presents a similar tableau of frozen movement in a timeless spring landscape. Like Botticelli, Milton used such a moment of stasis to heighten and universalize his mythic material, until the dance itself represents something ritual and holy, an iconographic embodiment of an eternal present, like the figures on Keats's urn.

Another pictorial technique Milton occasionally employs in *Paradise Lost* resembles what has been called, in chapter 1, the tableau and text method of ordering a narrative passage. The reader progresses from scene to scene; at length, an explication or moral commentary is provided. The best example of such a tableau and text mode in *Paradise Lost* occurs in Book XI, during Adam's visionary glimpse into the future, when he witnesses the events that culminate in the slaying of Abel by Cain.

> His eyes he op'n'd, and beheld a field,
> Part arable and tilth, whereon were Sheaves
> New reapt, the other part sheep-walks and folds;
> I' th' midst an Altar as the Land-mark stood
> Rustic, of grassy sward; thither anon

13. "On the Language of *Paradise Lost:* Its Elizabethan and Early Seventeenth-Century Background," *Language and Style in Milton, A Symposium in Honor of the Tercentenary of Paradise Lost,* ed. Ronald David Emma and John T. Shawcross (New York, 1967), p. 68. Hulme also finds this timeless quality in the famous Vallombrosa passage (*P.L.* I.301–13), referring to its "immobilized scenic quality" (*ibid.,* p. 79).

A sweaty Reaper from his Tillage brought
First Fruits, the green Ear, and the yellow Sheaf,
Uncull'd, as came to hand; a Shepherd next
More meek came with the Firstlings of his Flock
Choicest and best; then sacrificing, laid
The Inwards and thir Fat, with Incense strew'd,
On the cleft Wood, and all due Rites perform'd.
His Off'ring soon propitious Fire from Heav'n
Consum'd with nimble glance, and grateful steam;
The other's not, for his was not sincere;
Whereat hee inly rag'd, and as they talk'd,
Smote him into the Midriff with a stone
That beat out life; he fell, and deadly pale
Groan'd out his Soul with gushing blood effus'd.

[XI.429–47]

In a series of scenes the drama plays itself out. Initially attention focuses on the bare altar in the center foreground of a
conventional pastoral landscape. Then, first Cain and after him
Abel bring their sacrificial offerings. The scenes which follow
describe, with visual particulars, the sacrifice itself and God's
response. The murder, in the final scene, is presented with a
Homeric regard for grisly detail. A. S. P. Woodhouse has compared the style of Book XI to Homer's technique for presenting
the shield of Achilles (*Iliad,* XVIII). Milton, says Woodhouse,
presents "a series of scenes, each animated, each presenting an
internal balance of contrasted elements, and each contrasting
in its turn with the others, precisely in the manner of the
Homeric panels."[14] Some of the scenic elements are almost
identical in both epics: the bucolic, peaceful setting of most of
Homer's panels and the scenes of violent death juxtaposed
upon the heretofore tranquil landscape are a prominent feature
of both.

Milton's tableaux, however, are followed by a "text" section
in which the implicit thematic elements in the scenes themselves are used as the basis for Michael's explicitly moral and
theological disquisition on death and judgment. Reacting to
the sight before his eyes, Adam cries out in anguish, and his

14. "Pattern in *Paradise Lost,*" *UTQ,* XXII (1953), 125.

angelic companion both comforts him and points out the significance of what he has just seen:

> O Teacher, some great mischief hath befall'n
> To that meek man, who well had sacrific'd;
> Is Piety thus and pure Devotion paid?
>   T' whom *Michael* thus, hee also mov'd, repli'd.
> These two are Brethren, *Adam,* and to come
> Out of thy loins; th' unjust the just hath slain,
> For envy that his Brother's Offering found
> From Heav'n acceptance; but the bloody Fact
> Will be aveng'd, and th' other's Faith approv'd
> Lose no reward, though here thou see him die,
> Rolling in dust and gore. To which our Sire.
>   Alas, both for the deed and for the cause!
> But have I now seen Death? Is this the way
> I must return to native dust? O sight
> Of terror, foul and ugly to behold,
> Horrid to think, how horrible to feel!

[XI.450–65]

Turning back from text to tableau again, it is important to reiterate that the multiscene style of presenting the crucial elements in a narrative flourished in the visual arts as well as in a verbal context like Homer's epic. Biblical stories were especially subject to this method of illustration. John Baptist Medina, Milton's first illustrator, used such a conflation, for instance, in some of his *Paradise Lost* pictures to show a series of events within one engraving.[15] Another especially memorable example, one which Milton may have seen in Italy, is the great bronze relief of Cain and Abel by Ghiberti, done for the doors of the Baptistery in Florence in about 1436. Ghiberti's subject, one of a series on biblical themes, is, like Milton's poetic passage, treated in six sequential episodes.

These extended landscape passages in *Paradise Lost* which

15. See "Satan in the Garden," the plate for Book IX which is reproduced in Part I of C. H. Collins Baker's two-part article, "Some Illustrators of Milton's *Paradise Lost*," *The Library*, 5th s., III (1948), pt. 1, 1–21; pt. 2, 101–19. See also Pointon, *Milton and English Art* (Toronto, 1970), pl. 3.

we have just examined are often too diffuse or varied to permit
the kind of particularity conducive to most other modes of
pictorialism. Certain of these more precise or limited effects,
however, contribute in important ways to the rich diversity of
Milton's great epic and therefore should be carefully considered
next.

In Book V of *Paradise Lost,* Raphael, whose Platonism is
quite apparent, asks Adam a hypothetical question:

> what if Earth
> Be but the shadow of Heav'n, and things therein
> Each to other like, more than on earth is thought?
> [V.574–76]

Having already explained to Adam that the limitations of the
human intellect will force him to "delineate" spiritual concepts
and events of heavenly history in "corporeal forms," Raphael
has ostensibly prepared the reader as well as Adam for the more
obvious incongruities involved in the overrealistic depiction of
the war in Heaven in Book VI. But the archangel's question has
a larger significance as well. In Milton's epic, which is designed
to work, like Dante's, on several levels simultaneously, every
image in the poem becomes at least potentially the raw material
of symbol. When these symbols are at all pictorial, they often
tend to be emblematic as well, especially if a moral or philosophical point is at issue. A good example is provided in Book
V, ll. 211–19, in which Adam and Eve are pictured at their accustomed agricultural tasks:

> On to thir morning's rural work they haste
> Among sweet dews and flow'rs; where any row
> Of Fruit-trees overwoody reach'd too far
> Thir pamper'd boughs, and needed hands to check
> Fruitless imbraces: or they led the Vine
> To wed her Elm; she spous'd about him twines
> Her marriageable arms, and with her brings
> Her dow'r th' adopted Clusters, to adorn
> His barren leaves.

This passage says a good deal more about proper and improper marital relationships than it does about gardening.[16] The fruit trees which display excessive growth are said to have "reach'd too far" and must be restrained and pruned back. Unless their "pamper'd," undisciplined boughs are checked, their fruitfulness will be impaired and their destined purpose thwarted to some degree. A lesson for Eve is shadowed forth here. It is her self-indulgent whim to stray from Adam's side and work alone which brings about her downfall. The "fruitless" state of the overgrown tree testifies to its violation of the proper order of nature; in prelapsarian Eden fruitfulness is abundant, never ceasing. Raphael greets Eve:

> Hail Mother of Mankind, whose fruitful Womb
> Shall fill the World more numerous with thy Sons
> Than with these various fruits the Trees of God
> Have heap'd this table.
>
> [V.388–91]

Though Eve's fruitfulness will remain after her sin, it will be blighted by the primordial curse which her unchecked and overreaching appetite—for independence from Adam and equality with him—has brought upon her. The contrasting emblematic depiction of a fitting relationship between man and wife suggests her role should have been like the vine's—dependent upon the elm's superior strength—she "to adorn" and he to support. Milton reiterates this point later on in Book IX. When Satan approaches the solitary Eve to tempt her, she is engaged in propping up the drooping heads of flowers with myrtle bands. She is called the "fairest unsupported Flow'r,/ From her best prop so far" (ll. 432–33). Through the images of tree, vine,

16. Peter DeMetz has traced the motif of the vine and elm in both classical and Christian art and literature. Its "essentially marital meaning" extends back to Catullus. Milton uses what has become by his time a cliché for "his own highly allusive ends": the image of a "true marital hierarchy" about to be perverted. See "The Elm and the Vine: Notes toward the History of a Marriage *Topos*," *PMLA*, LXXIII (1958), 521–32. Shakespeare also used the elm and vine metaphor as an image of the marital relationship. See *The Comedy of Errors*, II.ii, 176–82.

and flower, then, Milton has employed visually striking, concrete equivalents to help express an intangible and abstract moral thesis. However, whereas in the vine imagery the moral point has been completely and fully stated in a pictorial emblem that is understandable by itself, the "fairest unsupported Flow'r" metaphor is still dependent upon a verbal explanation of its moral point. Here, unlike the emblematic vine-elm passage, the flower image cannot stand alone.[17] Eve as the fairest flower in a field of fragrant, colorful blooms is effectively poetic, but Milton has to point the explicit moral, telling us she is "From her best prop so far." Metaphoric tenor and vehicle merge completely as they do in painting only in the tree and vine image, not in the flower image, though both make the same thematic point.

Milton often employs allegorical imagery, making allusive use of pictorial emblems in the form of mythic, natural, or abstract personifications. These animate his heroic landscapes, subtly furthering the delineation of a mood and helping to objectify a dominant theme. In the "Hail wedded Love" passage of Book IV, a good example is this charmingly Ovidian portrait of Cupid:

> Here Love his golden shafts imploys, here lights
> His constant Lamp, and waves his purple wings,
> Reigns here and revels;
>
> [IV.763–65]

Such a presence, the attendant spirit of Adam and Eve's nuptial bower, tells Milton's audience much about the state of their love. In Renaissance depictions of mythological or literary

17. The myrtle bands, however, were probably invested with greater symbolic significance for Milton's contemporaries who were likely to know that myrtle was used as a sign of love, both in Roman mythology (the myrtle tree was sacred to Venus) and in Christian symbolism. Thus, the iconographical message of Milton's imagery is that Eve (flower) should, at this moment of approaching temptation, have been supported by Love (myrtle bands). She is vulnerable standing alone. See George Ferguson, *Signs and Symbols in Christian Art* (New York, 1966), p. 34.

lovers (Venus and Adonis, Armida and Rinaldo), Cupid is traditionally present. If love flourishes, he is equipped as above with golden arrows and, often, a burning lamp or torch. On the other hand, the death of love can be iconographically represented by an extinguished lamp or torch or by a grieving Cupid with folded wings. If hatred should displace love, Cupid's "golden shafts" are transformed into arrows of lead.[18] Given such visual clues, we may, with Thomas Kranidas, regard the embrace of Adam and Eve as, in a sense, "emblematic," noting the angels who guard the pair as they sleep and provide for them "a kind of ornamental frame."[19]

Sometimes Milton uses a pictorial allegorical train which is simply decorative, designed to add a richer texture to the fabric of the poem and to help sustain a mood so delicate and evanescent that it almost has to be suggested indirectly. When Eve addresses Adam in the following passages, night has come and the two are preparing to retire to their Bower.

> With thee conversing I forget all time,
> All seasons and thir change, all please alike.
> Sweet is the breath of morn, her rising sweet,
> With charm of earliest Birds; pleasant the Sun
> When first on this delightful Land he spreads
> His orient Beams, on herb, tree, fruit, and flow'r,
> Glist'ring with dew; fragrant the fertile earth
> After soft showers; and sweet the coming on
> Of grateful Ev'ning mild, then silent Night
> With this her solemn Bird and this fair Moon,
> And these the Gems of Heav'n, her starry train:
> But neither breath of Morn when she ascends
> With charm of earliest Birds, nor rising Sun
> On this delightful land, nor herb, fruit, flòw'r,
> Glist'ring with dew, nor fragrance after showers,

18. A good discussion of the iconography of Cupid personifying Love can be found in Erwin Panofsky, *Studies in Iconology* (1939; New York, 1962), chap. 4.

19. See *The Fierce Equation, A Study of Milton's Decorum,* Studies in English Literature, Vol. X (The Hague, 1965), p. 140. There is, in the composition of William Blake's illustration to this scene, such a concept of the angels as forming part of the "frame" that sets off the two central figures.

> Nor grateful Ev'ning mild, nor silent Night
> With this her solemn Bird, nor walk by Moon,
> Or glittering Star-light without thee is sweet.
>
> [IV.639–56]

The images of the Sun and Morn, of the Evening, Night, and Moon, are each struck off so economically and in such traditional terms that the inattentive reader is likely to miss the subtle effect of the train of natural personifications passing, as it were, before the two lovers.[20] These, inhabiting the timeless world before the Fall, watch time and season in their repetitive and circular movement but are not themselves touched by change. There is a suggestion in these lines that for Adam and Eve the shift from day to night and the seasonal variations (the latter still an unrealized concept in the Earthly Paradise of continual spring and fall) are only designed to provide a pleasing diversity of sight and sound. No time is inimical; "all please alike." Night is not the black and evil darkness in which Satan dwells but a period of beauty, peace, and rest, illuminated by moonlight and jewellike stars.

> Now came still Ev'ning on, and Twilight gray
> Had in her sober Livery all things clad;
> Silence accompanied, for Beast and Bird,
> They to thir grassy Couch, these to thir Nests
> Were slunk, all but the wakeful Nightingale;
> She all night long her amorous descant sung;

20. E. T. Dubois has characterized certain French poetic landscapes of the seventeenth century in terms that are often equally applicable to Milton's landscapes in *Paradise Lost,* especially in lines like those just cited: "What characterizes Baroque poetry is its own peculiar view of nature as closely linked with man, endowed with his emotions and sharing in them; but the Baroque poet goes further than the pathetic fallacy. Nature, or perhaps rather the forces of nature take on a human shape, something helped by a conventional mythology but one which is recast by the poet into a more personal and dramatic form. Nature is an important element of Baroque poetry running beside the love theme with which it is closely linked. Landscape in many poems is no mere background but the theme" ("Some Aspects of Baroque Landscape in French Poetry of the Early Seventeenth Century," *JAAC,* XIX [1961], 253).

> Silence was pleas'd: now glowed the Firmament
> With living Sapphires: *Hesperus* that led
> The starry Host, rode brightest, till the Moon
> Rising in clouded Majesty, at length
> Apparent Queen unveil'd her peerless light,
> And o'er the dark her Silver Mantle threw.
>
> [IV.598–609]

Milton's eye for chiaroscuro effects is quite painterly in this gorgeously baroque night landscape through which move the personified figures of Twilight and Moon. The serving-maid aspect of the first provides a dramatic contrast to the splendor of the queenly moon; the effect is stately and processional.

It is striking how baroque Milton becomes in his visual images when he leaves earth behind. If Eden is the Earthly Paradise, it is also the first English garden, and its naturalness charmed every eighteenth-century gardenist.[21] Conversely, Milton's vault of Heaven is all art—the moon rises like a goddess or like an apotheosized Marie de' Medici painted on the ceiling of a seventeenth-century palace.[22] In Milton's cosmic landscapes the impulse to personification becomes much more intense. Natural phenomena are transformed into sacred symbols which manifest concealed divinity—"Hail holy Light." Light-dark contrasts are exploited to the full; significantly, in the visual arts as well as in poetry, night scenes with a strongly dramatic play of light and shadow were not much appreciated or even often attempted before the seventeenth century.[23] Milton's

21. The influence of *Paradise Lost* on the development of the natural garden is well known to modern scholars. Horace Walpole, for example, credits Milton's "prophetic eye of taste" with having discovered and anticipated "modern gardening." In the "romantic" age, Byron once observed with ironic relish that "Pope was the principal inventor of that boast of the English, modern gardening. He divides this honor with Milton." See Ida Langdon, *Milton's Theory of Poetry and Fine Art* (New Haven, 1924), pp. 51–55.

22. The rising movement and cloudy throne are very similarly handled in Cortona's *The Triumph of Glory* on the ceiling of the salon of the Barberini Palace.

23. There are some exceptions, of course. Michelangelo, the great innovator, is an obvious one. But night paintings did not become relatively common until the seventeenth-century work of

Paradise Lost landscapes display this new appreciation for night shading and for moonlight.

> now reigns
> Full Orb'd the Moon, and with more pleasing light
> Shadowy sets off the face of things;
>
> [V.41–43]

This is undeniably an amateur's eye; the contrasting effect of light and shadow "sets off the face of things," but how, precisely, Milton does not say. He has an equally appreciative eye for the setting sun—a favorite time for landscape painters; one thinks especially of Claude. A passage in Book IV describes the setting sun's effect upon the alabaster gate of Paradise:

> Meanwhile in utmost Longitude, where Heav'n
> With Earth and Ocean meets, the setting Sun
> Slowly descended, and with right aspect
> Against the eastern Gate of Paradise
> Levell'd his ev'ning Rays: it was a Rock
> Of Alabaster, pil'd up to the Clouds,
> Conspicuous far, winding with one ascent
> Accessible from Earth, one entrance high;
> The rest was craggy cliff, that overhung
> Still as it rose, impossible to climb.
>
> [IV.539–48]

This landscape has both more detail and more sophistication. The dramatic effect of setting sun on a sheer face of rock mass, dazzling white and towering to the clouds, and the ruggedness of the "craggy cliff" provide a strikingly varied composition.

Both poetic landscapes above use the light-dark imagery for effects that are intended to be simply decorative; despite the second's greater elaboration of visual detail, its function in the poem is as purely ornamental as is the first example cited. In most parts of the poem, however, light and dark carry a moral, evaluative connotation that is obvious and is constantly reiterated. Hell, that place of "No light, but rather darkness

---

Elsheimer, Rubens, Rembrandt, and Salvator Rosa demonstrated their effectiveness and power.

visible" and Satan who lives in an eternal night are juxtaposed
with God who is himself Light and dwells in a Heaven of
dazzling brightness.

> Fountain of Light, thyself invisible
> Amidst the glorious brightness where thou sit'st
> Thron'd inaccessible, but when thou shad'st
> The full blaze of thy beams, and through a cloud
> Drawn round about thee like a radiant Shrine,
> Dark with excessive bright thy skirts appear
> Yet dazzle Heav'n, that brightest Seraphim
> Approach not, but with both wings veil thir eyes.
>
> [III.375–82]

Evil and good, sorrow and joy—throughout the epic these are
objectified in this dark-light imagery. Josephine Miles has discovered that an adjectival shift from good-bad to light-dark
occurred in English poetry after the Elizabethans and the metaphysicals, becoming especially noticeable in the work of Milton
for whom "descriptive detail, sensuous scenic detail became a
chief material of poetry." [24] Miss Miles asserts that *"bright* and
dark, as representative descriptive adjectives superseded *true*
and *false* as representative judgmental adjectives, and heaven
and earth began to shine forth pictorially in their depth and
height, air and mass, light and shadow." [25] The moral connotations of light-dark imagery coupled with this stronger impulse
toward the pictorial combine to effect the kinds of poetic landscapes in the epic which, in chapter 1, were labeled emblematic.
Often, however, the judgmental weight of Milton's light imagery
yields precedence to the intensity of its emotional impact. At
such times, the primarily moral equivalences suggested by light
or dark project larger, more symbolic correspondences.

The apex of light-dark symbolism in *Paradise Lost* is reached
in passages of visionary and mystical beauty in which the cosmic
landscape, Heaven itself, the dwelling place of God who is
Light, is so completely drenched in brightness that it becomes
pure radiance ("Bright effluence of bright essence increate").

24. "From Good to Bright: A Note in Poetic History," *PMLA,*
LX (1945), 770.
  25. *Ibid.*

Often it cannot be poetically or pictorially delineated in any completely rational and fully coherent terms; Milton seems to search for image after image, rejecting or questioning each that occurs to him as insufficient, in some way false or incomplete. At this most intense level, light imagery operates in the way we have designated as sacramental. It represents by pictorial, metaphoric means what cannot be rendered simply by verbal means. The first fifty lines or so which begin Book III reveal the "sacramental" quality of Milton's light; it becomes finally an attempt to make the deity incarnate in a landscape of the mind.

> thou Celestial Light
> Shine inward, and the mind through all her powers
> Irradiate, there plant eyes, all mist from thence
> Purge and disperse, that I may see and tell
> Of things invisible to mortal sight.
>
> [III.51–55]

Milton's physical blindness has paradoxically illuminated his inner vision; having had once "to venture down/ The dark descent, and up to reascend," he may now, like the shades of epic heroes, walk privileged in Elysian Fields, at least in spirit.

> Yet not the more
> Cease I to wander where the Muses haunt
> Clear Spring, or shady Grove, or Sunny Hill,
> Smit with the love of sacred Song; but chief
> Thee *Sion* and the flow'ry Brooks beneath
> That wash thy hallow'd feet, and warbling flow,
> Nightly I visit:
>
> [III.26–32]

Milton's juxtaposition of Mount Parnassus and Mount Sion is very apt for a baroque artist. Both are presented as ideal landscapes, the classical pagan one meeting and mingling with its sacred and Hebraic equivalent to give an intensified image of the Earthly Paradise. Milton the epic poet inhabits a spiritual Eden, won by dint of long apprenticeship and harsh suffering.

Much has already been written of the structural design implicit in Milton's vertical movement in the poem. The risings and fallings—of Satan from Hell, of the traitorous angels down into Hell, of the angelic visitants to Eden, of the planetary bodies—are almost constantly a feature of cosmic landscape. It seems superfluous to do more than reiterate that the same universality of vertical movement exists in baroque art, where soaring angels, ascending souls, and plunging demons become, by the seventeenth century, visual clichés.[26] Such dramatic movement is characteristic of similar landscape passages in other poetry besides Milton's. Mrs. E. T. Dubois analyzes its effect in French poetry of the seventeenth century, choosing the label "cosmic landscape" to identify

> a picture of nature where the elements of the earth and the universe on a large scale are so constantly drawn together. The poet animates the elements of water, sun, air, and earth . . . brings them to interplay, encloses them in his own mood, and builds and draws a picture on two planes. The horizontal plane of the surface of the earth is intersected by a vertical line which links it individually and collectively to some power beyond, thus presenting a deistic vision of the world.[27]

Milton's vision is, of course, theistic rather than deistic, but the pictorial effects of his cosmic landscapes operate in the same baroque fashion as those of his French contemporaries.

When the student of literary pictorialism must finally leave *Paradise Lost,* it is with the conviction that much remains unexamined and that many potentially rewarding leads still wait to be followed. Milton's variety and wealth seem inexhaustible; one ends at last by echoing Rose Macaulay's half-admiring, half-exasperated remark: "this huge, baroque, classic, romantic,

26. Some of the more striking examples of such vertical movement of bodies on a grand scale which Milton might have seen include Michelangelo's *Last Judgment* and Rubens' *Apotheosis of James I* at Whitehall. The latter is described as a "vortex of twisting, mounting, spiral rhythms, in which these monumental figures [James and allegorical representations of Justice, Religion, Victory, and Wisdom] are caught up to the dazzling gold and blue of limitless height. . . ." (see Oliver Millar, "Rubens: The Whitehall Ceiling," The Fortieth Charlton Lecture on Art [London, 1958], p. 20).

27. "Baroque Landscape in French Poetry," p. 260.

Catholic, Protestant, devil-haunted, learned, amusing, deriva-tive, unique fairy-tale." [28]

Paradise Regained

Examining scholarly and critical writings on *Paradise Regained*, one soon becomes aware of the extent to which it has, for three hundred years, borne the fate of most sequels. Inevitably com-pared to *Paradise Lost*, it has almost invariably suffered in such a comparison. Even its defenders—and these have become both more numerous and more discriminating—have failed to agree on so basic a question as the poem's genre. But whether we call it a "brief epic" like the Book of Job or a "drama of the mind," certain characteristics of the work are clearly apparent. These must be considered before Milton's use of landscape can be dis-cussed.[29]

The first point relevant to the present study is that most of *Paradise Regained* reveals itself to the reader conceptually rather than pictorially. Its method is dialectical, not metaphori-cal, for the most part. Exceptions to this prevailingly nonvisual mode occur in those sections which focus briefly on the actual moment of temptation itself, as well as in one or two passages at the beginning and end of the poem which place Christ in the setting of the desert wilderness and, later, make his final triumph over Satan more vivid by means of dramatically visualized descriptive passages. The rest of the poem consists of argument which is rhetorically subtle and dramatic in a purely intellec-tual sense, but hardly visual, let alone pictorial. In these lengthy

28. Cited in Logan Pearsall Smith, *Milton and His Modern Critics* (Boston, 1941), p. 128.
29. Barbara Lewalski has succinctly reviewed the various modern opinions on the genre of *Paradise Regained*. They range from her own view that it is a short biblical epic, to the belief that it is a kind of mental or psychological drama (Douglas Bush, Arnold Stein) ; these two interpretations appear to be currently the most popular. Other theories suggest that *Paradise Regained* is a moral allegory (Howard Schultz, E. M. W. Tillyard), a "rhetorical argu-ment" like *Religio Laici* (Kenneth Muir), or a "formal meditation on the gospel account of Christ's temptation" (Louis Martz). See *Milton's Brief Epic* (Providence, R.I., 1966), pp. 6, 359 n.

speeches, so artfully contrived, it is impressive to watch Milton, the master of rhetoric, at work—even if Milton, the poet of sensuous beauty, infrequently reveals himself.

Also contributing to the comparative lack of pictorial passages in this later epic is its derivation from a tradition that is austere and Hebraic instead of classical and Hellenic. In *Paradise Lost* the genealogy of the classic epic tradition often reveals itself in a kind of opulence recalling such Renaissance inheritors of the tradition as Ariosto, Tasso, and Spenser. Of course the fact that setting does dictate style to a great degree in both epics must be taken into account. Eden, Heaven, and Hell demand the splendidly baroque treatment that they indeed receive; a desert wilderness, on the other hand, requires the poet to employ muted, even stark, descriptive techniques. When the sensuous and opulent image does occur in *Paradise Regained* (in the banquet scene, for instance), it almost always carries negative moral connotations which are detrimental to a sustained accumulation of pictorial imagery.

Yet Milton himself seems to have realized that the impact of his epic argument would be increased if, at strategic intervals, he interrupted his dialogue to introduce passages of descriptive power. To address the eye as well as the ear by means of images that would represent and objectify the rhetorical argument seems to have been the purpose of the banquet scene, a Miltonic innovation. The temptation from the mountaintop also serves this purpose; Rome and Athens embody the different kinds of appeals—to power and wealth or to wisdom and contemplation —which Satan, with "persuasive Rhetoric/ That sleek't his tongue," was about to use to tempt Christ. Milton's poetic strategy was wise, for after finishing *Paradise Regained* and laying the book aside, few remember the particulars of the elaborate verbal duel between Christ and Satan. Instead, those scenes that remain in the mind are the ones in which Milton clothed his ethical and abstract arguments in image.

In Book I, before focusing upon Christ in the desert, Milton injects a poetic preamble which takes the reader from the Fall to the Baptism of Christ and his subsequent withdrawal into the desert. Milton lingers over a few scenes in these opening three hundred lines—Christ's Nativity and the Baptism itself—

but these are nonvisual and bookish, clearly suggesting a derivation from the biblical account rather than from any pictorial
versions of these two often-painted scenes. The first important
pictorial landscape is the desert itself, "A pathless Desert, dusk
with horrid shades" (I.296), in which, the reader is told, it is
easy to become lost. One begins to suspect this desert has affinities with Vergil's sacred wood in which hangs the golden
bough and with Dante's dark wood. The stage is being set for a
time of testing and trial, although certain features of the barren
landscape remind us that this desert wanderer is immune from
the kinds of human vulnerability which threatened Aeneas and
Dante:

> Full forty days he pass'd, whether on hill
> Sometimes, anon in shady vale, each night
> Under the covert of some ancient Oak,
> Or Cedar, to defend him from the dew,
> Or harbour'd in one Cave, is not reveal'd;
> Nor tasted human food, nor hunger felt
> Till those days ended, hunger'd then at last
> Among wild Beasts: they at his sight grew mild,
> Nor sleeping him nor waking harm'd, his walk
> The fiery Serpent fled, and noxious Worm,
> The Lion and fierce Tiger glar'd aloof.[30]
>
> [I.303–13]

The oak and cedar are sacred trees; at night (in the desert a
hostile, menacing time) Christ takes cover beneath them, there
to be defended, Milton says, "from the dew." [31] The mildness of
the beasts is significant; one sign of the Fall in *Paradise Lost* is

30. All quotations from *Paradise Regained* will be taken from the
edition prepared by Merritt Y. Hughes (New York, 1937).
31. Both oak and cedar became, in the Christian era, symbols of
Christ, although both were held to be holy in pre-Christian times too.
The oak was one of the trees traditionally believed to have provided
the wood for the cross of Christ; it "is also a symbol of the strength
of faith and virtue, and of the endurance of the Christian against
adversity." The cedar stands for "beauty and majesty" (Song of
Songs), and the prophet Ezekiel used it "as a symbol of the Messiah
and His Kingdom" (Ferguson, *Signs and Symbols in Christian Art*,
pp. 35, 29).

127

the behavior of the animals, the larger, more fierce carnivores turning suddenly upon those small and defenseless (X.710–15) and posing a potential threat to man himself. Also significant, of course, are the signs of Christ's future victory over sin and death, symbolized by the fleeing serpent and worm. Despite these details, Christ's forty days seem an indefinite rather than a specific period of time, left deliberately vague of particulars. Between temptations he remains in the wilderness, physically immune to danger but surrounded by evil portents:

> for now began
> Night with her sullen wing to double-shade
> The Desert; Fowls in thir clay nests were couch't;
> And now wild Beasts came forth the woods to roam.
>   [I.499–502]

Having surmounted, with little drama or debate, the first temptation in which Satan appears to him in the guise of "an aged man in Rural weeds," [32] Christ remains in the desert, planning his future ministry as the stage is set for the second and third trials. While Christ awaits Satan's next visit, he meditates "wand'ring this woody maze." The landscape continues to be an exemplification of the epic hero's mental and psychological condition; as Arnold Stein has observed, in this section "the images are those of profound, labyrinthine self-search." [33] Traditionally, theologians have insisted that Christ was really subject to temptation, that his testing was, at least to a degree, genuine enough. Since the struggle was an interior one, Milton has the problem of externalizing his protagonist's inner con-

---

32. Elizabeth Pope notes that artists and writers who depict Satan in human form generally choose one of three or four alternatives (an aged hermit, a poor and elderly man, a rich old man, a handsome young man). Miss Pope gives examples for each of the four traditional guises in the visual arts. Many come from the extra-illustrated Kitto Bible or from old woodcuts, though Botticelli's Sistine fresco shows the devil as an aged hermit and Titian has portrayed him as a handsome young man. *Paradise Regained: The Tradition and the Poem* (Baltimore, 1947), p. 44.

33. *Heroic Knowledge: An Interpretation of Paradise Regained and Samson Agonistes* (Minneapolis, 1957), p. 53.

flicts. Until the lengthy debates begin between Christ and Satan, this problem is largely surmounted by giving a great symbolic weight to the wilderness imagery. Here again, as in Vergil and Dante, landscape is used sacramentally. Sometimes, however, the landscape ceases to be a sign or manifestation of mysterious truths, human and divine, becoming instead moral and emblematic.

In Book II, after a restless night in which he dreams of being fed by Elijah and Daniel, Christ is awakened by "the Herald Lark" to find himself still hungry and alone. He climbs a hill to look for signs of human habitation.

> Up to a hill anon his steps he rear'd,
> From whose high top to ken the prospect round,
> If Cottage were in view, Sheep-cote or Herd;
> But Cottage, Herd or Sheep-cote none he saw,
> Only in a bottom saw a pleasant Grove,
> With chant of tuneful Birds resounding loud.
> Thither he bent his way, determin'd there
> To rest at noon, and enter'd soon the shade
> High rooft and walks beneath, and alleys brown
> That open'd in the midst a woody Scene;
> Nature's own work it seem'd (Nature taught Art)
> And to a Superstitious eye the haunt
> Of Wood-Gods and Wood-Nymphs;
>
> [II.285–97]

The seemingly fair landscape that Christ discerns below him is, for all its Golden Age loveliness, a sinister and false paradise like the gardens of Armida and Alcina, or Spenser's Bower of Bliss. The contrast with the barren wilderness is startling, and, in the last few lines, the scene is set for the reappearance of the Tempter. This time he is "seemlier clad/ As one in City, or Court, or Palace bred." After a preliminary speech filled with Satanic sophistry, the banquet scene immediately follows.

> Our Saviour lifting up his eyes beheld
> In ample space under the broadest shade
> A Table richly spread, in regal mode,
> With dishes pil'd, and meats of noblest sort
> And savour, Beasts of chase, or Fowl of game,

129

In pastry built, or from the spit, or boil'd,
Gris-amber-steam'd; all Fish from Sea or Shore,
Freshet, or purling Brook, of shell or fin,
And exquisitest name, for which was drain'd
Pontus and *Lucrine* Bay, and *Afric* Coast.
Alas how simple, to these Cates compar'd,
Was that crude Apple that diverted *Eve!*
And at a stately side-board by the wine
That fragrant smell diffus'd, in order stood
Tall stripling youths rich-clad, of fairer hue
Than *Ganymede* or *Hylas;* distant more
Under the Trees now tripp'd, now solemn stood
Nymphs of *Diana's* train, and *Naiades*
With fruits and flowers from *Amalthea's* horn
And Ladies of th' *Hesperides,* that seem'd
Fairer than feign'd of old, or fabl'd since
Of Fairy Damsels met in Forest wide
By Knights of *Logres,* or of *Lyones,*
Lancelot or *Pelleas,* or *Pellenore;*
And all the while Harmonious Airs were heard
Of chiming strings, or charming pipes, and winds
Of gentlest gale *Arabian* odours fann'd
From their soft wings, and Flora's earliest smells.

[II.338-65]

The likeness of this passage to Armida's banquet in *Jerusalem Delivered* has been sufficiently stressed by Milton scholars and cannot be disputed. Like the original in Tasso's epic poem, Milton has chosen gorgeous, sensuous images and woven them together with allusive references that evoke a wealth of mythic material, fabulous and legendary. One is reminded as well of the splendid banquet scenes of Venetian art, paintings like those of Paolo Veronese (1528–88) whose *Feast in the House of Levi* dazzles the eye with its magnificence and whose *Marriage at Cana* includes the sort of musical motif that appears in Milton's lines. Every sense is besieged with luxurious delights. The polarities implicit in the opulence of this scene and the austerity of Christ's desert setting contribute mightily to its visual and dramatic impact.

Failing to move Christ by the appeal to the senses that the banquet scene represents, his antagonist in Book IV shows him

two great cities, Rome and Athens, each symbolically representing another sort of temptation. In these sections of the poem,
Milton returns to the prospect or extensive view that he has
repeatedly employed in both epics to achieve the panoramic
effects so congenial to his art.[34] Satan, first tempting Christ with
worldly glory, takes him to a mountaintop and by means of an
"optic skill/ Of Vision" shows him Rome. When Christ remains
unmoved, the Tempter, supposing him more susceptible to
contemplation and learning than imperial glory, shows him
Athens. The mood and atmosphere of both cities is clearly expressed in the landscape. The two passages are given below,
first Rome, then Athens.

> He brought our Saviour to the western side
> Of that high mountain, whence he might behold
> Another plain, long but in breadth not wide;
> Wash'd by the Southern Sea, and on the North
> To equal length back'd with a ridge of hills
> That screen'd the fruits of the earth and seats of men
> From cold *Septentrion* blasts, thence in the midst
> Divided by a river, of whose banks
> On each side an Imperial City stood,
> With Towers and Temples proudly elevate
> On seven small Hills, with Palaces adorn'd,
> Porches and Theatres, Baths, Aqueducts,
> Statues and Trophies, and Triumphal Arcs,
> Gardens and Groves presented to his eyes,
> Above the highth of Mountains interpos'd:
> . . . .
>   there the Capitol thou seest,
> Above the rest lifting his stately head
> On the *Tarpeian rock,* her Citadel
> Impregnable, and there Mount *Palatine*
> The Imperial Palace, compass huge, and high
> The Structure, skill of noblest Architects,
> With gilded battlements, conspicuous far,

34. Milton's "continued attraction to the cosmic" is seen by Kester
Svendsen as enhancing much of the imagery of both *Paradise Lost*
and *Paradise Regained.* Svendsen comments on the way that "images
of sweep and distance enlarge the canvas" of the epics. *Milton and
Science* (Cambridge, Mass., 1956), p. 47.

Turrets and Terraces, and glittering Spires.
Many a fair Edifice besides, more like
Houses of Gods (so well I have dispos'd
My Aery Microscope) thou mayst behold
Outside and inside both, pillars and roofs
Carv'd work, the hand of fam'd Artificers
In Cedar, Marble, Ivory or Gold.

[IV.25–39, 47–60]

Look once more ere we leave this specular Mount
Westward, much nearer by Southwest, behold
Where on the *Aegean* shore a City stands
Built nobly, pure the air, and light the soil,
Athens, the eye of *Greece,* Mother of Arts
And Eloquence, native to famous wits
Or hospitable, in her sweet recess,
City or Suburban, studious walks and shades;
See there the Olive Grove of *Academe,*
Plato's retirement, where the *Attic* Bird
Trills her thick-warbl'd notes the summer long;
There flow'ry hill *Hymettus* with the sound
Of Bees' industrious murmur oft invites
To studious musing; there *Ilissus* rolls
His whispering stream;

[IV.236–50]

The Rome section begins with a careful series of details: the
western side of the mountain, a plain long but not wide, a ridge
of hills on the north. All of this precision, however, does not
contribute to any real sense of the visual. It is as though Milton
were working with line and not using color. The scene remains
general, even unreal; it begins to take on its own identity only
when the series of architectural forms is introduced. These
masses of classical architecture and sculpture are noble and
prominent on the hilly landscape—"proudly elevate." They
suggest the dignity and splendor of the Roman ideal, both in
the largeness of scale ("compass huge, and high") and the aura
of wealth ("gilded battlements") which are designed to impress
the beholder. Conveniently, Satan's "Aery Microscope," or tele-
scope, operates magically to permit a sight of the inside of these
great buildings "like/ Houses of Gods," adorned with rich carv-

132

Plate 8 N. Poussin. *Landscape with the Body of Phocion Carried Out of Athens*

Collection of the Earl of Plymouth, Oakly Park, Shropshire. Photograph by permission of the Courtauld Institute of Art, London

ings in precious materials. The latter are not described; Milton has moved from the panoramic view to a closer vantage point about midground, but he has carefully kept the impression nonparticularized enough to remain general.

This technique finds a visual counterpart in many of the heroic landscapes of N. Poussin, especially in a picture like *Landscape with the Body of Phocion Carried Out of Athens* (plate 8) which uses landscape to express the artist's theme and his attitude toward the subject portrayed.[35] In the background is the city of Athens; classical temples, monuments, and public buildings are separated from the foreground figures by a river. Trees balance the composition at either side. The landscape is shadowed and no flowers bloom; as usual in Poussin, it functions as an expression of the painting's mood, in this case one of mourning. A similar background of architecturally harmonious buildings, separated from the foreground figures by a river, occurs in other Poussin pictures, notably the *Gathering of the Ashes of Phocion, Healing the Blind of Jericho,* and *Madonna with a Basin.* Roger de Piles has described this characteristic composition as follows:

> The heroick style is a composition of objects, which, in their kinds, draw, both from art and nature, everything that is great and extraordinary in either. The situations are perfectly agreeable and surprising. The only buildings are temples, pyramids, ancient places of burial, altars consecrated to the divinities, pleasure-houses of regular architecture: and if nature appear not there, as we every day casually see her, she is at least represented as we think she ought to be. This style is an agreeable illusion, and a sort of inchantment, when handled by a man of fine genius, and good understanding, as Poussin was, who has so happily expressed it.[36]

If Milton's Roman landscape, like those Roger de Piles describes above, is "an agreeable illusion, and a sort of inchantment," such a description is even more applicable to the next passage in which Satan exhibits Athens to Christ. Here the

35. See chapter 1, pp. 13–14.
36. Cited in Benjamin Rowland, Jr., *The Classical Tradition in Western Art* (Cambridge, Mass., 1963), pp. 270–71.

heroic strain is muted, however, and the dominant impression is of an idyllic Golden Age landscape. To contrast better with Rome, the gentle, pastoral elements rather than urban features are catalogued: the "studious walks and shades," "Olive Grove," singing birds and murmuring bees, flowery hill, and stream. It has a dreamlike loveliness, the result of a baroque piling on of perfection after perfection, using allusive references to increase the impression of a paradise of the mind and spirit. Although it is not pictorial (there are certainly more auditory than visual stimuli in the last few lines), Satan's admonitions to "Look once more," "behold," and "See there" sustain the illusion that this landscape of perfection has substance and a kind of reality. For men like Milton and Poussin, employing in their art a seventeenth-century classical baroque, the "real" was less important than the ideal, and landscape was a tool of iconography through which poet and painter expressed concepts and emotions. It did not exist, as in the nineteenth century, for itself alone.

The view from the pinnacle of the temple in Jerusalem is similar to the Rome and Athens passages, but much more brief. The most interesting aspect of this last temptation, from the visual point of view, is Satan's fall from the heights and Christ's final triumph. Satan's fall was not a feature of the literature on the Temptation of Christ, but by Milton's time it was a firmly established tradition in the iconography of visual representations, especially in old woodcuts and prints on biblical subjects.[37]

> So Satan fell and straight a fiery Globe
> Of Angels on full sail of wing flew nigh,
> Who on their plumy Vans receiv'd him soft
> From his uneasy station, and upbore
> As on a floating couch through the blithe Air,
> Then in a flow'ry valley set him down
> On a green bank, and set before him spread
> A table of Celestial Food, Divine,
> Ambrosial, Fruits fetcht from the tree of life,
> And from the fount of life Ambrosial drink,

37. See Pope, *Paradise Regained*, pp. 10–11.

> That soon refresh'd him wearied, and repair'd
> What hunger, if aught hunger had impair'd,
> Or thirst; and as he fed, Angelic Quires
> Sung Heavenly Anthems of his victory
> Over temptation, and the Tempter proud.
>
> [IV.581–95]

The familiar baroque preoccupation with forms plunging downward or floating in mid-air is apparent in the lines above. Like a figure from a Last Judgment fresco, Satan plummets down to Hell while Christ, cloud-borne by angels, comes to rest in an earthly paradise landscape where he is refreshed by heavenly food and drink. As a final touch, angelic choirs celebrate his triumph; in a conventionally composed painting of the scene they would fill the sky or upper air above the figure of Christ in his landscape setting.[38] For an epic containing little more action than a series of dramatized debates between Christ and Satan, the baroque theatricality of the landscapes contributes a good deal to the pictorialization of themes that would otherwise be almost wholly abstract, ethical, and intellectual.

Milton's pictorialism, though it is at times inexpertly rendered, vaguely delineated, and overly general, is an important aspect of his art. When an attempt is made to relate his epic landscapes to the lofty, striving expression of Renaissance and baroque painting, additional evidence emerges for the renewed appreciation of Milton as a strongly visual poet. Especially in *Paradise Lost* the many-faceted quality of his visual imagination is illustrated. His work there in some instances echoes Rubens' dynamism and sensuous color, Bernini's nervous movement and emotional impact, Poussin's heroic forms and grave dignity, and Michelangelo's or Titian's chiaroscuro. Although his inevitable allegiance in epic poetry is traditional and classical, he is too late for the purer classicism of the High Renaissance; his landscape imagery betrays his affinities for a more baroque mode. A man of the changing, turbulent seventeenth century, one style could not contain him.

38. Renaissance and baroque paintings on two horizontal planes, one earthly and the other celestial, are, of course, numerous. Among the most well known is Raphael's *Disputà* in the Vatican.

Plate 9 Rubens, *The Birth of Louis XIII*   Alinari—Art Reference Bureau

~ 4 ~

Dryden's Decorative Landscapes: Harmonizing the Classical and the Baroque

$\mathcal{D}$ryden's poetic landscapes are characterized by the same classical and baroque elements that marked the style of Milton's literary pictorialism, however different the artistic purposes of the two poets. Dryden, the courtier, tended far more often than Milton to affect the decorative baroque in ways that recall the extravagant homage offered to prelate and prince alike in the visual arts of the seventeenth century.

This florid example from *Britannia Rediviva* resembles a mythologized baroque portrait by Rubens (see plate 9):

> Departing Spring cou'd only stay to shed ⎫
> Her bloomy beauties on the Genial Bed, ⎬
> But left the manly Summer in her sted, ⎭
> With timely Fruit the longing Land to chear,
> And to fulfill the promise of the year.
> Betwixt two Seasons comes th' Auspicious Heir,
> This Age to blossom, and the next to bear.
>
> [ll. 12–18]

It is conventional in season emblems to follow earlier mythological traditions that depict Spring as feminine and flower

139

laden, while Summer appears as a youthful, vigorous man bearing fruits. The lines above depict the infant prince between the personified seasons. So portrayed, he acquires, by association, an aura of divinity like that of the infant Bacchus in history paintings treating the popular subject of the Birth and Nurture of Bacchus. Even Dryden's more emblematic images tend to be baroque: ornate rather than spare, heightened rather than naturalistic, generalized, with few details (though there are exceptions to the tendency to avoid the specific), suspended in space and carefully arranged, as in this example from Dryden's translation of Ovid's *Metamorphoses,* Book XII:

> Full in the midst of this Created Space,
> Betwixt Heav'n, Earth, and Skies, there stands a Place,
> Confining on all three; with triple Bound;
> Whence all Things, tho' remote, are view'd around;
> And thither bring their Undulating Sound.
> The Palace of loud Fame, her Seat of Pow'r;
> Plac'd on the Summet of a lofty Tow'r;
>
> . . . .
>
> Error sits brooding there; with added Train
> Of vain Credulity; and Joys as vain:
> Suspicion, with Sedition join'd, are near;
> And Rumors rais'd, and Murmurs mix'd, and Panique Fear.
> Fame sits aloft; and sees the subject Ground;
> And Seas about, and Skies above; enquiring all around.[1]
>
> [ll. 56–62, 83–88]

Clearly Dryden's version, though lacking in visual particulars, betrays more spatial awareness than does a literal rendering of

1. Compare Dryden's translation with that by Frank Justus Miller in the Loeb Classics edition of Ovid's *Metamorphoses* (London and New York, n.d.), II, 183–85: "There is a place in the middle of the world, 'twixt land and sea and sky, the meeting-point of the three-fold universe. From this place, whatever is, however far away, is seen, and every word penetrates to these hollow ears. Rumour dwells here, having chosen her house upon a high mountain-top. . . . Here is Credulity, here is heedless Error, unfounded Joy and panic Fear; here sudden Sedition and unauthentic Whisperings. Rumour herself beholds all that is done in heaven, on sea and land, and searches throughout the world for news."

the original. With a painterly eye he exploits the suspension of the palace in space and the careful grouping of the allegorical personifications around and below the central figure of Fame, preeminent over all in her tower.

A similar treatment of vast unbounded space occurs in *Annus Mirabilis* when, after the great fire has raged unchecked in London for four days, even the planetary bodies and angelic spirits are sympathetically affected.

> And now four days the Sun had seen our woes,
>   Four nights the Moon beheld th' incessant fire:
> It seem'd as if the Stars more sickly rose,
>   And farther from the feav'rish North retire.
>
> In th'Empyrean Heaven, (the bless'd abode)
>   The Thrones and the Dominions prostrate lie,
> Not daring to behold their angry God:
>   And an hush'd silence damps the tuneful sky.
>
> [verses 278–79]

Dryden's angry deity finally takes pity on London to the extent of putting out the fire by miraculous intervention.

> An hollow crystal Pyramid he takes,
>   In firmamental waters dipt above;
> Of it a brode Extinguisher he makes,
>   And hoods the flames that to their quarry strove.
>
> [verse 281]

With "lifted hands" the King "thanks him low on his redeemed ground." This sort of direct commerce between heaven and earth, between the deity and his subject—whether saint or king —is a common feature of baroque art. One is especially reminded of the series by Rubens of Marie de' Medici and Henry IV now in the Louvre. The sense of movement downward from above is often balanced by the response heavenward from below, in this example focusing on the uplifted hands of the King. In some cases the central emphasis involves a more dramatic upward soaring like that of the Virgin in Titian's *Assumption* in the Frari church in Venice or, in a more secular vein, the already cited apotheosis of James I, again by Rubens, on the ceiling of the banqueting salon at Whitehall.

141

Later in the same poem, *Annus Mirabilis,* the allegorical figure of London is portrayed: "New deifi'd she from her fires does rise." Her former state, like that of a lowly shepherdess "Who sate to bathe her by a River's side," is contrasted with her new glory:

> Now, like a Maiden Queen, she will behold,
> From her high Turrets, hourly Sutors come:
> The East with Incense, and the West with Gold,
> Will stand, like Suppliants, to receive her doom.
>
> [verse 297]

Earl Miner has singled out this passage as an instance of Dryden's pictorialism, remarking that it makes use of the "palette and genre of heroic painting." [2] Certainly the composition, the central queenly figure raised above the procession of regal suitors bearing their rich gifts, imbues the scene with dignified grandeur. The narrative element is present but frozen into stasis. The structural counterpoint operates effectively to contrast the horizontal line of suitors with the strong vertical assertion of turret and queen. All these aspects of the passage bear out Miner's judgment that the section comprises a poetic history painting. One thinks especially of Veronese's magnificent allegorical fresco, *Venice Crowned Queen of the Sea,* in the Doges' Palace, Venice.

A final example will help to illustrate further how widely and repeatedly Dryden chose to emphasize both the vertical movement so typical of baroque art and the frequent use of two planes in a scene, the heavenly and the earthly, connected by a dramatically visualized figure, plunging or rising from one plane to another. In Book IX of the *Aeneid,* Apollo, fearful that young Ascanius, in the absence of Aeneas, will risk his safety while the Trojans are being besieged by the forces of Turnus, comes to earth, assumes a mortal's disguise, and conducts the young prince to safety.

2. "The 'Poetic Picture, Painted Poetry' of *The Last Instructions to a Painter,"* in *Andrew Marvell: A Collection of Critical Essays,* ed. George deF. Lord (Englewood Cliffs, N.J., 1968), p. 169.

> *Apollo* then bestrode a Golden Cloud,
> To view the feats of Arms, and fighting Crowd; }
> And thus the beardless Victor, he bespoke aloud: }
>
> . . . .
>
> *Troy* is too narrow for thy Name. He said,
> And plunging downward shot his radiant Head;
> Dispell'd the breathing Air, that broke his Flight,
> Shorn of his Beams, a Man to Mortal sight.
> Old *Butes* Form he took, *Anchises* Squire,
> Now left to rule *Ascanius*, by his Sire:
>
> [ll. 873–75, 884–89]

One need only contrast Dryden's treatment of these lines with
that of a good modern translation [3] to appreciate to what extent
the seventeenth-century poet has yielded to contemporary taste
by endowing the Homeric staple of a god's intervention on
earth with the strong sense of swooping or soaring movement
characteristic of much baroque art (see plate 10).

Dryden's classicism, as ingrained and pervasive as his inclination to the baroque, often prompts him to compose the ingredients of his ideal landscapes in a fashion more ordered,
static, and self-contained than that illustrated in the passages
above. At times a less exuberant style may be more conducive
to his material, causing him to temper theatrical and hyperbolic
tendencies in order to gain an effect that is primarily one of restrained simplicity. Such classicism is more apparent in his
Vergil translations and certain of the *Fables* than it is in his
occasional verse or in the odes. His best work, like Milton's,
often succeeds in combining classical and baroque elements
through a realization of certain inherently complementary
qualities in the two styles. By examining Dryden's landscapes
in conjunction with those of Milton, this classical-baroque fusion can be effectively analyzed and illustrated.

3. The translation of Rolfe Humphries (New York, 1951, p. 256)
attempts to capture the pithy economy of the original, a feat Dryden
and his contemporaries thought impossible in English.

> And he left the heaven,
> Came through the stir of air, and sought Iulus,
> Disguised as ancient Butes, armor-bearer,
> Once to Anchises, a guardian at his threshold,
> Later Ascanius' servant.

Plate 10 Annibale Carracci,   Alinari—Art Reference Bureau
Mercury Giving the Golden Apple to Paris

Dryden and Milton

It has long been recognized that Dryden, Janus-like, looks both forward to Pope and back at Milton. His position as Corneille to Pope's Racine, however, has been much more stressed by literary scholars than has his deep affinity for Milton's later poetic.[4] The lines Dryden wrote for Tonson's folio edition of *Paradise Lost* in 1688 should not be dismissed as little more than a characteristically hyperbolic tribute from one who, even in an age of fulsome flattery, excelled most of his peers in this dubious art.

> Three *Poets*, in three distant *Ages* born,
> *Greece, Italy,* and *England* did adorn.
> The *First* in loftiness of thought Surpass'd;
> The *Next* in Majesty; in both the *Last*.
> The force of *Nature* cou'd no farther goe:
> To make a *Third* she joynd the former two.
>
> [Lines on Milton]

These lines reflect the endless seventeenth- and eighteenth-century debate on original genius versus formal perfection that pitted Homer against Vergil and Michelangelo against Raphael. Dryden's poem asserts that Milton combined in his work the supreme inventive power of Homer and the "exact propriety"[5] of Vergil. Neither classical poet alone possessed for Dryden this sort of ideal balance though, needless to say, he vastly admired both. Vergil was the more "perfect," Dryden concedes, but looking back over his own career late in life, he regretted not having translated more of Homer than the first book of the *Iliad* and a passage from the sixth.[6] Homer's dash and fire, like

---

4. An exception to this tendency is Anne Davidson Ferry's study of the similarities between *Paradise Lost* and *Absalom and Achitophel* and between *Samson Agonistes* and *All for Love*. See *Milton and the Miltonic Dryden* (Cambridge, Mass., 1968). Earlier Morris Freedman had explicated the parallels between Milton's epics and *Absalom and Achitophel*. See "Dryden's Miniature Epic," *JEGP*, LVII (1958), 211–19.

5. "Preface to *Sylvae*," *Essays*, ed. Watson, II, 22.

6. "Preface to the *Fables*," *ibid.*, 274.

Michelangelo's, was often contrasted with the repose and formal perfection typical of Vergil and Raphael. Englishmen of the seventeenth century recognized and responded to both approaches to art. Such polarities help to define and illuminate different facets of the sometimes complementary and sometimes contradictory pull in Dryden between the classical and the baroque styles, each so characteristic of his age.[7]

Milton's great epics in part represented to Dryden, therefore, the harmonious mingling of fundamentally antithetical classic and baroque forms.[8] In the seventeenth century, baroque exuberance could add a requisite boldness and imaginative élan to works of both verbal and visual art whose aesthetics were ostensibly predicated on unassailably classical principles. In *Paradise Lost* especially, Milton had succeeded in grafting his highly individualized "grand style" with its Latinate vocabulary and sonorous blank verse rhythms on to the classic structure of the epic with its universal themes, traditional devices, and regular partitions. Given the artistic security of Milton's classical structure in *Paradise Lost,* Dryden felt confident in stressing the boldness of its imagery and the necessity for such boldness in both heroic poetry and its sister art of painting. He cited Horace's assertion that "painters and poets have always had

7. Jean H. Hagstrum has pointed out that "no account of Dryden can be satisfactory that does not consider both the classical-Renaissance and the Counter Reformation-baroque in his poetic genius. These antithetical elements existed in his mind and art from the beginning" (*The Sister Arts* [Chicago, 1958], p. 178).

8. Imbrie Buffum gives the date 1660 for the advent of baroque into England, associating it especially with the later Milton. See *Studies in the Baroque from Montaigne to Rotrou* (New Haven, 1957), p. viii. He agrees with Margaret Bottrall, who earlier made a similar judgment. See "The Baroque Element in Milton," *English Miscellany*, I (1950), 31–42. Mario Praz is ambivalent, calling Crashaw, Milton, and Dryden baroque in a recent article ("Baroque in England," *MP*, LXI [1964], 178–79), and preferring to stress Milton's classicist tendencies in an earlier essay ("Milton and Poussin," *Seventeenth-Century Studies Presented to Sir Herbert Grierson* [Oxford, 1938]). Josephine Miles also argues for the inclusion of Milton's later works in the classical tradition that includes Dryden and Pope. See *Eras and Modes in English Poetry*, 2d ed., rev. and enl. (Berkeley and Los Angeles, 1964), p. 46.

an equal right to audacity." [9] The effect of powerful "tropes and figures" upon an audience's emotional response has been studied since Aristotle; "therefore is rhetoric made an art." [10] Dryden argues for the acceptance of certain types of figures which metaphysical poetry had overstressed and thereby spoiled for later seventeenth-century tastes: "catachresis and hyperbole have found their place amongst them [those tropes and figures which universally delight]; not that they were to be avoided, but to be used judiciously, and placed in poetry as heightenings and shadows are in painting, to make the figure bolder, and cause it to stand off to sight." [11]

This combination of the classical and baroque can be attributed in part to the influence of Torquato Tasso on the heroic poem and in part to the growing responsiveness of poets to what came to be called the sublime.[12] Tasso's aesthetic, congenial to both Milton and Dryden, stressed the importance of the marvelous and the monumental; it rejected the mannerism of Ariosto, just as the English poets had repudiated the metaphysicals. Instead it attempted essentially to restore a vital classicism that could still be genuine and yet meaningful to a new age. The great task that challenged the Counter Reformation artist was that of assimilating and reconciling the anticlassical tendencies of the preceding age with the perennial classicism that was still exalted. Poets confronting this dilemma were, like Tasso, sometimes aware of its effects in the visual arts. Dryden, who had read Bellori, was perfectly capable of understanding why the latter had hailed the contribution of Annibale Carracci to seventeenth-century painting. Annibale had "classicized" the baroque of Bernini and Cortona, successfully mingling styles heretofore considered entirely antithetical; [13]

9. "The Author's Apology for Heroic Poetry and Poetic License," prefixed to *The State of Innocence*, in *Essays*, ed. Watson, I, 206.
10. *Ibid.*, p. 201.
11. *Ibid.*
12. Dryden's debt to Tasso is a sizable one according to John C. Sherwood. See "Dryden and the Critical Theories of Tasso," *Comparative Literature*, XVIII (1966), 351–59. Also see Praz, "Baroque in England," p. 177.
13. The similarities and differences of the two can be readily perceived and appreciated by viewing Pietro's ceiling painting in

Poussin, whose series of paintings on the Sacraments was admired by Dryden, had carried this classicizing bent even further. What was not refined out, however, even in Poussin was the predilection for the vast and majestic as reflected in heroic men and ideal nature.

George Watson asserts that Dryden's "Apology for Heroic Poetry and Poetic License" is the document that marks his "discovery of Longinus." [14] Boileau's translation is dated 1674; Dryden's *The State of Innocence* and its preface were published in 1677, though Dryden may have written his opera as early as 1673.[15] Clearly Dryden associates the baroque elements in Milton with the Longinian sublime. In the "Apology," Dryden acknowledges his debt to his predecessor, calling *Paradise Lost* "one of the greatest, most noble, and most sublime poems which either this age or nation has produced." He castigates the false critics of his day, "illiterate, censorious, and detracting people," who fail to appreciate Milton's genius.[16] They should read Longinus, "after Aristotle, the greatest critic amongst the Greeks," who "has judiciously preferred the sublime genius that sometimes errs to the middling or indifferent one which makes few faults, but seldom or never rises to any excellence." [17]

---

the great salon of the Barberini Palace and comparing it with Annibale's brilliant work for the salon ceiling of the Farnese Palace.

14. *Essays*, ed. Watson, I, 195.

15. *Ibid*. James M. Osborn dates the completion of *The State of Innocence* as 1674, the same year as the Boileau translation. See *John Dryden: Some Biographical Facts and Problems* (New York, 1940), p. 29.

16. *Essays*, ed. Watson, I, 196. H. James Jensen has shown that Dryden usually uses the term *sublime* rhetorically rather than aesthetically and that often it is synonymous with *elevated*. On at least one occasion, however, he uses it in the later sense employed in the eighteenth century. Much of what Dryden admires in *Paradise Lost* is what became the aesthetic sublime, even if Dryden's technical vocabulary in the late seventeenth century was not equal to the task of precise definition. For Jensen's discussion of Dryden's sublime, see *A Glossary of John Dryden's Critical Terms* (Minneapolis, 1969), p. 111.

17. "Apology," *Essays*, ed. Watson, I, 197.

We have tended to associate the sublime more specifically with the eighteenth century of Burke's *Enquiry* than with the seventeenth century of Milton's and Dryden's baroque. They appear, however, surprisingly similar within the context of English poetry of the Restoration and eighteenth century. Martin Price, discussing the multiple applications of the term *sublime* in eighteenth-century literature, religion, and psychology, suggests that "the sublime tended to be a name for those experiences whose power seemed incommensurate with a human scale or with formal elegance. Because the experiences were of many kinds, yet all of them seeming to defy the limits of form, the term itself produced esthetic confusion." [18] The inability to accept the limitations of a form within which one must somehow express intensely felt emotions born of powerful experiences is an artistic dilemma shared by both baroque and sublime painters and poets. We can, of course, explain this periodic artistic frustration by accepting the theory that postulates perennial oscillation in the arts from classical statement to anticlassical reaction, but such inclusive categories blur some suggestive parallels between the earlier baroque and the later sublime. For instance, Price has a tendency to define the sublime in terms that are equally applicable to the earlier baroque: he views the former as "an experience of transcendence, a surpassing of conventions or reasonable limits, an attempt to come to terms with the unimaginable." One crucial exception, however, seems to point forward to the Romantics, especially Coleridge, rather than back to Milton and Dryden's baroque, that is, "the dissolution of the image." At the sublime moment, "the visible object was eclipsed or dissolved." [19]

The baroque image, floating or soaring into the empyrean, undergoing an apotheosis into a new, often divine form, or moving through dazzling light and deep shadow, is perpetually on the edge of dissolution, or, if not dissolution, at least meta-

18. "The Sublime Poem: Picture and Powers," *Yale Review*, LVIII (1969), 194.

19. *Ibid.*

morphosis.[20] Is Bernini's Daphne, at the moment we view her, girl or tree? Is Milton's Satan a reptilian monstrosity or a fallen angel? Is Dryden's Anne Killigrew a woman or the goddess-patron of the sister arts? The baroque metamorphosis is still alive enough to parody in Pope's day. Is Belinda's lock a curl or a constellation? However we answer we must agree that the image in some form is still visible before us. It must suggest the possibility of being eclipsed, but the threat must never become the reality. Baroque art tenaciously retains the visible element, whether poetic image or painted form, but so transmutes it that it grows into a meaning larger and more mysterious than it first possessed. Mario Praz calls such images organic, asserting that they become "actual symbols" which unify the work of art and give it its specifically baroque character.[21] Such a symbol is Milton's Eden; Dryden, in *The State of Innocence,* also structures his poetic opera around this central image.[22]

In the passage which follows, Raphael "descends to Adam [newly created] in a cloud," explains his creation, and tells him of Eve; as they "ascend to soft musick" toward the earthly paradise where Adam is to dwell, Raphael describes it:

> A Mansion is provided thee, more fair
> Than this; and worthy Heav'n's peculiar care:
> Not fram'd of common Earth, nor Fruits, nor Flowers,
> Of vulgar growth; but like Celestial Bowers:
> The Soil luxuriant, and the Fruit Divine,
> Where golden Apples on green Branches shine,
> And purple Grapes dissolve into Immortal Wine.

20. Imbrie Buffum associates movement with metamorphosis in a discussion of the baroque preoccupation with change and flux, illustrating the point with examples from Rubens and Bernini. See *Studies in the Baroque from Montaigne to Rotrou,* pp. 44–45.

21. "Baroque in England," p. 176.

22. Alan Roper has demonstrated how pervasive in Dryden's later poetry is the imagery of the Garden of Eden, although it is hard to agree with his remark that "the matter of Eden makes significant appearance only in the mature poetry from 1680 onwards. . . ." (*Dryden's Poetic Kingdoms* [London, 1965], p. 106). It seems likely that *The State of Innocence* contributed vitally to the persistence of the Eden image in Dryden's poetry.

For Noon-day's heat are closer Arbors made;
And for fresh Ev'ning Air, the op'ner glade.
Ascend: and, as we go,
More wonders thou shalt know.[23]

[II.i]

Both Milton's Eden and Dryden's allude directly or indirectly
to virtually every other paradisal setting in legend or literature.
Milton tends to make this reference specifically, calling up associations that link Eden with classical ideal landscapes ("Not
that faire field of Enna, . . . nor that sweet Grove/ Of
Daphne . . ."), while Dryden prefers to suggest such analogies
through image. Adam goes forth to meet Eve in a *locus
amoenus* whose "Celestial Bowers" recall those earthly versions
by Ariosto, Tasso, and Spenser. The sensuous setting carries
suggestive undertones; Dryden's Eve, more coquettish than
Milton's, is not Armida, but she is cousin to that Cleopatra
for whom the world was well lost.[24] The Golden Age landscape
of untilled earth abundantly bringing forth fruits is a familiar
image in classical literature as well as a popular subject in
Renaissance and baroque art. In the Garden of Hesperides,
like Eden, golden apples shine enticingly against the surrounding darker foliage. The purple grapes, dissolving into wine,
while adding more lush extravagance and color to Dryden's
poetic palette, are another instance of what we have labeled
the "metamorphosizing" tendency of baroque imagery. The
extravagance and opulence characteristic of the baroque landscape (see plate 11) is given full rein in the Edenic passages
which simultaneously evoke the biblical Earthly Paradise and
the classical Golden Age:

23. John Dryden, *The State of Innocence, and Fall of Man: An
Opera* (London, 1684). All subsequent citations will refer to this
edition.
24. Dryden's Eve greatly resembles Tintoretto's fleshly beauty
(*Adam and Eve*, Academy Gallery, Venice), languorously encircling
the Tree of Knowledge with one arm while, with the other hand,
she offers the fatal apple to an understandably reluctant Adam. She
also evokes, by association, Tiepolo's series of paintings of Armida
and Rinaldo in just such an ideal enclave as the paradisal garden
above.

151

Plate 11 Cortona, *The Golden Age*   Alinari—Art Reference Bureau

Adam: When to my Arms thou brought'st thy Virgin-Love,
       Fair Angels sung our Bridal Hymn above:
       Th' Eternal nodding shook the Firmament,
       And conscious Nature gave her glad Consent.
       Roses unbud, and ev'ry Fragrant Flower,
       Flew from their stalks, to strow thy Nuptial Bower:
       The furr'd and feather'd kind, the Triumph did pursue,
       And Fishes leapt above the streams, the passing Pomp
         to view.

       . . . .

Eve: Blest in our selves, all pleasures else abound;
       Without our care, behold th' unlabour'd Ground,
       Bounteous of Fruit, above our shady Bowers
       The creeping *Jess'min* thrusts her fragrant Flowers;
       The *Myrtle, Orange,* and the Blushing *Rose,* ⎫
       With bending heaps so nigh their blooms disclose, ⎬
       Each seems to smell the flavor which the other blows: ⎭
       By these the *Peach,* the *Guava,* and the *Pine,* ⎫
       And creeping 'twixt 'em all, the mant'ling *Vine* ⎬
       Does round their trunks her purple clusters twine. ⎭

                                                    [III.i]

An animated, decorated landscape is presented, replete with personified natural and angelic presences, suffused with odors and colors, and vitalized with a constant movement which, in such a heavily descriptive passage, is paradoxically contained and negated into stasis.

Dryden's version of Milton's epic teaches us to appreciate the boldness of his images. Using a form like opera, which naturally lends itself to the baroque treatment, Dryden took full advantage of the freedom the genre permitted. There are, however, indications that he considered his work primarily as poetry rather than theater. (It was never staged, and Sir Walter Scott, like Dr. Johnson, suggests that Dryden never expected it to be produced.) Dryden's characteristic classical baroque style is here weighted on the side of the baroque, whereas in his slightly later *All for Love* (1677), the classical elements predominate. Although his canvas was narrower than Milton's, inevitably so in an ostensibly dramatic rather than epic work, and his heroic couplets were smoother and more "regular" than Milton's blank verse, the classical aspects of

The State of Innocence are subordinated to the baroque appreciation for vastness, movement, spectacle, and panorama. Uriel points out man's dwelling place to Lucifer:

> On yonder Mount; thou seest it fenc'd with Rocks,
> And round th' ascent a Theatre of Trees,
> A Sylvane Scene, which rising by degrees,
> Leads up the Eye below, nor gluts the Sight
> With one full Prospect, but invites by many,
> To view at last the whole:
>
> [II.ii]

It is obvious that many of Dryden's effects are designed to recall the elaborate, dazzling Italian masques staged by Bernini in Rome or by Parigi in Florence during the early decades of the seventeenth century. Dryden's experience in the theater must have made him familiar with the work of Inigo Jones, who had studied in Italy and who had been known to plagiarize Parigi's effects more than once.[25]

The most fully developed example of the bold baroque use of an image which has come to assume the larger reverberations of symbol and myth occurs in Dryden's Act III. In scene i, as a prelude and prefiguration of the actual Fall of Eve in Act IV, her dream, instigated by Satan, is visualized.

> A Vision, where a Tree rises loaden with Fruit; four Spirits rise with it, and draw a Canopy out of the Tree; other Spirits dance about the Tree in deform'd shapes; after the Dance an Angel enters with a Woman, habited like Eve.

> Angel, singing:
> Look up, look up; and see

25. Enid Welsford emphasizes Jones's love of landscape, his original intention of studying landscape in Italy, and the extent to which his subsequent interest in masque scenery reveals this first artistic ambition (*The Court Masque* [New York, 1962], p. 173). About 467 of Jones's sketches for masque scenery survive, according to Henry and Margaret Ogden (see *English Taste in Landscape in the Seventeenth Century* [Ann Arbor, 1955], p. 21). Welsford stresses the "strong family likeness between all the landscapes of Renaissance poets, painters, and masque writers" (p. 312); Dryden's work reveals a knowledge of that tradition.

> What Heav'n prepares for thee;
> Look up, and this fair Fruit behold,
> Ruddy it smiles, and rich with streaks of Gold.
> The loaden Branches downward bend,
> Willing they stoop, and thy fair hand attend.
> Fair Mother of Mankind, make haste,
> And bless, and bless thy Senses with the taste.
>
> Woman: No: 'tis forbidden, I
> In tasting it shall die.
>
> Angel: Say who injoyn'd this harsh Command?
>
> Woman: 'Twas Heav'n; and who can Heav'n withstand?

The Vision section is a piece of poetic strategy that reveals Dryden's baroque propensity to manipulate temporal sequences. It is an anticipation of the Fall in a timeless dream state which looks forward to the actual Fall, the real beginning of time, and the end of Eden's eternal present. Here, in a perverted *hortus conclusus* setting, a grotesque parody of the Annunciation is enacted. Woman and angel confront each other in a garden setting. The ruddy, gold-streaked apples on the bough of the forbidden Tree bend toward Eve, parodying the homage to Mary of the chaste lily, a common feature of classical Annunciation iconography. The biblical greeting by the angel, "Blessed art thou among women," is echoed in the lines above as Eve is enjoined to "bless, and bless thy Senses with the taste." Eve's sensual self-indulgence will bring posterity's curse upon the "Fair Mother of Mankind," while Mary, the new Eve, can state, "All generations shall call me blessed."

The Vision scene continues. To help persuade the pseudo-Eve to eat, the following ruse is enacted:

The Angel takes the Fruit, and gives to the Spirits who danc'd; they immediately put off their deform'd shapes, and appear Angels.

Angels, singing:
> Behold what a change on a sudden is here!
> How glorious in Beauty, how bright they appear!
> From Spirits deform'd they are Deities made,
> Their Pinions, at pleasure, the Clouds can invade,

155

Convinced, Eve eats with pleasure; the resultant effect, she says, "enlightens my Eyes, and enlivens my Mind." The scene ends with these stage directions: "Two Angels descend; they take the Woman each by the hand, and fly up with her out of sight. The Angel who sung, and the Spirits who held the Canopy, at the same instant sink down with the Tree."

The Expulsion scene which ends Dryden's *The State of Innocence* is a cruel reversal of the apparently triumphant conclusion of the Vision scene. The warrior angels who descend are adamant and threatening. Raphael advises Adam and Eve:

> Thus arm'd, meet firmly your approaching ill:
> For, see, the Guards, from yon' far eastern Hill
> Already move, nor longer stay afford;
> High in the Air, they wave the flaming Sword,
> Your signal to depart: Now, down amain
> They drive, and glide, like Meteors through the Plain.
>
> [V.ii]

There is a baroque preoccupation with dramatic light effects in this scene. The fiery intensity of this light (emanating from the angels and the flaming sword) suggests an effectively apocalyptic transformation of the landscape. Earlier, Raphael's descent to the guilty pair is similarly described by Eve:

> Eastward as far as I could cast my Sight,
> From op'ning Heavens, I saw descending Light.
> It's glitt'ring through the Trees I still behold:
> The Cedar tops seem all to burn with Gold.
>
> [V.i]

Eve's subsequent farewell to her paradise garden is no less affecting for baroque embellishments like angelic musicians and animated flowers.

> Farewel, you happy shades!
> Where Angels first should practice Hymns, and String
> Their tuneful Harps, when they to Heav'n wou'd sing.
> Farewel, you Flow'rs, whose Buds with early care
> I watch'd, and to the chearful Sun did rear:
> Who now shall bind your stems? or, when you fall
> With Fountain Streams, your fainting Souls recall?
>
> [V.ii]

The lost Eden and the lost Golden Age meet and fuse in a retrospective ideal dramatically at variance with the post-lapsarian reality Raphael describes in the concluding lines.

> The rising Winds urge the tempestuous Air;
> And on their Wings deformed Winter bear:
> The Beasts already feel the change; and hence;
> They fly, to deeper Coverts for defence:
> The feebler Herd before the stronger run;
> For now the War of Nature is begun:
>
> [V.ii]

Time and mutability, at variance with the immortal and unchanging perfection of Eden, now subject man to the vicissitudes of life in a fallen world, to an endless struggle in a Hobbesian environment, to suffering and death.[26] The "war of nature" has defaced the landscape of paradise.[27]

The State of Innocence has been treated brusquely by critics since the seventeenth century; they have viewed it as a tawdry vulgarization of the great epic poem that was its model. Milton's legendary and condescending permission to the younger poet to "tag my verses if you will" was not, however, taken by Dryden as license to commit artistic mayhem on *Paradise Lost*. As poetry, Dryden's effort may be second rate; it is certainly hurried, often sloppy, and occasionally silly. But fine poetic passages abound, and if Dryden does not do the sort of justice to his original that he did to Shakespeare's *Antony and Cleopatra*, his poetic opera is still a far from despicable effort. That *All for Love* exhibited its author's classicist tastes, while *The State of Innocence* is predominantly baroque, makes one suspect

26. Dryden's debt to Hobbes in *The State of Innocence* has been pointed out by Bruce King. See "The Significance of Dryden's *State of Innocence*," *SEL,* IV (1964), 371–91.

27. This idea is repeated in the prologue to *The Unhappy Favorite,* providing yet another poetic example of the England as Eden theme.

> Our land's an *Eden,* and the Main's our Fence,
> While we Preserve our State of Innocence;
> That lost, then Beasts their Brutal Force employ,
> And first their Lord, and then themselves destroy:
> What Civil Broils have cost we know too well,
> O let it be enough that once we fell, . . .
>
> [ll. 27–32]

it may have been easier to order, refine, and restructure Shakespeare's sprawling masterpiece than it was to whittle down Milton's immense epic and, at the same time, emphasize its baroque elements.

After having examined the baroque ideal landscape of Eden in *The State of Innocence,* we can sum up the ingredients which constitute it. It is fundamentally decorative rather than didactic or apocalyptic. Its imagery functions as a kind of pictorial rhetoric, designed to stimulate the visual imagination and move the aesthetic passions. Dryden's landscapes are not ethical emblems like Marvell's. Though he makes use of the emblematic tradition, he does so primarily to enrich and embellish the descriptive beauty of his poetic landscapes and only secondarily to function as the vehicle for a moral or spiritual meaning. Like Milton, Dryden used a wholly different form for his openly didactic or satiric works. Unlike Milton's, however, Dryden's poetic landscapes rarely, if ever, attempt the anagogical or sacramental level. (A possible exception may be the opening lines of *Religio Laici* with their grave beauty and Vergilian echoes.) [28] Dryden recalls Homer, Ovid, and, among English poets, Chaucer at times, in using landscape imagery largely to strengthen a poem's aesthetic effect while creating a symbolic idea.

Dryden's decorative landscapes do possess a distinctly baroque quality which differentiates them from those of his predecessors, with the exception of some of Milton's. We have seen that this baroque element derives first from an emphasis in his poetic imagery upon movement, often swooping or soaring motion that attempts an uneasy balance with the dominant pictorial stasis. Second, a baroque quality is often gained by emphasizing opulence and vastness, the accumulation of rich or ornate effects on a large canvas, creating a designedly theatrical impression. Third, Dryden likes to personify, and hence visualize for his contemporaries, both natural phenomena and abstract qualities.[29] Finally, though this aspect is harder to

28. See Jeanne K. Welcher, "The Opening of *Religio Laici* and Its Virgilian Associations," *SEL,* VIII (1968), 391–96.
29. The strongly visual impact upon classical sensibilities of personifications which seem general and abstract to modern readers

isolate and illustrate, Dryden's baroque images frequently reflect the obsession with transience and temporality, with illusion, flux, and metamorphosis so characteristic of baroque art. The next section attempts to isolate and describe the more classical side of Dryden's complex, multifaceted response to the currents of seventeenth-century art, at times artificially isolating it from the baroque, insofar as it is possible to do so, in order to identify the two separate strands or traditions which, in much of his most successful later poetry, are artfully blended to create a unified aesthetic impression.

Dryden and Vergil

Readers in an age like our own, which puts a high value on originality, may react negatively to the statistic that translations constitute two-thirds of Dryden's poetry. Dryden's contemporaries responded quite differently, regarding the translations, especially the Vergil which took three years to complete, as "the climax of his poetic career." [30] This admiration endured throughout the classical period. Pope modeled his Homer upon Dryden's Vergil, while Dr. Johnson praised Dryden for providing "just rules and examples of translation" and for showing his successors "the true bounds of a translator's liberty." [31] Dryden's method of paraphrase, a judicious compromise between the literalness of metaphrase and the license of imitation, permitted him to render the text before him as he believed it would have been handled had the original been written in English for seventeenth-century readers. Since he took comparatively few liberties with Vergil (treating the *Aeneid* especially with proper deference), it is more rewarding to examine the qualitative nature of Dryden's changes than their quantity or extent.

---

has been fully established in the well-known studies by Professors A. S. P. Woodhouse, Bertrand Bronson, Earl Wasserman, and Chester Chapin.

30. William Frost, *Dryden and the Art of Translation,* Yale Studies in English, Vol. 128 (New Haven, 1955), p. 1.

31. "Dryden," in *Lives of the English Poets,* ed. George Birkbeck Hill, 3 vols. (Hildesheim, 1968), I, 422, 469.

The most interesting additions (the succinctness of the Latin made condensation unlikely) [32] are those in which Dryden attempts to reveal beauties implicit but hidden in the original. Often these are pictorial; painterly details are added to flesh out the spare economy of Vergil's lines which had a visual impact upon readers in Dryden's day despite their brevity. Appropriately enough Dryden used analogies from the visual arts to clarify for his readers his approach to translation.

> Translation is a kind of drawing after the life; where every one will acknowledge there is a double sort of likeness, a good one and a bad. 'Tis one thing to draw the outlines true, the features like, the proportions exact, the colouring itself perhaps tolerable; and another thing to make all these graceful, by the posture, the shadowings, and chiefly by the spirit which animates the whole. I cannot without some indignation look on an ill copy of an excellent original: much less can I behold with patience Virgil, Homer, and some others, whose beauties I have been endeavouring all my life to imitate, so abused, as I may say to their faces, by a botching interpreter.[33]

Dryden's application of the tenets of ideal imitation to the business of translation is amplified in a later passage, to a point where his theories strikingly anticipate those of Sir Joshua Reynolds in the sister art. Having made the point that a translator must present his original in the best possible light, he goes on to add the important qualifier that the unique flavor of a poet must not be so smoothed out in the translation as to result in an overgeneralized, essentially vapid beauty.

> It was objected against a late noble painter [supposedly Sir Peter Lely] that he drew many graceful pictures, but few of them were like. And this happened to him, because he always studied himself more than those who sat to him. In such trans-

32. Dryden acknowledges that Vergil had a gift, surpassing Homer's, for compression and economy of utterance. See "To Lord Radcliffe," in *Essays,* ed. Watson, II, 167. Also, Vergil "studies brevity more than any other poet" (Preface to the *Aeneid, ibid.,* p. 246).
33. Preface to *Sylvae, ibid.,* pp. 19–20.

lators I can easily distinguish the hand which performed the
work, but I cannot distinguish their poet from another.[34]

Evidence that Dryden, in his mind's eye, visualized segments
of Vergil's texts as history paintings or sculptures can be found
in the preface to the translation of Dufresnoy, written, it will be
remembered, during the period of the Vergil translation. In the
Aeneid, the fruitless attempt made by Lausus to save his father
Mezentius incurs Aeneas' pity and admiration. Dryden vis-
ualizes him: "in the posture of a retiring man who avoids the
combat, he stretches out his arm in sign of peace, with his right
foot drawn a little back, and his breast bending inward, more
like an orator than a soldier." [35] An epic description evokes in
the translator's mind an antique statue which is not really
present in either poetic version. Dryden's pictorializing tendency is here "characteristic of the motion of the neoclassical
mind" which "is constantly freezing the motions of nature and
of antecedent literary art into the picturesque." [36] Dryden's preoccupation with Vergil also prompted him to emphasize the
parallels between epic poetry and the visual arts, especially
painting, whereas Dufresnoy had stressed the parallel between
painting and drama.[37] At times this sister arts comparison results in dubious if suggestive equations, such as the notion
that figurative language is to the poet what color as well as
light and shadow are to the painter.[38]
Undeniably Dryden endeavored to expend his talents and
energies most lavishly on the *Aeneid* translation. He had reservations about Vergil as a pastoral poet and expressed some of
them in his dedication of the eclogues to Hugh, Lord Clifford.
Dryden's admiration for the *Pastorals* was selective rather than
totally uncritical. In the dedication he singles out for approbation an iconic passage in the third pastoral (ll. 55–70), the description of some carved bowls, enlarging Vergil's text with
small but visually suggestive details. The following couplet, for

34. *Ibid.,* p. 21.
35. *Ibid.,* p. 197.
36. Hagstrum, *The Sister Arts,* p. 188.
37. *Essays,* ed. Watson, II, 181.
38. *Ibid.,* pp. 203, 206.

example, goes beyond the original in picturing Orpheus, lyre in
hand, surrounded by the forest animals as he laments his lost
Eurydice:

> Where *Orpheus* on his Lyre laments his Love,
> With Beasts encompass'd, and a dancing Grove: [39]
>
> [III.69–70]

Dryden's scene resembles a painting by Roelandt Savery
(1576–1639), *Orpheus Charming the Animals,* which was probably widely known through engraved versions.[40] It is appropriate, perhaps, that these more rustic passages in the pastorals
suggest Northern rather than Italian visual analogues.

There is an extended catalogue of flowers in the second
pastoral which contrasts with the floral passages in *The State
of Innocence.* It is decidedly not baroque; its visual qualities
are heightened by judicious touches of color or tone ("white,"
"purple," "pale," "iron blue") and texture ("downy,"
"glossy") rather than by a preoccupation with movement, allegorical presences, or dramatic and exaggerated effects.

> Come to my longing Arms, my lovely care,
> And take the Presents which the Nymphs prepare.
> White Lillies in full Canisters they bring,
> With all the Glories of the Purple Spring:
> The Daughters of the Flood have search'd the Mead
> For Violets pale, and cropt the Poppy's Head:
> The Short *Narcissus* and fair Daffodil,
> Pancies to please the Sight, and Cassia sweet to smell:
> And set soft Hyacinths with Iron blue,
> To shade marsh Marigolds of shining Hue.
> Some bound in Order, others loosely strow'd,
> To dress thy Bow'r, and trim thy new Abode.
> My self will search our planted Grounds at home,

39. "And for us too Alcimedon made two cups . . . and in the
middle set Orpheus and the following woods:" trans. J. W. MacKail,
Virgil's Works (New York, 1934), p. 271.

40. Among the landscape illustrations reproduced in Ogden and
Ogden's *English Taste in Landscape in the Seventeenth Century* are
several by Savery, engraved by Aegidius Sadeler. The Sadelers were
prolific engravers and their work circulated widely.

For downy Peaches and the glossie Plum:
And thrash the Chestnuts in the Neighb'ring Grove,
Such as my *Amarillis* us'd to love.

[II.59–74]

This unpretentious passage has a simplicity which is less characteristic of the descriptive parts of the fourth, or messianic, eclogue. The latter appears to have stimulated Dryden to attempt a more showy version of his original.

> But when Heroick Verse his Youth shall raise,
> And form it to Hereditary Praise;
> Unlabour'd Harvests shall the Fields adorn,
> And cluster'd Grapes shall blush on every Thorn.
> The knotted Oaks shall show'rs of Honey weep,
> And through the matted Grass the liquid Gold shall creep.
> . . . .
>   O foster son of *Jove!*
> See, labouring Nature calls thee to sustain
> The nodding frame of Heav'n, and Earth, and Main;
> See to their Base restor'd, Earth, Seas, and Air,
> And joyful Ages, from behind, in crowding Ranks appear.

[IV.31–36, 59–63]

Aside from the inherent hyperbole of the Vergilian original, a further consideration may have motivated Dryden to add a touch of baroque splendor to his translation. Earl Miner believes that in its original version of 1684 it had been designed to compliment Queen Anne, then still a princess, upon the birth of her first child. The infant was stillborn, however, on April 30, 1684.[41] The association of the restoration of the monarchy and the return of the Golden Age is common enough in Dryden's poetry, as is the analogy between Augustan Rome and Stuart England (see, for example, the conclusion of *Astraea Redux*). Dryden's baroque tendencies are especially stimulated by the stylistic demands of his occasional and panegyric verse, as the section below on the odes will illustrate.

With the exception, then, of the fourth eclogue, Dryden's ideal landscapes in the *Pastorals,* when pictorial at all, strive

41. "Dryden's Messianic Eclogue," *RES*, n.s., XI (1960), 299–302.

for an unaffected simplicity at variance with the baroque and
suitable for a genre which was thought appropriate mainly
for fledgling poets. Dryden followed Boileau's advice for the
pastoral in the *Art of Poetry,* which he himself adapted from
the French:

> As a fair Nymph when Rising from her bed,
> With sparkling Diamonds dresses not her head;
> But, without Gold, or Pearl, or costly Scents,
> Gathers from neighb'ring Fields her Ornaments:
> Such, lovely in its dress, but plain withal,
> Ought to appear a Perfect *Pastoral:*
>
> [Canto II.231–36]

Dryden's *Georgics* translation is another matter; it has vividness and energy. Throughout the *Georgics,* Dryden frequently
responds to the stimulus for pictorial amplification that his
original provides. The variety of landscapes therein—from
sunny fields to stormy seas—appears to have exercised more
appeal upon the translator than did the bland monotony of the
pastoral terrain. Given greater opportunity to display this
poetic virtuosity, without, however, lapsing from "paraphrase"
into "imitation," Dryden obviously enjoyed himself. A passage
in the first book describing natural phenomena, accompanied
by preternatural manifestations, as portents of dire events, has
both echoes of Shakespeare and anticipations of the eighteenth-
century terrible sublime.

> Earth, Air, and Seas, with Prodigies were sign'd,
> And Birds obscene, and howling Dogs divin'd.
> What Rocks did *Ætna's* bellowing Mouth expire
> From her torn Entrails! and what Floods of Fire!
> What Clanks were heard, in *German* Skies afar,
> Of Arms and Armies, rushing to the War!
> *Dire Earthquakes rent the solid* Alps *below,*
> *And from their Summets shook th' Eternal Snow.*
> Pale Specters in the close of Night were seen;
> And Voices heard of more than Mortal Men.
> In silent Groves dumb Sheep and Oxen spoke;
> *And Streams ran backward, and their Beds forsook:*

164

The yawning Earth disclos'd th' Abyss of Hell:
The weeping Statues did the Wars foretel;
And Holy Sweat from Brazen Idols fell.
Then rising in his Might, the King of Floods,
Rusht thro' the Forrests, tore the lofty Woods;
And rolling onward, with a sweepy Sway,
Bore Houses, Herds, and lab'ring Hinds away.
Blood sprang from Wells, Wolfs howl'd in Towns by Night,
And boding Victims did the Priests affright.
Such Peals of Thunder never pour'd from high;
Nor forky Light'nings flash'd from such a sullen Sky.
Red Meteors ran a-cross th' Etherial Space;
Stars disappear'd, and Comets took their place.[42]

[I.634–58]

The passage, composed in about equal parts of vivid visual effects and histrionic rant, recalls the style of the heroic dramas. Dryden has indulged himself here to an extent he would not consider permissible in the *Aeneid*. He has achieved a sustained, cumulative rhetorical impact that is, to a large degree, dependent upon investing fairly stereotyped signs and portents in the Vergilian original with a heightened sense of *enargeia*. The fascination with Alps and meteors betrays the seventeenth-

42. A more literal prose translation provides the following version of the lines above. A few lines in each translation have been italicized to facilitate comparison. "Yet at that season earth too and the plains of sea, and unclean dogs and ominous birds gave presage. How often did we see Etna flooding the Cyclopean fields with the torrent bursting from her furnaces, and rolling forth balls of flame and molten rocks! Germany heard the clash of armour fill the sky; *the Alps quaked with unwonted shocks.* Moreover a voice was heard of many among silent groves, crying aloud, and phantoms pallid in wonderful wise were seen when night was dim; and cattle spoke, a monstrous thing: *rivers stop and earth yawns;* and ivory sheds tears of mourning and bronzes sweat in the temples. Eridanus, king of rivers, whirled whole forests away in the wash of his raging eddies, and swept herds and stalls together all across the plains. Neither at that same time did boding filaments ever cease to show themselves in disastrous victims, or blood to ooze from wells, and high cities to echo night-long with howling of wolves. *Never elsewhere did more lightnings fall from clear skies, or ghastly comets so often blaze."* See MacKail, *Virgil's Works*, p. 307.

century poet, involuntarily, perhaps, responding as much to Longinus as to Vergil.

The heightened, poeticized sort of classical landscape that will concern us in the *Aeneid* first makes its appearance in the third book of the *Georgics,* in an iconic passage given much painterly amplification by Dryden. Vergil, the Roman poet, announces at the beginning of Book III that he is weary of choosing Greek themes for his verse; he wishes instead to derive his inspiration from Roman sources. Like his countrymen who conquered Greece in battle, he will take back to Rome what spoils he chooses, using these relics of the older culture, however, merely to decorate, not to dominate, his native setting. Mantua, not Arcadia, will provide the ideal landscape in which to build a temple of art, raised to honor Caesar and celebrating in its design and furnishings the glory of Rome.

> I, first of *Romans,* shall in Triumph come
> From conquer'd *Greece,* and bring her Trophies home:
> With Foreign Spoils adorn my native place;
> And with *Idume's* Palms, my *Mantua* grace.
> Of *Parian* Stone a Temple will I raise,
> Where the slow *Mincius* through the Vally strays:
> Where cooling Streams invite the Flocks to drink:
> And Reeds defend the winding water's brink.
> Full in the midst shall mighty *Cæsar* stand:
> Hold the chief Honours; and the Dome command.
> Then I, conspicuous in my *Tyrian* Gown,
> (Submitting to his Godhead my Renown)
> A hundred Coursers from the Goal will drive:
> The Rival Chariots in the Race shall strive.
>
> [ll. 15–28]

Here is a landscape such as Poussin might well have painted. We see in imagination a well-ordered canvas: the classic temple of prized Parian marble, adjacent to it the meandering stream which bisects the valley and attracts the flocks to its waters. The prominent figure of the poet commands the foreground, waiting to do honor to Caesar by instituting magnificent games involving a hundred chariots in a race. When the games are

concluded, Vergil describes a procession to Caesar's temple, led
by the poet himself, olive-crowned and bearing gifts.

> The passing Pageants, and the Pomps appear.
> I, to the Temple, will conduct the Crew:
> The Sacrifice and Sacrificers view;
> From thence return, attended with my Train,
> Where the proud Theatres disclose the Scene:
> Which interwoven *Britains* seem to raise,
> And shew the *Triumph* which their *Shame* displays.
> High o're the Gate, in Elephant and Gold,
> The Crowd shall *Cæsar's Indian* War behold;
> The *Nile* shall flow beneath; and on the side,
> His shatter'd Ships on Brazen Pillars ride.
> Next him *Niphates* with inverted Urn,⎫
> And dropping Sedge, shall his *Armenia* mourn;⎬
> And *Asian* Cities in our Triumph born.⎭
> With backward Bows the *Parthians* shall be there;
> And, spurring from the Fight, confess their fear.
> A double Wreath shall crown our *Cæsar's* Brows;
> Two differing Trophies, from two different Foes.
> *Europe* with *Africk* in his Fame shall join;
> But neither Shore his Conquest shall confine.
> The *Parian* Marble, there, shall seem to move,
> In breathing Statues, not unworthy *Jove.*
> Resembling Heroes, whose Etherial Root
> Is *Jove* himself, and *Cæsar* is the Fruit.
> *Tros* and his Race the Sculptor shall employ;
> And He the God who built the Walls of *Troy.*
> Envy her self at last, grown pale and dumb;
> (By *Cæsar* combated and overcome)
> Shall give her Hands; and fear the curling Snakes
> Of lashing Furies, and the burning Lakes:
> The pains of famisht *Tantalus* shall feel;⎫
> And *Sisyphus* that labours up the Hill⎬
> The rowling Rock in vain; and curst *Ixion's* Wheel.[43]⎭
>
> [III.34–66]

All the artistry, whether of tapestry, pillar, or sculpture, proclaims Caesar's might and Rome's supremacy. Dryden has

43. Compare with MacKail's translation, *Virgil's Works,* pp.
323–24.

permitted himself to add some finishing touches to Vergil's potentially pictorial but unstylized scene. "Niphates driven in rout" becomes an emblematic mourner "with inverted Urn,/ And dropping Sedge." Caesar's statue, crowned with "a double Wreath," dominates the center of Dryden's canvas and receives the trophies of the vanquished. Europe and Africa—again the suggestion of emblematic representation is present—are part of his train. This repeated emphasis on Caesar as the focus of the temple scene is absent in Vergil, but it provides Dryden with a more carefully structured composition. The other elements of the picture—attendant statues of heroic proportions seeming almost alive and a personified Envy "grown pale and dumb"— are also provided with pictorial details not found in Vergil. The result is a vivid "history painting," created by a poet of strongly visual imagination who inevitably responded to the stimulus of an iconic passage in his original. In rendering it into English, he made of it the kind of poetic painting his age most valued, suggesting the classical grandeur of the antique in the art of Nicolas Poussin.

At the close of this passage Vergil addresses Maecenas, his patron, promising that his "maturer Muse" shall, in time, choose "a Nobler theme" than rural husbandry. That vow he fulfilled in the *Aeneid;* it is this work which most challenged Dryden's talents as a translator and made him wish he had four years for correcting to add to the three he spent composing.[44]

In the first place, the *Aeneid* is a heroic poem; its end is to delight, but it must also "form the mind to heroic virtue by example."[45] The poet (or his translator) is not allowed even

---

44. Preface to the *Aeneid,* in *Essays,* ed. Watson, II, 235–36. Dryden's diffidence should not obscure the fact that his long acquaintance with Vergil extended back to his schoolboy days at Westminster under Dr. Busby. Modern scholars (J. M. Bottkol, Helene Maxwell Hooker, and L. Proudfoot) have vindicated him from numerous accusations of ignorance and of plagiarism, while admitting that he did not always work his hardest nor scruple to take what help he could from earlier translators—in that period, a practice not regarded with the same opprobrium it elicits now.

45. *Ibid.,* p. 224.

temporarily to abandon the steep path leading to the literary heights for more congenial and relaxing valleys. "Even the least portions" of such poems "must be of the epic kind." [46] A becoming gravity, a sustained nobility must permeate the whole work. At the same time, however, the poet must never lapse into stilted artificiality; he must follow nature. "Nothing but nature can give a sincere pleasure; where that is not imitated, 'tis grotesque painting; the fine woman ends in a fish's tail." [47] The nature that is the poet's guide is, of course, ideal nature: it may be learned as Vergil has learned from Homer or as modern painters learn from Raphael; it must not be slavishly copied.

It was the quality of Vergil's language—lofty, elegant, yet vivid—that Dryden tried to render into English.[48] Since the original continually suggested pictures to the translator, he tried to communicate that pictorial quality to the English reader unable or unwilling to consult the source. That these pictures often took the form of history paintings is not to be wondered at; history painting, like epic, was the most noble form in its genre, and the two were natural equivalents. Inevitably most of these poetic pictures have a landscape setting in the *Aeneid*. Ostensibly background, these landscapes suggest much more; they reflect the classical perception of nature, both external and human. The epic landscape has importance not only for its literal, narrative role in the life of the epic hero, but also for its symbolic function, the way it represents emotional and psychological values in the poem.

In Book I, for example, Aeneas and his companions battle a storm at sea. Though eventually Neptune calms the winds, the ships are scattered. Aeneas' ship takes refuge in a nearby harbor on the Libyan coast.

46. *Ibid.*
47. *Ibid.*, p. 229.
48. Dryden had early formed the habit of employing Vergil's diction and allusions whenever he wished to elevate the style of his own poetry. See Reuben Brower, "Dryden's Epic Manner and Virgil," in *Essential Articles for the Study of John Dryden,* ed. H. T. Swedenberg, Jr. (Hamden, Conn., 1966), pp. 466–92, and Reuben Brower, "Dryden's Poetic Diction and Virgil," *PQ*, XVIII (1939), 211–17.

> Within a long Recess there lies a Bay,
> An Island shades it from the rowling Sea,
> And forms a Port secure for Ships to ride,⎤
> Broke by the jutting Land, on either side: ⎬
> In double Streams the briny Waters glide.⎦
> Betwixt two rows of Rocks, a Sylvan Scene
> Appears above, and Groves for ever green:
> A Grott is form'd beneath, with Mossy Seats,
> To rest the *Nereids,* and exclude the Heats.
> Down thro' the Cranies of the living Walls
> The Crystal Streams descend in murm'ring Falls.
> No Haulsers need to bind the Vessels here,
> Nor bearded Anchors, for no Storms they fear.[49]

[I.228–40]

Two aspects of this poetic landscape are striking: the first is the precision with which it is designed in terms of its larger structural elements; the second is the relatively few detailed particulars within this perfectly balanced composition. Dryden has emphasized the "double Streams" and the "two rows of Rocks" which make both sides of his picture perfectly symmetrical. This left-right symmetry is counterbalanced by the upper and lower levels of the "Sylvan Scene." There, groves of

49. For a convenient comparison of passages cited, the modern translation by Rolfe Humphries follows:
> In a bay's deep curve
> They find a haven, where the water lies
> With never a ripple. A little island keeps
> The sea-swell off, and the waves break on its sides
> And slide back harmless. The great cliffs come down
> Steep to deep water, and the background shimmers,
> Darkens and shines, the tremulous aspen moving
> And the dark fir pointing still. And there is a cave
> Under the overhanging rocks, alive
> With water running fresh, a home of the Nymphs,
> With benches for them, cut from the living stone.
> No anchor is needed here for weary ships,
> No mooring-cable.

William Frost comments briefly on the difference between Dryden and Humphries in this passage, noting justly that "readers of the classics in any age will of course see the objects described in them partly through the lenses of their own sensibility," especially in the case of "Nature" in the sense of "landscape" (*Dryden and the Art of Translation,* pp. 42–43).

trees define the upper area of the seacoast while a grotto is described below. The "Crystal Streams" which "descend in murm'ring Falls" emphasize the vertical elements in the composition, while serving also to repeat the motif of flowing water, thereby unifying this part of the picture with the twin streams flowing at left and right. None of this concern for careful, balanced arrangement of spatial masses is discernible in Vergil's original (see ll. 157–69). Dryden, however, is much less interested in vivid particulars than is Vergil; the towering peaks of the cliffs, the play of sunlight and shadow on the wooded landscape, and the more minute observation of the trees are all missing in Dryden's version. Why should the larger outlines of his landscape be rendered with such a sensitive regard for exact effects and the smaller details be sketched in with what seems a decidedly perfunctory air?

It is likely that Dryden wanted to retain a measure of epic generality that he sensed in the original but which might in English have been lost, resulting in an over-particularized impression, if translated literally. A certain degree of abstractness is one way to preserve a necessary idealizing distance between the object and the viewer. The significance of this landscape in the affairs of Aeneas is clear. It is what Renato Poggioli calls a "pastoral oasis," defined by Renssalaer W. Lee as "a period of refreshment and recreation in the midst of the heavy business and manifold cares of life." [50] The image of a safe, secluded harbor is reinforced by a landscape that suggests the Golden Age, with "Groves for ever green," a shady grotto where nereids rest, and murmuring "Crystal Streams." Dryden, in the next few lines, refers to this place as a "happy Harbour" and a "welcome Land." An idyllic refuge can be particularized into a commonplace rural setting all too easily. Dryden is determined not to let that happen. Wordsworth's famous remark, in a letter to Scott in 1805, is relevant here: "Whenever Vergil can be fairly said to have his *eye* upon his object, Dryden always spoils the passage." It is this abstracting tendency of Dryden's,

50. "Erminia in Minneapolis," in *Studies in Criticism and Aesthetics, 1660–1800,* ed. Howard Anderson and John S. Shea (Minneapolis, 1967), p. 38.

one suspects, that elicited Wordsworth's negative evaluation of his translation. Dryden, in his turn, would have abhorred Wordsworth's "Dutch" vignettes of rustic life and would have considered his sensibilities wholly unsuited to translating Vergil acceptably for cultivated seventeenth-century readers.

Where it suits his purposes to do so, Dryden is as capable of adding or amplifying details as he is of minimizing them elsewhere. The details he chooses to focus on, however, are not realistic; Wordsworth would never have considered them "nature." They are artificial and decorative, employed to heighten the visual impact of the original by using designedly elevated images which reinforce the ideal landscape of the epic.

> *Cymothoe, Triton,* and the Sea-green Train
> Of beauteous Nymphs, the Daughters of the Main,
> Clear from the Rocks the Vessels with their hands;
> The God himself with ready Trident stands,
> And opes the Deep, and spreads the moving sands;
> Then heaves them off the sholes: where e're he guides
> His finny Coursers, and in Triumph rides,
> The Waves unruffle and the Sea subsides.[51]
>
> [I.205–12]

These lines, which precede the longer passage just cited, describe the rescue of Aeneas' ships and the calming of the sea by Neptune and his minions. In Dryden's version they are much enlarged over the original which is succinct and unadorned. Purely Dryden's are the train of nymphs and their activities, and there is no mention in the original of Neptune's "finny Coursers." Dryden's periphrasis would have been regarded by his readers as perfectly Vergilian in tone, even if it were his own addition, though it was exactly the kind of emendation that provoked the contempt of nineteenth-century critics. Modern

51. Rolfe Humphries' version of these lines (I.144–47 in the original) is:

> Cymothoe and Triton,
> Heaving together, pulled the ships from the reef,
> As Neptune used his trident for a lever,
> Opened the quicksand, made the water smooth,
> And the flying chariot skimmed the level surface.

scholars realize that the function of the periphrasis was to elevate and to pictorialize an English term that would have been considered flat and, if not low, at least undistinguished in an epic. Dryden wanted to help his readers visualize Neptune's appearance in this seascape; so he provides him with "finny Coursers," a periphrastic equivalent of fish.

Neptune's commanding figure, dominating the waves from his sea chariot, was a popular subject in Renaissance art. The most epic or heroic treatment may be Poussin's *The Triumph of Neptune*,[52] in which the god, surrounded by sea nymphs, Triton, and *putti,* casts an amorous glance at Galatea in her chariot beside his own. Though three powerful horses draw his vehicle, hers is harnessed to four dolphins being guided by Cupid. Here is a precedent for Dryden's "finny Coursers," a detail that Poussin borrowed from Raphael's *Galatea,* an influential and highly regarded picture. It would not have been unreasonable to expect cultivated Englishmen reading Dryden's passage to form a mental image of a scene very like those depicted in the paintings of Raphael and Poussin.

Unlike the baroque landscapes discussed earlier, the classical landscape possesses a more serene stability and projects an impression of order and containment. A greater sense of repose and dignity arises from the absence of theatrical effects and restless movement inherent in so much baroque art. Poussin's painting offers an especially appropriate analogue to Dryden's Vergil, for Poussin tried to be consciously Vergilian in his own medium, imitating the antique and revering the ideal form of Roman art. Poussin's greatest popularity in England came in the late seventeenth and early eighteenth centuries, the height of the classical period. In the 1680s and 1690s he was thought a history painter, rather than a landscapist, because of the austere, elevated, and cerebral nature of his work.[53] Even the mood of his paintings is Vergilian: Charles Dempsey comments upon the frequent "inimitable evocation of lingering melancholy"

52. In the Philadelphia Museum of Art. Reproduced in Anthony Blunt, *Nicolas Poussin,* 2 vols. (New York, 1967), Vol. II, pl. 91.
53. Ogden and Ogden, *English Taste in Landscape in the Seventeenth Century,* p. 107.

in his pictures.[54] One having even a casual acquaintance with Poussin's work is reminded of it continually when reading Dryden's Vergil.

Dryden's painterly touches are more remarkable in the descriptive parts of the *Aeneid* than in the iconic passages. These —like the walls of Dido's Carthaginian temple, Cloanthus' prize vest, and Aeneas' shield—are translated closely with only a slightly amplified pictorialism. Dryden's landscape touches, on the other hand, are very often enlarged and rendered more visually decorative:

> And now the rising Morn, with rosie light
> Adorns the Skies, and puts the Stars to flight:
> When we from far, like bluish Mists, descry
> The Hills, and then the Plains of *Italy*.
>
> [III.682–85]

William Frost, in noting this passage, credits Dryden with "a newly created simile," the phrase "like bluish mists." [55] He does not, however, relate it to painting and to the invariable practice of landscapists from Patenir to Claude of painting distant mountains and background vistas a luminous, delicate blue.

Enough illustrations have been given to help us form a clear concept of Dryden's classical ideal landscapes. We may summarize by noting first that they are still predominantly decorative, like their more baroque equivalents in *The State of Innocence*. They are also, however, less theatrical and more self-contained, functioning not as pictorial rhetoric but as painterly objectifications in landscape of elevated epic moods and themes. They strive for stasis, not movement, and use recognizable iconographic and emblematic motifs from Renaissance art to punctuate poetic images. But we must reiterate that only in a very few instances do they exhibit any thoroughgoing technical understanding of landscape composition such as that found in the poetic landscapes of Pope and Thomson. In the next sections we shall begin to see how Dryden has blended both kinds of landscape—baroque and classical—in

54. "The Classical Perception of Nature in Poussin's Earlier Works," *JWCI*, XXIX (1966), 247.
55. *Dryden and the Art of Translation*, p. 48.

the odes and *Fables,* achieving in his most successful poems the unification of these apparently disparate modes of seventeenth-century art.

Dryden's Poetry of Praise

Though occasional poetry usually deserves the low critical esteem it frequently receives, Dryden's panegyrics sustain an impressively high level. The appeal of this poetry is aesthetic rather than affective, Dr. Johnson's strictures on *Lycidas* to the contrary. Such art offers, therefore, an opportunity for a poet to exercise the formal elegancies of his craft, to celebrate or to mourn in a fitting, public manner those occasions that demand a suitable commemoration. Inevitably, the emphasis for both poet and audience is upon the way this end is achieved; the how and not the why becomes the main issue. Dryden's age subscribed to the covering over of "lamentable reality" by the "persistent exemplification of the ideal." [56] As a result, verisimilitude usually yielded place to artifice in the poetry of praise.

Such art has returned to both critical and popular favor. In painting, a good case for the formalist aesthetic has been made by Roger Fry on behalf of Poussin, whose stylistic likeness to Dryden has already been pointed out. Fry grants that Poussin's subjects are the traditional ones, which seem insipid and artificial to twentieth-century tastes, but, he says, that fact only frees us to focus on form. "Once he [Poussin] got to work his intense feeling for formal harmonies became his chief occupation, as indeed it remains for us, now that we no longer respond to the rhetoric of Poussin's time, the real meaning of his work . . . the endless variety and daring originality of his pictorial architecture." [57]

Dryden's odes and panegyrics permitted him the same kind of scope as Poussin for achieving striking stylistic effects within

56. James Kinsley, "Dryden and the Art of Praise," in *Essential Articles for the Study of John Dryden,* p. 547.

57. *French, Flemish and British Art* (New York, 1951), p. 20. Cited in Solomon Fishman, *The Interpretation of Art: Essays on the Art Criticism of John Ruskin, Walter Pater, Clive Bell, Roger Fry, and Herbert Read* (Berkeley and Los Angeles, 1963), p. 132.

a formal framework. Both poet and painter concentrated on the image or icon as the principal vehicle for exploiting the potentials of their forms. Dryden's odes permitted him liberties similar to those he had enjoyed in another permissive genre, the opera. As a result we shall expect to see once again the baroque techniques and motifs that operated in *The State of Innocence.*

Ideal landscape in the poetry of praise functions both as a decorative, ornamental adjunct to the person being honored and as a metaphor of his fortunes and qualities. Dryden addresses Charles II in *Astrea Redux:*

> That Star that at your Birth shone out so bright
> It stain'd the duller Suns Meridian light,
> Did once again its potent Fires renew
> Guiding our eyes to find and worship you.
>
> [ll. 288–91]

Charles as a Christ-figure strains credulity, but Dryden's intent is not blasphemous. Rather, he is attempting to invest a significant occasion like the king's return with all of the august and solemn associations he can muster. Invariably exaggeration plays a recognized role in this process. Arthur Hoffman stresses what he calls the "incarnational" aspects of some of Dryden's poems of praise, "where the object of praise is enlarged beyond the frame of nature and epic" and the imagery moves from "the dominion of Nature" to "the qualified permanence of the symbols of art." [58] Such a preference for art over nature or, more accurately, such a transformation of nature into art is congenial to baroque pictorialization, tending as it does to the theatrical and hyperbolic. When Dryden wants to tell us that Charles's ship made slow progress because of failing winds and a slow sea, he does so like this:

> The winds that never Moderation knew
> Afraid to blow too much, too faintly blew;
> Or out of breath with joy could not enlarge
> Their straightned lungs, or conscious of their Charge.

58. *John Dryden's Imagery* (Gainesville, Fla., 1962), p. 98.

176

> The British *Amphitryte* smooth and clear
> In richer Azure never did appear;
> Proud her returning Prince to entertain
> With the submitted Fasces of the Main.
>
> [ll. 242–49]

Here is a fairly typical baroque canvas. Emblematic figures surround and ornament the central element in the picture, Charles's ship. Above it the wind gods with distended cheeks help propel the boat shoreward. Amphitrite, the nereid wife of Neptune, waits to greet the king, looking her best as even a goddess would wish to do on such an occasion.

These effects are repeated in a later poem to the Duchess of Ormond which was a dedication to her, in verse, of Dryden's Chaucer translation, "Palamon and Arcite." The Duke and Duchess had just returned from a trip to Ireland and the expectation (confirmed finally in 1703) was that the Duke would shortly be named Lord Lieutenant of that country.

> When Westward, like the Sun, you took your Way,
> And from benighted *Britain* bore the Day,
> Blue *Triton* gave the Signal from the Shore,
> The ready *Nereids* heard, and swam before,
> To smooth the Seas; a soft *Etesian* Gale
> But just inspir'd, and gently swell'd the Sail;
> *Portunus* took his Turn, whose ample Hand ⎫
> Heav'd up his lighten'd Keel, and sunk the Sand, ⎬
> And steer'd the sacred Vessel safe to Land. ⎭
> The Land, if not restrain'd, had met Your Way,
> Projected out a Neck, and jutted to the Sea.
> *Hibernia,* prostrate at Your Feet, ador'd,
> In You, the Pledge of her expected Lord;
>
> ["To Her Grace the Dutchess of Ormond," ll. 42–54]

Again both mythologized and personified nature transforms the seascape into an exercise in the decorative baroque. Several scholars have associated Dryden's baroque images with Rubens' iconography, and that correspondence should be reiterated here. *The Disembarking of Marie de Medici at Marseilles* in the Louvre series shows the nereids who swam before the ship,

177

the sea and wind gods who protected it, and the splendid figure of Marie receiving the homage of the French. In Dryden's poem, the Duchess of Ormond is, like Marie, metamorphosized into a deity. The ship she sails upon is a "sacred Vessel," and she is adored by personified Hibernia prostrate before her. She resembles Apollo, and her vessel, like the chariot of the sun, deprives Britain of the light of her presence as it journeys westward. The movement of the land to greet the incoming boat is a motif resurrected from *Astraea Redux:*

> Behold th' approaching cliffes of *Albion;*
> It is no longer Motion cheats your view,
> As you meet it, the Land approacheth you.
> The Land returns, and in the white it wears
> The marks of penitence and sorrow bears.
>
> [ll. 251–55]

While this sort of exaggeration is a baroque constant, it is not as strained and inflated when Dryden's patron is a less exalted personage and when the poet is not quite so conscious of playing the courtier or laureate. Such is the case with his ode to Anne Killigrew where artistic tact and delicacy operate to great effect, perhaps because "the Accomplisht Young LADY" is, in reality, an unpretentious figure. The same simplicity that ennobled the verses to Oldham operates here to the extent of toning down and giving a measure of classical restraint to the poem's baroque imagery. In the process of writing the ode, Dryden's creative intelligence had to deal simultaneously with the fact of Anne and the decorative setting into which he was placing her.

The consciousness of the gulf between his subject and the role he was investing her with in the ode appears to affect the tone Dryden takes toward Anne, especially in the first stanza. The "Youngest Virgin-Daughter of the Skies" is pictured half humorously in the celestial regions, in alternatively considered cosmic landscapes, each more remote and grandly extensive.

> Whether, adopted to some Neighbouring Star,
> Thou rol'st above us, in thy wand'ring Race,

178

Or, in Procession fixt and regular,
Mov'd with the Heavens Majestick pace;
Or, call'd to more Superiour Bliss,
Thou tread'st, with Seraphims, the vast Abyss:

[i.6–11]

Whatever her exalted position in the heavenly choir, Anne is urged to cease her "Celestial Song" and listen to the poet's earthly harmonies in her praise.

Dryden pays predictable tribute to his heroine's ancestry, both actual and figurative. Her father and, by implication, her uncles are gracefully complimented, while she is allied in spiritual kinship with "all the Mighty Poets" of classical antiquity. The earlier stanzas of the ode celebrate her poetic achievement as well as her moral excellence and intellectual growth, leaving the last half for a commemoration of her accomplishments in the sister art of painting and her symbolic relevance, moral and artistic, to the age which she has adorned. The whole poem is replete with painterly images; we may instance in stanza iii Anne's birth translated into a baroque nativity scene complete with angelic musicians. The separation between the real Anne and her allegorical significance as goddess-patron of the sister arts is maintained throughout the poem, as are superficially contradictory but essentially complementary qualities of her mind and character. Gradually we are led to perceive in Anne's duality a metaphor for the ideal state of the arts, both poetic and pictorial. They are, or should be, like Anne, both human and divine, deriving from nature, unspoiled by art (in the pejorative sense of that word), directed toward moral as well as aesthetic ends, and infused with lofty spirituality and intellectual vigor.

In the complex form of the ode, multiplicity can all too easily fail to attain the necessary, overriding unity it ultimately requires to harmonize its disparate aspects. Dryden's unifying element is Anne herself. The apparent contradictions reveal paradoxically her essential harmony, as Dryden's imagery, often taken from the landscape of classical literature, testifies.

> Her *Arethusian* Stream remains unsoil'd,
> Unmixt with Forreign Filth, and undefil'd,
> Her Wit was more than Man, her Innocence a Child!
>
> [iv.68–70]

Another example describes Anne:

> So cold herself, whilst she such Warmth exprest,
> 'Twas *Cupid* bathing in *Diana's* Stream.
>
> [v.86–87]

The climax of the poem occurs in stanza vi, a section twice as lengthy as the stanzas that precede and follow it, the apex of the poem's pyramidal structure. In the beginning of this passage, Anne is portrayed as extending her sway over two realms in a highly developed and elaborated image. Painting is a "plenteous Province" and a "Fief" which she claims by conquest. The last half of stanza vi describes her paintings as being all landscapes (a tribute to the growing popularity of the genre), despite the fact that she seems, in real life, to have specialized in portraits, with a few still life and history paintings also recorded.[59] Stanza vii does pay tribute to her abilities as a portraitist, but Dryden's primary poetic emphasis focuses decidedly upon the landscapes in stanza vi.

> Her Pencil drew, what e're her Soul design'd,
> And oft the happy Draught surpass'd the Image in her Mind.
> The *Sylvan* Scenes of Herds and Flocks,
> And fruitful Plains and barren Rocks,
> Of shallow Brooks that flow'd so clear,
> The Bottom did the Top appear;
> Of deeper too and ampler Flouds,
> Which as in Mirrors, shew'd the Woods;
> Of lofty Trees with Sacred Shades,
> And Perspectives of pleasant Glades,
> Where Nymphs of brightest Form appear, ⎫
> And shaggy Satyrs standing neer, ⎬
> Which them at once admire and fear. ⎭

59. Horace Walpole, *Anecdotes of Painting in England,* 4 vols. (Strawberry Hill, 1762–71), III, 25. Walpole's information about Anne Killigrew comes in part from Anthony à Wood as well as other unnamed contemporaries.

> The Ruines too of some Majestick Piece,
> Boasting the Pow'r of ancient *Rome* or *Greece,*
> Whose Statues, Freezes, Columns broken lie,
> And though deface't, the Wonder of the Eie,
> What Nature, Art, bold Fiction e're durst frame,
> Her forming Hand gave Feature to the Name.
> So strange a Concourse ne're was seen before,
> But when the peopl'd Ark the whole Creation bore.
>
> [vi.106–26]

These scenes poetically reproduce the ideal landscapes of Nicolas Poussin, the Italianate French painter.[60] Living in a baroque age, Poussin's artistic instincts were predominantly classical, but his work represents a restatement of classical ideals which recognized and assimilated aspects of the baroque rather than wholly repudiating it. It appears that Anne's landscapes, like Anne herself, are designed by the poet to suggest these harmonizing, reconciling qualities inherent in the canvases of "learned Poussin." Like the Ark, they contain "the whole Creation," including antithetical elements—"fruitful Plains and barren Rocks," "shallow Brooks" and "ampler Flouds," "Nymphs" and "shaggy Satyrs." The last juxtaposition recalls the contrast Dryden has drawn earlier, in stanza iv, between the purity of Anne, likened to the nymph Arethusa, and the profligate playwrights of "this lubrique and adult'rate age." Finally, it is not unreasonable to connect the majestic ruins, "though deface't, the Wonder of the Eie," with the tribute to classical poets in stanza ii. Anne is associated with the arts of that noble age rather than with those of her own time, fallen to low estate. In the latter part of the poem, she is also presented as a guide whose salvific influence may restore to the arts an age as golden as those she paints.

The last image of Anne and her fellow poets on the Day of

60. The similarity of Dryden's landscapes to those of Poussin has been commented upon by Jean Hagstrum. See *The Sister Arts,* p. 202. Earl Miner has also linked the passage in stanza vi to the "French style of 'classical' painting" and the schools of Claude Lorrain and Nicolas Poussin. See *Dryden's Poetry* (Bloomington and London, 1967), pp. 259–60.

Judgment, rising, "Like mounting Larkes, to the New Morning," reduces to a single vivid simile the concept of Anne Killigrew's role as patron of the sister arts. The simple, classical image of the lark who "at break of day sings hymns at heaven's gate" is fused with the baroque energy and movement of the dead souls bursting from their tombs and soaring aloft. She has become the symbol of a reconciling force operating on two levels, the aesthetic and the moral, recalling other artists to Nature and ideal imitation while reminding them of their responsibility "to form the mind to heroic virtue by example." Anne's classical simplicity in this poetic portrait is displayed more advantageously with the aid of Dryden's ornately baroque frame.

The Fables

Looking retrospectively at the landscapes of Dryden's *Fables* from the vantage point of the eighteenth century, we are struck by the ways in which so many anticipate later poetic exercises in the beautiful and the sublime. "The Wife of Bath: Her Tale" offers a haunted wood that recalls Spenser and looks forward to Thomson's *Castle of Indolence:*

> In this despairing State he hap'd to ride
> As Fortune led him, by a Forest-side:
> Lonely the Vale, and full of Horror stood
> Brown with the shade of a religious Wood:
> When full before him at the Noon of night,
> (The Moon was up and shot a gleamy Light)
> He saw a Quire of Ladies in a round,
> That featly footing seem'd to skim the Ground:
> Thus dancing Hand in Hand, so light they were,
> He knew not where they trod, on Earth or Air.
>
> [ll. 209–18]

Boccaccio also seems to have frequently inspired Dryden to attempt the sublime. Gothic novelists as well as poets writing in the next century must have admired the atmosphere of de-

182

licious horror that permeated the landscapes of "Sigismonda and Guiscardo" and "Theodore and Honoria." In the former tale, Dryden describes the lovers' secret meeting place, a cave "dug with vast Expence" into "a Mount of rough Ascent and thick with Wood." The description of the cave's entrance is amplified:

> Its Outlet ended in a Brake o'ergrown
> With Brambles, choak'd by Time, and now unknown.
> A Rift there was, which from the Mountains Height
> Convey'd a glimm'ring and malignant Light,
> A Breathing-place to draw the Damps away,
> A Twilight of an intercepted Day.
>
> [ll. 113–18]

The remote and inaccessible nature of the terrain, the thickly overgrown vegetation, the mountainous height, and the malign gleam of moonlight are all stock ingredients of the "sublime" terrain. Although, as usual, Dryden has not structured his poetic composition in the careful painterly fashion that we expect to find in later emulators of Salvatorian effects, the raw materials of a Rosa landscape are all there.

The hero's stroll at dawn through a haunted wood in "Theodore and Honoria" provided Dryden with another opportunity made to order for a poetic venture into the sublime:

> It happ'd one Morning, as his Fancy led,
> Before his usual Hour, he left his Bed;
> To walk within a lonely Lawn, that stood
> On ev'ry side surrounded by the Wood:
> Alone he walk'd, to please his pensive Mind,
> And sought the deepest Solitude to find:
> 'Twas in a Grove of spreading Pines he stray'd;
> The Winds, within the quiv'ring Branches plaid,
> And Dancing-Trees a mournful Musick made.
> The Place it self was suiting to his Care,
> Uncouth, and Salvage, as the cruel Fair.
>
> [ll. 72–82]

This descriptive passage is elaborated further in subsequent lines, ultimately becoming a highly developed, minutely detailed landscape. It was capable a century later of eliciting an enthusiastic comment from Sir Walter Scott, who often attempted similarly pictorial landscapes in his own work.

> Nothing can be more highly painted than the circumstances preliminary of the apparition; the deepening gloom, the falling wind, the commencement of an earthquake; above all, the indescribable sensation of horror with which Theodore is affected, even ere he sees the actors in the supernatural tragedy. The appearance of the female, of the gaunt mastiff by which she is pursued, and of the infernal huntsman, are all in the highest tone of poetry, and could only be imitated by the pencil of Salvator.[61]

Robert Bell, Dryden's editor in the mid-nineteenth century, has stressed the originality of passages like the one quoted above, asserting that none of the "preparatory circumstances" of the scene which so delighted Scott were to be found in Boccaccio's original; Dryden is credited with having "elevated" his material in translating it.[62]

It is more accurate to call Dryden's translations of Chaucer and Boccaccio examples of "imitation" rather than "paraphrase," though Dryden did not so consider them. Less overawed by his original than had been the case with Vergil's works, Dryden often pruned, embroidered, or restructured his model, until the results reflected his own tastes and those of his age as much as they reproduced Chaucer and Boccaccio in modern English verse. W. H. Williams has estimated, for example, that only about seven lines in Dryden's "Palamon and Arcite" are adopted from Chaucer's "Knightes Tale" unchanged except for modernized spelling.[63] Though the reasons for such thoroughgoing revisions were various, they did not indicate a contempt for his originals. Indeed, Earl Miner

61. Quoted in *The Poetical Works of John Dryden,* ed. Robert Bell, 3 vols. (London, 1862), III, 120.
62. *Ibid.*
63. " 'Palamon and Arcite' and the 'Knightes Tale,' " *MLR,* IX (1914), pt. 1, 162.

credits Dryden with being "the first to conceive of Chaucer as a classic." [64] The Preface to the *Fables* reveals that Dryden even preferred his English predecessor to Ovid, the classical poet whom Chaucer most resembled.[65] Both Chaucer and Boccaccio, however, had suffered the disadvantage of writing when their respective vernaculars were in a relatively undeveloped state. Dryden believed that in order to enable his countrymen to share his own admiration for these literary figures, it was necessary for him to adapt their language and style to the more elevated seventeenth-century standards. By briefly investigating the nature of his changes, we are easily able to perceive and to understand the taste that motivated them.

An especially interesting focus for investigation is "Palamon and Arcite." It is probably the most successful of the *Fables,* and there is evidence to suggest that Dryden accorded it a special dignity in his own estimate of Chaucer's works, considering it "of the epic kind, and perhaps not much inferior to the *Ilias* or the *Æneis*." [66] He seems to have approached "The Knightes Tale" in much the same spirit that he approached Shakespeare's *Antony and Cleopatra,* and the result is, like *All for Love,* a more symmetrically conceived, more elegantly phrased, and more pictorially imagined version than the original which inspired it. W. H. Williams stresses Dryden's many embellishments, noting that "Dryden is especially fond of filling in an outline, or elaborating a sketch into a picture." [67] These additions, however, occur within a poetic structure which has been carefully revised and curtailed to produce a "clearer narrative line" and a strong sense of unity of place.[68] Dryden's version is divided into three books, giving it a more balanced epic or dramatic structure than it possessed in Chaucer's comparatively loose four-part division. These changes result in a

---

64. "Chaucer in Dryden's *Fables,*" *Studies in Criticism and Aesthetics, 1660–1800,* p. 71.
65. See *Essays,* ed. Watson, II, 271.
66. *Ibid.,* p. 290.
67. " 'Palamon and Arcite' and the 'Knightes Tale,' " pt. 2, p. 312.
68. Miner, "Chaucer in Dryden's *Fables,*" p. 68.

work in which highly developed, often baroque pictorializations achieve maximum effect by being contained within a tight classical framework. Dryden's design is severely restrained; his colors are exuberantly vivid.

In Book I Emily walks in the castle garden, unaware that she is observed first by Palamon and later by Arcite also, as, imprisoned in the castle tower, they gaze down upon her. The hour is dawn, and Dryden anticipates Claude Lorrain's penchant for sketching a sunrise landscape.

> *Aurora* had but newly chas'd the Night,
> And purpl'd o'er the Sky with blushing Light,
>
> [ll. 186–87]

Although it is a literary stereotype, especially in epics, to indicate the coming of day by a reference to Aurora, nonetheless there are indications here that Dryden expected to evoke a picture in his readers' minds. There are no corresponding lines in Chaucer's original, but at least a score of Renaissance and baroque paintings of the seventeenth-century Englishman's pantheon depicted the dawn by showing Aurora flying in the heavens before the chariot of Apollo and displacing the figure of Night. The emphasis on color and on the effects of light and shadow is painterly, and a baroque sense of movement is suggested by "chas'd." A few lines later we are shown Emily picking flowers. All but the last two lines are Dryden's alone.

> At ev'ry Turn, she made a little Stand,
> And thrust among the Thorns her Lilly Hand
> To draw the Rose, and ev'ry Rose she drew
> She shook the Stalk, and brush'd away the Dew:
> Then party-colour'd Flow'rs of white and red
> She wove, to make a Garland for her Head:
>
> [ll. 191–96]

This scene contrives somehow to create a medieval impression upon the reader. An image of the Virgin in a *hortus conclusus* is suggested by the artless maiden gathering flowers in her Edenic garden with her "Lilly Hand." At the same time, the redness of the roses recalls Venus as does the flower crown with which Emily adorns herself. In the poem she emblematically but clearly represents chastity; her patroness is Diana. She is also the prize of love, and Palamon, who prays, significantly, to Venus, eventually wins her. The reader who knows the whole story sees, then, in this first glimpse of Emily her two disparate but complementary aspects symbolized in the garden landscape. This last is both *hortus conclusus* and *locus amoenus;* the virginal white of the lady's hand provides a dramatic contrast to the amorous red of the roses she plucks.

The implication of all of this imagery is clarified in the temple section of Book II. Here in an elaborate iconic passage Dryden describes, with pictorial amplification, three altars to Mars, Venus, and Diana. Chaucer's original is followed but much extended.

> Before the Palace-gate, in careless Dress,
> And loose Array, sat Portress Idleness:
> There, by the Fount, *Narcissus* pin'd alone;
>
> [ll. 500–502]

Here, for example, the difference between Chaucer's original and Dryden's translation is that the latter places his emblematic figures in a landscape, grouping them in a picture, while Chaucer is content simply to make a list.

> Nat was foryeten the porter, Ydelnesse,
> Ne Narcisus the faire of yore agon,
>
> [ll. 1940–41]

Chaucer gives his Venus a wreath of red roses, but Dryden adds green myrtle, a plant traditionally associated with Venus and with lovers. Chaucer tells us Cupid is blind; Dryden pictorializes this information, saying, "his Eyes were banded o'er." In Dryden's version the temple of Mars is provided with a landscape background (Dryden uses the word "landscape"; Chaucer, of course, does not) that is, for the most part, an enlarged version of Chaucer's original. Where Chaucer simply states in passing, however, that the temple is situated "downward from an hille," Dryden designs an elaborate exercise in the sublime which culminates in the picture of a "Mountain . . . Threat-

187

ning from high," overlooking the forest "Beneath the lowring Brow."

The same preoccupation in Dryden with enlarging the landscape setting provides the temple of Diana with a Claudian contrast to the Salvatorian setting assigned to Mars. Chaucer tells us only the following before going immediately on to list the mythic figures surrounding Diana.

> Depeynted been the walles up and doun
> Of hyntyng and of shamefast chastitee.
>
> [ll. 2054–55]

Dryden's landscape is much fuller:

> A Sylvan Scene with various Greens was drawn,
> Shades on the Sides, and on the midst a Lawn:
> The Silver *Cynthia,* with her Nymphs around,
> Pursu'd the flying Deer, the Woods with Horns resound:
>
> [ll. 619–22]

In this work Dryden, late in his career, was still only beginning to be able to develop a landscape scene knowledgeably, in terms of relating its description to the techniques of landscape composition in painting. "Various Greens" is vague, but the poet has learned now to shade the "side screens" of his verbal canvas and suggest the play of light. Of greater importance, he has developed the ability to employ the landscape description more flexibly by pictorializing it until it functions both as an important element in its own right and as an objectification of a mood or an individual.

Painters of the sixteenth and seventeenth centuries were in the process of demonstrating to their contemporaries that ideal landscape was important in just this way—both in itself and as the extension of an individual or group. Titian's Charles V in a brooding, oppressive wood, Rubens' Marie de' Medici in a nymph-strewn sea, Poussin's St. John on the austere Patmos shore—all create the same interacting effect that Dryden strove for less surely in his poetic landscapes. Though no virtuoso at achieving a precisely realized painterly quality, Dryden was the sensitive, responsive product of a visual age. In his manipulations of both baroque and classical effects, he displayed his own aesthetic awareness, as much intrinsic as learned, of how fruitfully these styles could be employed, separately or in combination, to enrich the landscapes of his poetry. Intuitively he knew it was the function of ideal landscape to transmute and heighten the "essential element" or "highest truth," whether "of beauty, of pathos, of power, [or] of grandeur," from the real, from which it ultimately derived.[69] For a more deliberate and sophisticated application of that thesis we must look to the next century and to Alexander Pope.

69. Josiah Gilbert, *Landscape in Art before Claude and Salvator* (London, 1885), p. 80.

Plate 12 Zuccarelli, *The Rape of Europa*

⌐ 5 ⌐

Pope's Ideal Landscapes: Pictorial Metaphors of Poetic Themes

𝒫rotestations are no longer necessary against the old heresy that Alexander Pope's work, if not essentially a stylistic exercise in classic prose, still remains the coolly cerebral testament of the Age of Reason and, as such, can rarely be expected to be simple, let alone sensuous or passionate. A generation of Pope scholars has effected a reeducation of the reader while accomplishing a reevaluation of the poetry, and we now recognize to what extent poetic statement is everywhere vivified and reinforced by image in Pope's work. We are also prepared now to concede that he is a poet of nature in the restricted, lowercase sense of that word when used to describe the writing of Wordsworth or Keats. Pope's richest and most durable metaphors derive from landscape, as Maynard Mack has recently demonstrated.[1] These poetic landscapes possess both variety and visual impact; they range from serene visions of a surprisingly Blakean new Jerusalem (*Messiah*) to prophetic

1. *The Garden and the City* (Toronto, 1969). Mack's use of the term *landscape* is not restricted to its narrow application as a term of art, but includes the "emblematic quality" of the poet's setting at Twickenham.

glimpses of imminent chaos and dark night (*The Dunciad*). Though such.diversity is well known to Pope scholars, it should be stressed at the outset of this chapter. Pope displays great flexibility in creating his well-stocked gallery of literary landscapes; he suits style to purpose with a sophistication and verve unknown in the work of any poet we have previously studied. Pope's landscapes are correspondingly varied; with subtle discrimination he adapts them to his purposes, whether these are primarily decorative (*Pastorals*), affective (*Eloisa to Abelard*), or moral (*Epistle to Bathurst*). Everywhere his poems betray evidence of a highly cultivated visual imagination stimulated by a lifelong familiarity with painting. More than twenty years have passed since Norman Ault stated that "Pope was the first of the great English landscapists in verse to compose his picture within the frame and paint it in the colours of nature." [2] Ault's assertion corrects the estimate of earlier scholars, like Elizabeth Manwaring, who had held that it was not until about 1726 that an attentive reader could discern, in the work of Thomson and Dyer, the conscious, skilled application of picturesque techniques in poetic descriptions of nature.[3] Though we have perceived that a significant number of painterly effects are demonstrable in the work of several "English landscapists" of the later seventeenth century, Ault's judgment remains valid, though it must be qualified. Pope should still be regarded as the first poet who consistently arranges his landscape ingredients in a fashion that attests to his thoroughgoing technical knowledge of pictorial design.

Variations on a Landscape Theme

The extent to which Pope's work, especially the earlier poems, is saturated with vivid color descriptions and epithets has been fully studied and categorized,[4] but in poetry as in painting

2. *New Light on Pope* (London, 1949), p. 81. All of chap. 5, pp. 68–100, is devoted to an examination of Pope's knowledge of painting.

3. *Italian Landscape in Eighteenth-Century England* (London, 1925), p. 96.

4. See especially Ault, *New Light on Pope,* pp. 82–100, as well as Marjorie Nicolson and G. S. Rousseau (*"This Long Disease, My*

Pope more often placed the primary emphasis on design, as this analogy illustrates.

> Yet if we look more closely, we shall find
> Most have the *Seeds* of Judgment in their Mind;
> Nature affords at least a *glimm'ring Light;*
> The *Lines,* tho' touch'd but faintly, are drawn right.
> But as the slightest Sketch, if justly trac'd, ⎫
> Is by ill *Colouring* but the more disgrac'd, ⎬
> So by *false Learning* is *good Sense* defac'd; ⎭
>
> [*An Essay on Criticism,* ll. 19–25] [5]

Such a stress on the importance of "line" is, of course, a predictable part of Pope's classical orientation, though his classicism, especially in the earlier years, is hardly confining or rigorous, or even, to purists, consistent. While it is the dominant mode in the poetry of his mature years, such an emphasis is to be expected from a poet who grew ever more concerned with the social and ethical dimension of poetry and used genres like the moral essay and Horatian epistle.

Pope early recognized the strong appeal of a complementary rather than opposing "romantick" tendency in himself. In a letter to Lady Mary Wortley Montague in 1716, he wrote: "The more I examine my own mind, the more Romantick I find myself. . . . Let them say I am Romantick, so is every one said to be that either admires a fine thing, or praises one." [6] The close connection between Pope's romanticism and a taste for certain kinds of landscape has been discerned by several scholars.[7] Here we must guard against a temptation to interpret the complexity of Augustan neoclassicism too simply and nar-

Life": Alexander Pope and the Sciences [Princeton, 1968], pp. 266–94). The latter have modified some aspects of Ault's earlier study and amplified others.

5. See also ll. 484–93.

6. *The Correspondence of Alexander Pope,* ed. George Sherburn, 5 Vols. (Oxford, 1956), I, 367.

7. Most recently by Nicolson and Rousseau who tentatively conclude that if Pope had not embarked upon his *Iliad* translation at a crucial time in his life, "he might have become a 'Romantic' poet. . . . His treatment of Homer is not infrequently 'romantic'" (*"This Long Disease, My Life,"* p. 235).

rowly. From Shaftesbury to Addison a liking for irregular "natural" landscape could and did peacefully coexist with the doctrine of ideal imitation. Pope, like many of his contemporaries, exhibits an attitude of "horticultural romanticism," to use A. O. Lovejoy's phrase, but "there is no real contradiction between his neoclassicism as a poet and his theory and practice as a gardener."[8] On the contrary, the principles of the English art of landscaping, developed during the eighteenth century, derived from the ideal landscapes evolved by painters of the Italian Schools from Giorgione and Titian to Claude and Nicolas Poussin.[9] As William Shenstone suggested, "Landskip should contain variety enough to form a picture upon canvas; and this is no bad test, as I think the landskip painter is the gardiner's best designer."[10] Pope himself once observed that "all gardening is landscape-painting."[11]

When Pope applied himself to his avocation of landscape gardening, like Shenstone, Thomson, and many another contemporary, he took his principles of composition from the art of landscape painting and created "a pretty landskip of his own possessions," to use Addison's phrase in *The Spectator* (No. 414, 1712). He was no slavish copyist, however; his own painter's eye judiciously gauged the final effect. It gave him pleasure to advise friends who were redesigning their estates in conformity with the new natural aesthetic. Joseph Spence has recorded one conversation in which Pope expatiated on his own innovative landscaping as if the Twickenham countryside

8. A. L. Altenbernd, "On Pope's 'Horticultural Romanticism,'" *Essential Articles for the Study of Alexander Pope,* ed. Maynard Mack (Hamden, Conn., 1964), p. 137.

9. E. H. Gombrich has traced the development of landscape painting, while asserting its priority over landscape "feeling." It is interesting to see a parallel to this development in England where the transformation of one's estate into an imitation of a landscape painting elicited rhapsodic responses to "nature." See "The Renaissance Theory of Art and the Rise of Landscape," in *Norm and Form* (London, 1966), p. 118.

10. Cited in B. H. Bronson, "When Was Neoclassicism?," in *Facets of the Enlightenment* (Berkeley and Los Angeles, 1968), p. 17.

11. Joseph Spence, *Anecdotes, Observations and Characters of Books and Men,* ed. James M. Osborn, 2 vols. (Oxford, 1966), I, 252.

were his canvas. "You may distance things by darkening them and by narrowing the plantation more and more toward the end, in the same manner as they do in painting, as 'tis executed in the little cypress walk to that obelisk [Pope's mother's memorial]." Not only the tricks of achieving perspective but also the management of chiaroscuro effects interested Pope the painter-landscapist: "The lights and shades in gardening are managed by disposing the thick grove-work, the thin, and the openings in a proper manner, of which the eye generally is the properest judge." [12] As one can readily perceive, the natural garden was a far from haphazard construction. It involved a certain degree of preliminary theorizing: the realization that variety and a measure of irregularity gave a more pleasing effect than the geometric uniformity of seventeenth-century gardens and that, though "rules" were a valuable guide, in landscape as in literature the greatest art lay in concealing them. Pope's *Guardian* essay (No. 173, 1713) which, for all its unpretentiousness, played a part in making the new tastes prevail,[13] argued for the beneficent effect of the natural landscape on the mind. "There is certainly something in the amiable Simplicity of unadorned Nature, that spreads over the Mind a more noble Sort of Tranquillity, and a loftier Sensation of Pleasure, than can be raised from the nicer Scenes of Art." [14]

12. *Ibid.*, p. 253. Spence notes the opposite of "distancing" was "contrasting" (see *Epistle to Burlington*, ll. 62–64). In this context it is well to remember Walpole's remark that "Pope undoubtedly contributed to form Kent's taste." Joseph Warton tells us that Kent borrowed the design of Twickenham for the Prince of Wales's garden at Carleton House. See *An Essay on the Genius and Writings of Pope*, 2 vols. (London, 1806), II, 175.

13. Pope's *Guardian* essay may well have been "the decisive influence upon Bathurst's original conception" at Cirencester. Pope's principles also affected Burlington's and Kent's plans at Chiswick. See James Lees-Milne, *Earls of Creation: Five Great Patrons of Eighteenth-Century Art* (London, 1962), p. 40.

14. *The Prose Works of Alexander Pope*, ed. Norman Ault (Oxford, 1936), p. 145. As the Augustan age became the "Age of Sensibility," it is easy to see this affective element increasingly stressed. Its role in the aesthetics of the earlier period is, however, far from insignificant. See Wallace Jackson, "Affective Values in Early Eighteenth-Century Aesthetics," *JAAC*, XXVII (1968), 87–92.

Of course "unadorned" did not mean to Pope's readers what it would mean to Wordsworth's. Pope's rural nature was judiciously rearranged to suggest the ideal landscapes of a literary tradition that went back to Homer's Garden of Alcinous in the *Odyssey*. Since these same literary sources had furnished inspiration to sixteenth- and seventeenth-century painters, the *ut pictura poesis* ramifications of landscape, both visual and verbal, were strongly entrenched. Inevitably, English landscape architecture reflected the literary orientation of those Italian painters who had gone to Vergil and Ovid for inspiration as often as they had consulted the work of their own predecessors. Pope's experience with painting, along with his translation of Homer and knowledge of the pastoral genre, combined to endow him with a vision of rural beauty (much indebted to the *locus amoenus*) that was both classical in its concern for the balanced arrangement of spatial masses and contemporary in its rejection of rigidity and formalism. As Geoffrey Tillotson has remarked, "And when he saw beautiful country, there was for Pope another human enrichment. He saw it with the eye of a painter." [15]

A final word remains to be said about the number and variety of Pope's poetic landscapes. Despite their differences, each can be recognized and classified within the pictorial tradition. Pope's choice in each case was dictated by conventions of generic propriety based upon the subject and purpose of his poem. After close study of these landscape poems, one suspects that Pope's categories derived at least as much from the generic traditions operable within the sister art of painting as they did from the conventions of poetry. Pope had available to him, in Richard Haydocke's English translation of 1598, the first systematic treatise on landscape, G. P. Lomazzo's *Trattato*, written in 1584. Using a sketchy and undeveloped system of categories derived from Vitruvius, Lomazzo had evolved a number of reasonably distinct types of landscape.

> Those who have shown excellence and grace in this branch
> of painting, both in private and public places, have discovered

15. *Pope and Human Nature* (Oxford, 1958), p. 103.

various ways of setting about it—such as fetid, dark under-
ground places, religious and macabre, where they represent
graveyards, tombs, deserted houses, sinister and lonesome sites,
caves, dens, ponds and pools; [secondly] privileged places
where they show temples, consistories, tribunals, gymnasiums
and schools, [or else] places of fire and blood with furnaces,
mills, slaughterhouses, gallows and stocks; others bright with
serene air, where they represent palaces, princely dwellings,
pulpits, theatres, thrones and all the magnificent and regal
things; others again places of delight with fountains, fields,
gardens, seas, rivers, bathing places and places for dancing.[16]

E. H. Gombrich finds "truly astonishing" the later development of these distinctions. "For Lomazzo's 'privileged places'
are clearly turned into the heroic landscape of Poussin, his
'places of delight' become the Pastoral of Claude, and his
'sinister dens' the subject matter of Salvator Rosa and Ma-
gnasco." [17] Pope is the first English poet to reveal in his own
work such a comparable sense of the variety of heroic and ideal
landscape categories. The "religious and macabre" places recall
the romantic settings of *Eloisa to Abelard* and the *Elegy to the
Memory of an Unfortunate Lady*. Scenes in the *Iliad* are suggested by the "places of fire and blood," while the confines of
Windsor Forest are evoked by Lomazzo's "privileged places."
Landscapes in the Epistles to Burlington and Bathurst are
often like those locales "bright with serene air" in the *Trattato,* just as the "places of delight" are the focus of Pope's
Pastorals and *Messiah*.[18] While there is no textual evidence to

16. Cited in Gombrich, "Renaissance Theory of Art," p. 120.
17. *Ibid.*
18. The durability of these categories and the subsequent development of other, more careful distinctions remained a continuing
phenomenon of landscape painting well into the nineteenth century.
J. M. W. Turner's *Liber Studiorum* gives labels to each of the painter's landscapes: "H. standing for Historical, Ms. for Mountainous,
P. for Pastoral, E. P. for Elevated Pastoral, Ma. for Marine and A.
for Architectural" (Gombrich, "Renaissance Theory of Art," p.
121). Later, John Ruskin categorized landscapes as Heroic, Classical,
Pastoral, and Contemplative, noting also two lesser forms, Picturesque and Hybrid. See *Modern Painters,* 5 vols. (New York,
1897), V, 250–51.

show that Pope was guided by Lomazzo's categories when he designed his poetic landscapes, it is certainly clear that he sensed the kinds of differences that these labels recognize.

The diversity and multiplicity of Pope's landscapes make them less easily susceptible than Dryden's to simple division along classical and baroque lines; they resist an all-inclusive descriptive label. The groupings that follow, therefore, are intended to be more suggestive than arbitrary. They will reveal the poet's development as a pictorialist and display the astonishing range and complexity of his landscape art.

From Decorative to Emblematic Pastoral

For Pope the Arcadian landscape was always to possess an emblematic significance expressive of his own most cherished artistic and moral principles. Martin Battestin asserts that of deepest importance to Pope was the Golden Age concept, "comprehending both the Christian's conception of Time and History, and within this context, the poet's conception of the relationship of Art to Nature." [19] In his *Discourse on Pastoral Poetry,* Pope reminds us that the art of poetry itself first flowered in a rural setting.[20] Even in urbanized eighteenth-century England, an apprentice poet could simultaneously rediscover that idyllic world and announce his own vocation. His exercise in pastoral was expected to be derivative; the echoes of Vergil (especially in Dryden's translation), of Spenser, and of Milton in young Alexander Pope's pastoral poetry constituted an acknowledgment of his debt to his literary forebears and his acceptance of the implicit challenge to

19. See "The Transforming Power, Nature and Art in Pope's Pastorals," *Eighteenth-Century Studies,* II (1969), 183. Battestin's view of the *Pastorals* is that Pope intends the artifice of their form to have a "redemptive function" and "the transforming power to restore to us a measure at least of grace and harmony . . . to remind us of the identity of Art and Nature that once obtained in Eden, in the Golden Age."

20. "The original of Poetry is ascribed to that age which succeeded the creation of the world: And as the keeping of flocks seems to have been the first employment of mankind, the most ancient sort of poetry was probably pastoral" (*Works,* I, 23).

infuse new life into old forms. In the pastoral, the setting itself rather than the activities of the shepherds is given primary emphasis. For this reason scenic description abounds, and the effect is strongly visual, often pictorial. In a series of pastoral poems, divisions are made on the basis of the months of the year or the seasons, thereby gaining the widest variety of landscapes possible. It is not surprising that seventeenth-century painters raided Vergil for pictures of ideal rural beauty. Pope's *Discourse* recognizes this stress on the pictorial and on variety when it states that "in each of them [eclogues] a design'd scene or prospect is to be presented to our view, which should likewise have its variety." He also recommends varying the times of day in pastoral poetry and shows himself adroit in capitalizing on the moods that are traditionally associated with seasons and times, from the joyful promise of a spring morning to the somber malaise of a winter night.

Pope's "Spring," the first pastoral, is centered upon a worn enough convention: two shepherds celebrate their loves in a contest of song. Predictably, one of the prizes is a drinking bowl, described by Daphnis:

> this Bowl, where wanton Ivy twines,
> And swelling Clusters bend the curling Vines:
> Four Figures rising from the Work appear,
> The various Seasons of the rowling Year;
> And what is That, which binds the Radiant Sky,
> Where twelve fair Signs in beauteous Order lye?
>
> [ll. 35–40]

Martin Battestin suggests that the art object in this iconic passage is "Pope's emblem for the Pastorals . . . themselves" and metaphorically indicates the relationship between art and ideal nature.[21] That relationship in these poems is extremely close; nature itself is imbued with a painterly aura which is designedly artificial. The decorative aspects of the Golden Age landscape are rendered with a deft rococo elegance that makes the pastoral setting as much an art object as the carved bowl vied for by the shepherds.

21. "The Transforming Power," pp. 192–93.

"Spring" suggests the *capriccio,* a style of landscape painting which by the eighteenth century had a primarily decorative aim in England. The earlier *capriccio* of the Italian Cinquecento was fantastic, often grotesque. Vasari, in 1568, recognized it as a genre "not subject to ordinary rules" but rather "a kind of painting full of license and absurdity, admired by the ancients as room ornaments." [22] From being a vehicle for eccentric visual jokes in the sixteenth century, its uses grew more varied in the seventeenth, taking essentially two directions. One was toward the satiric, where *capriccio* met and mingled with caricature; this style reached its culmination in the eighteenth-century work of Goya, especially in his print cycle *Los Caprichos,* 1796–98. The other developmental direction for the *capriccio* was toward an increased emphasis on the pleasingly decorative with the consequent reduction of most grotesque elements to the merely playful. This second type of *capriccio* was associated with Venetian rococo. Created by Marco Ricci (1676–1720), it was continued throughout the greater part of the eighteenth century on a smaller, more delicate scale by Francesco Zuccarelli (1702–88), who was associated with the Royal Academy in the years following its founding in 1768.

Though Venetian in origin, the decorative *capriccio's* popularity and the high repute of its painters soon made it an international genre, especially in European court circles, including England, where the Riccis, Marco and Sebastiano, lived from 1712 to 1716. [23] Sebastiano's allegorical wall paintings on pastoral themes adorned the staircase at Burlington House and were undoubtedly familiar to Pope. Reuben Brower and Giorgio Melchiori have agreed upon the resemblance between Pope's pastoral landscapes and those of Zuccarelli; [24] they can

22. Cited in the *Encyclopedia of World Art* (New York, 1964), V, 351.

23. Decio Gioseffi, *Canaletto and His Contemporaries* (Bergamo, 1964), p. 13. Also see Germain Bazin, *Baroque and Rococo* (New York, 1964), pp. 179–80.

24. See Reuben A. Brower, *Alexander Pope, The Poetry of Allusion* (London, 1963), p. 24, and Giorgio Melchiori, "Pope in Arcady: The Theme of *Et in Arcadia Ego* in his Pastorals," *The*

as plausibly be related to the whole context of the Venetian rococo, especially to the decorative landscape paintings of the Riccis. A few lines will illustrate Pope's talents for delicate and beguiling artifice.

> Soon as the Flocks shook off the nightly Dews,
> Two Swains, whom Love kept wakeful, and the Muse,
> Pour'd o'er the whitening Vale their fleecy Care,
> Fresh as the Morn, and as the Season fair:
> The Dawn now blushing on the Mountain's Side,
>
> [ll. 17–21]

The pastoral terrain is treated like an actual landscape painting by the poet, intent upon pictorializing the scene. The sheep, a mass of vivid white in the clear morning sunlight, are "pour'd" over the vale while, in the distance, the mountainside reflects the pinkish tones of the dawn sky. As in Zuccarelli's work, domestic animals are used decoratively; the texture and color of their coats are effectively exploited. Though the compositional elements are familiar—indeed, trite—shepherds, sheep, fields, and hills, Pope's eye is fresh and sharply observant. As in the later *Rape of the Lock,* a quality of fantasy mingles pleasingly with descriptions of natural beauty.

> Here the bright Crocus and blue Vi'let glow;
> Here Western Winds on breathing Roses blow.
> I'll stake yon' Lamb that near the Fountain plays,
> And from the Brink his dancing Shade surveys.
>
> [ll. 31–34]

The self-regarding lamb, attentive to the choreography of his own gamboling, is exactly the kind of detail that transforms Pope's spring pastoral into a verbal *capriccio.* The lamb's playfulness also recalls Zuccarelli, who affects such motifs. In *The Rape of Europa,* for instance, a *putto* and a garlanded goat frolic together in the lower right corner of the canvas.

English Miscellany, XIV (1963), 85. Brower's book was first published in 1959. He and Melchiori also perceive similarities between Pope's landscapes and Poussin's, a parallel that will be discussed later in this chapter.

Clumps of brightly colored flowers, like those in Pope's lines, punctuate the same picture's foreground (see plate 12).[25] In these early landscapes "the colors are more painterly than natural" as well, serving to heighten the decorative effect: [26] "And lavish Nature paints the Purple Year" (l. 28). Both the verb "paints" and the adjective "Purple" (from the Latin derivation meaning "vivid") [27] further underscore Pope's strategy of description in which "Flow'rs adorn the Ground" (l. 43) and "Glories gild the Shore" (l. 75).

Though in terms of ideal landscape the "high point of the pastorals" [28] is reached in "Summer," man's state has grown less happy. The lovelorn shepherd of the second pastoral vainly implores his beloved to come to him.

> Oh deign to visit our forsaken Seats,
> The mossie Fountains, and the Green Retreats!
> Where-e'er you walk, cool Gales shall fan the Glade,
> Trees, where you sit, shall crowd into a Shade,
> Where-e'er you tread, the blushing Flow'rs shall rise,
> And all things flourish where you turn your Eyes.
>
> [ll. 71–76]

The familiar lines conjure up *loci amoeni* by Watteau and Boucher or the landscape of Correggio's *Leda and the Swan,* leafy paradises designed for amorous joys where all nature is attuned to the lovers' mood. Pope's shepherd mourns, however; within his "Heart Eternal Winter reigns" (l. 22). Out of harmony with his surroundings, he recalls Marvell's Damon the Mower, wandering the noontide fields sultry with the day's heat, himself burning with unrequited love. Though "soon the Sun with milder Rays descends" and relieves the discomfort of midday, there is "no Relief for Love" (ll. 88–89).

25. This painting is reproduced in Arno Schönberger and Halldor Soehner, *The Rococo Age, Art and Civilization of the 18th Century,* trans. Daphne Woodward (New York, 1963), pl. 188. Also see Gioseffi, *Canaletto,* pls. 45, 46, 47.

26. Hagstrum, *The Sister Arts* (Chicago, 1958), p. 215.

27. See Arthur Johnston, " 'The Purple Year' in Pope and Gray," *RES,* n.s., XIV (1963), 389–93.

28. Brower, *Alexander Pope,* p. 22.

On me Love's fiercer Flames for ever prey,
By Night he scorches, as he burns by Day.

[ll. 91–92]

The theme of love, ended or forsaken, is continued in "Autumn," the melancholy deepening as two shepherds at twilight hymn past loves, one "faithless," the other "absent." The lighthearted songs in praise of their two mistresses composed earlier in spring sunlight by the swains of the first eclogue are ironically recalled in the gathering darkness of the third. The suggestion of transience and the decorative veneer, only half concealing a far from superficial theme, are qualities again suggestive of Watteau, Pope's contemporary, who only a few years after the publication of the *Pastorals* painted his two Cythera pictures. The first, *The Island of Cythera,* depicts a bright morning landscape, much like Pope's "Spring," where lovers, assisted by a dozen winged cupids, line up to board the vessel which will take them to the island of Cythera, the locale associated with Venus whose name is frequently invoked in the *Pastorals* as well. The second, a later and more famous picture, on display at the Louvre, shows *The Departure from Cythera;* reluctant couples board the ship which will remove them from this island devoted to love's pleasures, returning them to the "real" world. As in the "Autumn" pastoral, day is ending and the darkening sky reinforces the muted but pervasive sadness which seems to suggest something more than the obvious mood of *post coitum tristis.* Both poet and painter depict a *locus amoenus.* The presence of water is a common element; Pope's pastoral landscape is located on the banks of the Thames, and Watteau's pictures portray a setting on the shore of a river or lake. Both also suggest the proximity of shady woods, from which "green retreats," in Watteau's second picture, the lovers appear to have come. Strikingly similar is the behavior of the lovers themselves. Their amorous glances and hesitant or eager gestures in Watteau's first painting find an echo in the ambivalent play of Pope's flirtatious girls in "Spring":

The sprightly *Sylvia* trips along the Green,
She runs, but hopes she does not run unseen,

> While a kind Glance at her Pursuer flies,
> How much at variance are her Feet and Eyes!
>
> [ll. 57–60]

In Watteau's *Departure from Cythera,* the very moment of parting is shown; but, as we have seen, Pope chooses in "Autumn" to focus on a later time in this progressive deterioration of lovers' relationships. The bereft shepherd mourns his now solitary state. Love which was joyfully anticipated in a spring-time Arcadia is unexpectedly transformed into love nostalgically recalled or cruelly betrayed in a landscape which in "Autumn" awaits the shadowy "Approach of Night." One shepherd histrionically contemplates suicide:

> Farwell ye Woods! adieu the Light of Day!
> One Leap from Yonder Cliff shall end my Pains.
>
> [ll. 94–95]

The darkness of Pope's scene, at the end of the third pastoral, reinforces the suggestion of man's mortality as sympathetic nature veils its light, lengthens its shadows, and sheds copious, but still highly decorative, dewy tears.

> The Skies yet blushing with departing Light,
> When falling Dews with Spangles deck'd the Glade,
> And the low Sun had lengthen'd ev'ry Shade.
>
> [ll. 98–100]

The bitterness and bite of Marvell's exercises in the pastoral form find no really comparable echo here in Pope. Differences between them in age and in attitude are ultimately more important than superficial similarities.

Although in "Winter" death becomes an actuality rather than a future threat, the focus of the poem is less upon the loss of Daphne than again on sympathetic nature's response to the event.[29] Her demise is mourned by two shepherds whose alter-

---

29. In a recent article David S. Durant has argued that in Pope's *Pastorals* emphasis gradually shifts from nature ("Spring") to man ("Winter"). (See "Man and Nature in Alexander Pope's *Pastorals,*"

nating songs more effectively pictorialize the response of the winter landscape than articulate their own conventional sorrow. Pope has leisure for fiction and, one suspects, little grief for Mrs. Tempest, to whose memory the poem is dedicated. Occasionally the poet's pleasure in delineating the midnight prospect causes him to abandon the elegiac tone altogether.

> Now sleeping Flocks on their soft Fleeces lye,
> The Moon, serene in Glory, mounts the Sky,
>
> [ll. 5–6]

Even when that tone is remembered, the decorative element in Pope's poetic landscape is so pervasive that the reader is more often moved aesthetically than emotionally.

> Now hung with Pearls the dropping Trees appear

> The silver Swans her hapless Fate bemoan,
> In Notes more sad than when they sing their own.

> The Trembling Trees, in ev'ry Plain and Wood,
> Her Fate remurmur to the silver Flood
>
> [ll. 31, 39–40, 63–64]

The hyperbole and artifice, the repetition of words like silver (and golden), and the constant, exquisitely visualized vignettes

---

SEL, 1500–1900, XI [1971], 469–85.) Certainly the gradual darkening of both the landscape and the spirits of the shepherds who inhabit it places increasing dramatic emphasis on suffering humanity, as the poem progresses from its light beginning to its more somber conclusion. I only question Durant's statement: "In the later poems, natural setting continues to be of use, but with rare exceptions it is only incidental" (p. 484). Classical ideal landscape in both poetry and painting always functions as a metaphor or icon of man's condition; it never exists simply to glorify "nature," as it will in the later romantic tradition. In Pope's poem setting objectifies and communicates the theme in "Winter" as fully as it does in "Spring." In the former section weightier themes inevitably have the effect of enlarging the role of the shepherds and focusing more of our attention upon them. Landscape, however, remains the dominant element throughout the *Pastorals.*

like those above are characteristic of "Winter." Though there
has been a progressive deterioration in man's state throughout
the four pastorals, the cumulative effect is not an unrelievedly
somber one.

A parallel between Pope's confrontation of death in Arcadia
and Poussin's landscape painting which treats the same theme
has been pointed out.[30] While both attempt a sense of Vergilian melancholy, Poussin's highly intellectual work possesses
a grave though not pessimistic complexity and an uncompro-
misingly classical style that differentiate it from Pope's.[31] Each
designs "a reproduction of properly arranged natural objects
imbued with a particular mood" and each is preoccupied with
the "theme of time." [32] However, there is a crucial difference in
style which becomes clear when we examine Pope's conclusion
to "Winter."

> But see! when *Daphne* wondring mounts on high,
> Above the Clouds, above the Starry Sky.
> Eternal Beauties grace the shining Scene,
> Fields ever fresh, and Groves for ever green!
> There, while You rest in *Amaranthine* Bow'rs,
> Or from those Meads select unfading Flow'rs,
> Behold us kindly who your Name implore,
> *Daphne,* our Goddess, and our Grief no more!

[ll. 69–76]

The apotheosis of Daphne and her translation to a celestial
Arcadia above the clouds suggests Tiepolo more than it does
Poussin. The rococo delicacy and charm endure; Daphne

30. Melchiori, "Pope in Arcady," pp. 83–93.
31. Pope most resembles Poussin, perhaps, in ll. 61–66 which describe "the trembling Trees" and "the silver Flood. . . ./ Swell'd
with new Passion. . . ." Poussin's *Winter* (*The Flood*) (see plate 4)
in his Seasons series portrays a scene like Pope's, including the use
of a night landscape seen by moonlight. Pope probably knew the
Seasons pictures; they were highly admired and often engraved.
His own pastoral poems are, however, usually closer in mood and
style to the more decorative Seasons series of his French contemporary, the imitator of Watteau, Nicolas Lancret (1690–1745).
32. Melchiori, "Pope in Arcady," p. 86.

eternally inhabits a bower much like Armida's. Both scale and style are reduced from Dryden's baroque grandeur in the apotheosis of Anne Killigrew.[33]

The "Time conquers all" speech by Thyrsis that concludes the poem seems almost intrusive, a conventional enough but anticlimactic conclusion. High sentence in the *Pastorals* is reduced to the slightly ponderous philosophizing of a youth still in his teens; it is image, not statement, that reveals the author's genius. While the impression Pope creates is certainly not trivial or specious, it is primarily decorative rather than moral. His ultimate achievement in the *Pastorals* is almost purely aesthetic and pictorial, as he himself suggested later in a slyly self-depreciating couplet in the *Epistle to Dr. Arbuthnot:* "Soft were my Numbers, who could take offence/ While pure Description held the place of Sense?"

Pope may have intended his *Messiah,* published in *The Spectator* in 1712, to be a belated coda to the *Pastorals* which had appeared three years earlier in Tonson's *Miscellanies*. In it he continues to use the Golden Age theme, while countering the motif of death in "Winter" with one of rebirth and renewal in *Messiah*. Though Vergil's Fourth Eclogue is his model, Pope incorporates in his imitation the prophecies of Isaiah, thought to refer to the birth of Christ. "Pope is . . . giving us an English version of the eclogue that Virgil might have written, could he have drawn on Isaiah rather than . . . on the sibylline prophecy."[34] A "sacred eclogue," as Pope labeled it, required more loftiness and polish than did an ordinary pastoral;

33. The word *rococo* has retained its unfavorable connotations even longer than has baroque. Too often it is used wholly disparagingly as a descriptive label for eighteenth-century *kitsch* devoid of any redeeming significance, stylistic or cerebral. Or else it is limited to suggesting the playful element in paintings like those of Fragonard or poems like Pope's *Rape of the Lock*. Perhaps, as Michael Levey says, it "is conceivably no more than the baroque tamed and cut down for a more civilized age" (*Rococo to Revolution* [New York, 1966], p. 15). But used with discrimination, it is a useful term for identifying a definable style neither baroque nor classical, though reflecting and reacting to both.

34. Robert Kilburn Root, *The Poetical Career of Alexander Pope* (Princeton, 1941), p. 61.

yet it could not sacrifice the graceful simplicity that was supposed to characterize the pastoral form.³⁵ The deliberate fusion
of Vergil and Isaiah was a bold idea, and to some, like Rev.
Whitwell Elwin, a nearly blasphemous one, but Pope has carried it off with remarkable ease, though undeniably Isaiah's
ruggedness has been toned down.

The mingling of classical and biblical strains is most successfully accomplished in terms of landscape imagery. The Golden
Age landscape accommodates the ingredients of biblical pastoral without strain.

> See Nature hasts her earliest Wreaths to bring,
> With all the Incence of the breathing Spring:
> See lofty *Lebanon* his Head advance,
> See nodding Forests on the Mountains dance,
> See spicy Clouds from lowly *Saron* rise,
> And *Carmel's* flow'ry top perfumes the Skies!
>
> [ll. 23–28]

The reiterated "See" directs the reader's response to each
element in a gradually unfolding landscape. The pictorial
revelation progresses logically from the figure of Nature in the
foreground; she is an allegorical votary bearing spring wreaths.
Then the tall cedar of Lebanon catches the imagination's eye
in midground, after which we are urged to see the forested
mountains in the background. These, in turn, direct attention
to the full extensiveness of Pope's prospect where Mount
Carmel's heights are partially obscured in clouds at the summit. Clearly this is still a pastoral landscape; in the lines
immediately following, the Messiah himself inhabits it and
"As the good Shepherd tends his fleecy Care" (l. 49). Again a
parallel may be found in Poussin's pictures of the seasons in the
Louvre (see plates 1–4). In both *Summer* (*Ruth and Boaz*) and

35. Pope would have known instances from the visual art of a
successful mingling of pastoral and religious themes, especially in
Renaissance paintings depicting the Holy Family. A particularly
attractive example is Raphael's *Madonna del Passeggio* (National
Gallery, Edinburgh) which perfectly captures this combination of
spiritual dignity and bucolic tranquillity.

Autumn (*The Spies with the Grapes of the Promised Land*), a single tree is prominent in midground while mountains and cloud formations are seen in the distance. *Spring* (*The Earthly Paradise*) suggests the verdurous, Edenic landscape of *Messiah*, a place of sunlight, groves, and the enameled colors of fruits and flowers. Just as Poussin's paintings of the four seasons have successfully combined scenes from the Old Testament with ideal landscape ingredients in a decidedly Vergilian style, so Pope in *Messiah* attempts the same task.

The elevated nature of his subject does impel Pope at times to affect a classical baroque style resembling Dryden's in the odes. Baroque moments in the poem are characteristic of those sections of heightened drama in which an instant of revelation is pictorialized. The elaborate use of emblematically pictured allegorical presences and sacred symbols invests the landscape with a sacramental rather than a purely decorative aura.

> From *Jesse's* Root behold a Branch arise,
> Whose sacred Flow'r with Fragrance fills the Skies.
> Th'Æthereal Spirit o'er its leaves shall move,
> And on its Top descends the Mystic Dove.
> Ye Heav'ns! from high the dewy Nectar pour,
> And in soft Silence shed the kindly Show'r!
> The Sick and Weak the healing Plant shall aid;
> From Storms a Shelter, and from Heat a Shade,
> All Crimes shall cease, and ancient Fraud shall fail;
> Returning Justice lift aloft her Scale;
> Peace o'er the World her Olive-Wand extend,
> And white-roab'd Innocence from Heav'n descend.
>
> [ll. 9–20]

The characteristic baroque movement both upward and downward is strikingly evident in the rising branch of the Jesse tree (a figure representing the Virgin Mary) as well as in the descending glide of the dove, a symbol of the Holy Spirit and a frequent iconographical detail in pictures representing the Annunciation. The shower which accompanies the dove's descent is probably intended to represent divine grace. Toward the end of the passage, Justice's lifting aloft her scale is balanced by the downward movement of "white-roab'd Innocence."

Astraea's presence in the scene echoes Vergil's Pollio eclogue, while the reference to the Jesse tree's sacred branch comes from Isaiah. Both Milton and, before him, Dante combine Christian and classical motifs in this way. Pope also makes us remember the use of a classical ruin or broken column in Nativity paintings of the Renaissance, designed to suggest the passing of the old pagan world and the coming of the new dispensation.

The Messiah's advent will effect a rejuvenation of the landscape; a new Golden Age will be born with him. Here again Vergil's imagery mingles harmoniously with Isaiah's.

> The Swain in barren Desarts with surprize
> Sees Lillies spring, and sudden Verdure rise;
> And Starts, amidst the thirsty Wilds, to hear
> New Falls of Water murm'ring in his Ear:
> On rifted Rocks, the Dragon's late Abodes,
> The green Reed trembles, and the Bulrush nods.
> Waste sandy Vallies, once perplex'd with Thorn,
> The spiry Firr and shapely Box adorn;
> To leaf-less Shrubs the flow'ring Palms succeed,
> And od'rous Myrtle to the noisome Weed.
> The Lambs with Wolves shall graze the verdant Mead,
> And Boys in flow'ry Bands the Tyger lead;
>
> [ll. 67–78]

Pope's vision of the new day is as vividly prophetic as William Blake's. At the end of his poem, it rises to a triumphant Miltonic crescendo of light:

> No more the rising *Sun* shall gild the Morn,
> Nor Evening *Cynthia* fill her silver Horn,
> But lost, dissolv'd in thy superior Rays;
> One Tyde of Glory, one unclouded Blaze,
> O'erflow thy Courts: The LIGHT HIMSELF shall shine
> Reveal'd; and *God's* eternal Day be thine!
>
> [ll. 99–104]

At the close of *Messiah,* Pope shows himself capable of using the Golden Age landscape of the eclogues for purposes that go beyond the gracefully decorative. The aesthetic goals are still important ones for the poet; the painterly artifice remains, as

210

does the preoccupation with formal elegance. There is a new intensity and heavy freight of meaning to Pope's images, however, that look forward to the revised *Windsor Forest* and beyond to the Horatian *Epistles*. England as Eden, the theme of poets from Shakespeare to Blake, is to become Pope's vision too, until his Tory satirist gloom extinguishes *Messiah's* cosmic blaze with the darkness of *The Dunciad*.

The *Pastorals* and *Windsor Forest,* whose last line echoes the opening of "Spring" (an imitation of Vergil's practice in the *Eclogues* and *Georgics*), were intended to be "companion pieces" originally,[36] although the only political allusions in the former are the brief references to King Charles's oak and the symbolic thistle and lily.[37] For all its patriotic accretions of 1713, however, *Windsor Forest* remains fundamentally a georgic.[38] Its most obvious literary ancestor is *Cooper's Hill* in which Denham also blended the topographical and the ideal, the loco-descriptive and the meditative strains. Helping to unify such potentially disparate elements is Pope's central symbol, Windsor Forest itself; its landscape is made to represent "Nature's one law of *concordia discors.*"[39]

> Here Hills and Vales, the Woodland and the Plain,
> Here Earth and Water seem to strive again,
> Not *Chaos*-like together crush'd and bruis'd,
> But as the World, harmoniously confus'd:
> Where Order in Variety we see,
> And where, tho' all things differ, all agree.
>
> [ll. 11–16]

On a purely pictorial level such an emphasis upon the overall harmony to be gained from superficially contrasting particulars results in a number of highly picturesque descriptions that anticipate effects in Thomson, Dyer, and ultimately the early Wordsworth.

36. Earl R. Wasserman, *The Subtler Language* (Baltimore, 1968), p. 109.
37. "Spring," ll. 86, 89–90.
38. See Wasserman, *The Subtler Language,* p. 102; and Brower, *Alexander Pope,* pp. 48–49.
39. Wasserman, *The Subtler Language,* p. 103.

> Here waving Groves a checquer'd Scene display,
> And part admit and part exclude the Day;
> As some coy Nymph her Lover's warm Address
> Nor quite indulges, nor can quite repress.
> There, interspers'd in Lawns and opening Glades,
> Thin Trees arise that shun each others Shades.
> Here in full Light the russet Plains extend;
> There wrapt in Clouds the blueish Hills ascend: [40]

> [ll. 17–24]

The eye is directed by the alternating "here" and "there" to focus on opposing yet complementary landscape features, familiar elements almost invariably the omnipresent staples of seventeenth-century ideal landscapes in painting. Here are the expected lawns and groves, broad plains and distant hills, but the most fully developed and reiterated contrasts in Pope's verbal canvas are those involving light and shadow, the painter's chiaroscuro, a peculiarly apt analogy for an Augustan poet to use. Over and over in his work, Pope expresses his favorite theme, one of reconciliation, balance, and synthesis, by resorting to this same analogy.

> This light and darkness in our chaos join'd,
> What shall divide? The God within the mind.
> Extremes in Nature equal ends produce
> In Man they join to some mysterious use;
> Tho' each by turns the other's bound invade,
> As, in some well-wrought picture, light and shade,
> And oft so mix, the diff'rence is too nice
> Where ends the Virtue, or begins the Vice.

> [*An Essay on Man,* II.203–10]

Light and shadow should blend together artfully to enhance the total effect; despite occasional impressions to the contrary, however, neither is really obscured by the other. Pope continues his analogy:

40. Dorothy M. Stuart has noted that Pope uses bluish and brownish tones in *Windsor Forest* to contrast with each other in the way Thomson will do later. "Landscape in Augustan Verse," *Essays and Studies by Members of the English Association,* XXVI (1940), 75. For an example, see the last two lines just cited.

> Fools! who from hence into the notion fall,
> That Vice or Virtue there is none at all.
> If white and black blend, soften, and unite
> A thousand ways, is there no black or white?
>
> [ll. 211–14]

Pope's metaphors are often designed to illustrate the vital difference between the harmonious confusion of "order in variety," in the lines cited above, and chaos, all things "together crush'd and bruis'd." The conclusion of *The Dunciad,* where darkness finally extinguishes all light in Pope's cosmic landscape, is such a chaos. How vital is the difference between that state and the one that views man's setting as "A mighty maze! but not without a plan"; Windsor Forest is such a maze.

> Bear me, oh bear me to sequester'd Scenes,
> The Bow'ry Mazes and surrounding Greens;
>
> [ll. 261–62]

The darker patches in its historical tapestry give the brightness of the present, under Queen Anne's reign, added luster. Christopher Salvesen has intimated that *Windsor Forest* gains greater implications for the reader by being punctuated with Wordsworthian "spots of time," though these are racial rather than personal.[41] The landscape of Windsor is, of course, uniquely conducive to the reinvoking of racial memories, to the extent that even simple description in Pope's poem takes on the reverberations of metaphor. This metaphoric dimension does not gain its powerful effect primarily from the poem's historical allusions. More important is Pope's ability to employ the richly associative ingredients of ideal landscape painting and hence to suggest eternal implications in the temporal scene before him. So past and present are, in turn, held up to view reflected in the mirror of the ideal. "The positive sense of the analogy with Eden develops from Pope's descriptions of the landscape and its affinities with art."[42] Pope himself

41. *The Landscape of Memory: A Study of Wordsworth's Poetry* (Lincoln, Neb., 1965), pp. 12–13.
42. Thomas R. Edwards, Jr., *This Dark Estate: A Reading of Pope* (Berkeley and Los Angeles, 1963), p. 6.

stressed this close relationship between art and his poem. While revising *Windsor Forest* in 1713, he wrote, "I am endeavouring to raise up around me a painted scene of woods and forests in verdure and beauty. . . . I am wandering through bowers and grottoes in conceit." [43]

The painted scenes that Pope creates glow with brilliant tints. Norman Ault observes that "Pope's conscious references to colour in *Windsor Forest* are carried to a pitch never before attained by any poet, in which the direct colour-words average as many as one to every seven lines." [44] The lines which describe the pheasant killed by the hunter (115–18) and the fish lured by the angler (142–45) are most often cited to illustrate the splendid opulence of Pope's palette. Both passages describe living creatures as if they were objects of art rather than natural phenomena: "painted Wings, and Breast that flames with Gold," "Fins of *Tyrian* Dye," "silver Eel," and "Carp, in Scales bedrop'd with Gold," all reveal Pope's tendency to ecphrasis and emphasis on the decorative element in these scenes. Such an accumulation of gorgeous effects results in the creation of landscapes that glitter with elegant artifice. Lodona, dissolving "In a soft, silver Stream," and Father Thames, whose "shining Horns diffus'd a golden Gleam," are associated with carefully composed prospects made deliberately unreal. Lodona's waters mirror forth the unchanging perfection of the reflected landscape, becoming the glass through which it is seen:

> Oft in her Glass the musing Shepherd spies
> The headlong Mountains and the downward Skies,
> The watry Landskip of the pendant Woods,
> And absent Trees that tremble in the Floods;
> In the clear azure Gleam the Flocks are seen,
> And floating Forests paint the Waves with Green.
> Thro' the fair Scene rowl slow the lingring Streams,
> Then foaming pour along, and rush into the *Thames*.
>
> [ll. 211–18]

---

43. Cited in Frederick Bracher, "Pope's Grotto: The Maze of Fancy," in *Essential Articles for the Study of Alexander Pope,* p. 108.
44. *New Light on Pope,* p. 87.

The design of Pope's landscape is revealed, in reverse order, from background (mountains, sky) to foreground (forests and flocks); the movement of the stream traversing the terrain unites the whole. The impression on the reader is one of evanescence and, except for the last line, an almost ethereal delicacy. The shimmering and tremulous movement of the water has a blurring, distancing effect upon the reflected scene, softening it in a decorative manner suggestive once again of the Venetian rococo style. The story of Lodona, as Joseph Warton has said, is "prettily Ovidian," but Pope has successfully revivified a worn genre.[45]

The allegorical figure of Father Thames dominates a different kind of landscape, one as grandly baroque as a frescoed ceiling by Antonio Verrio. In a poetic picture created to endure long after "Verrio's Colours fall," Pope's river god is enthroned above his tributary brethren. The iconic urn he leans upon reveals a moon rising above the silver tides of his own waters and the city of London in sculptured gold. The god wears a "sea-green Mantle" and turns "azure Eyes" toward Windsor's domes and turrets. The pictorial effect is elaborate, almost Eastern in the way of much Venetian art. It is certainly a contrast to the sparely emblematic personifications at the end of the poem: Envy with her snakes, Persecution with "her broken Wheel," and Rebellion with her chain.

The rich variety of *Windsor Forest's* landscapes testifies to their creator's fertile pictorial imagination. Pope began his poem "with an intimation of lost Eden" and ended it with a glimpse "of a Paradise to be regained." [46] Such visions of unchanging, eternal peace and order were "emblematic visions within the mind" to the poet's contemporaries,[47] fearful, like Pope himself, that the newly won Pax Anna might not endure. Nor did it, and in Pope's later poems, whenever rural life is celebrated the theme of retirement from society as a conse-

---

45. *An Essay on the Genius and Writings of Pope,* I, 23.

46. Maynard Mack, "On Reading Pope," *College English,* VII (1946), 272.

47. Morris Golden, "The Imaging Self in the Eighteenth Century," *Eighteenth-Century Studies,* III (1969), 26.

quence of disillusionment with it casts a melancholy shadow on the bright pastoral world.

Even in those eighteenth-century Edens created by Pope and his contemporaries, often men of wealth and taste, there were intrusive reminders of the fallen world. In an age of great estates being constantly "improved" by extensive landscaping in the new style, dismayingly few, Pope felt, respected the integrity of the land or the obligations due its inhabitants. The poet's *Epistle to Bathurst* postulates that even one great lord who perfectly realized his responsibilities and observed them might make "Honour linger ere it leaves the land." The image of honor fleeing like Astraea at the end of the Golden Age epitomizes Pope's censure of those whose avarice or ostentation, like the Cottas', was an equal blight on the rural beauty of the English countryside. The imitation and re-creation of the ideal landscape of epic poetry and Renaissance art should not be attempted for purposes of sheer display. The land so rejuvenated could become a fragile, fragmentary representation of the Earthly Paradise; its lord, therefore, was expected to function very much like a secular Good Shepherd. Such a rare individual was the Man of Ross:

> Who hung with woods yon mountain's sultry brow?
> From the dry rock who bade the waters flow?
> Not to the Skies in useless columns tost,
> Or in proud falls magnificently lost,
> But clear and artless, pouring thro' the plain
> Health to the Sick, and solace to the swain.
> Whose Cause-way parts the vale with shady rows?
> Whose Seats the weary Traveller repose?
> Who taught that heav'n-directed spire to rise?
> The MAN of ROSS, each lisping babe replies.
>
> [*Ep. to Bathurst*, ll. 253–62]

The Man of Ross is a godlike artificer who can actually create his own microcosmic universe. His impact on the land is reminiscent of the deity's effect in Pope's *Messiah* eclogue: he brings health, solace, rest, and order to his world. In an almost miraculous fashion, he causes water to flow "From the dry rock," as Moses did, and shades the "mountain's sultry brow"

216

with woodlands. Earl Wasserman has pointed out that "the seemingly hyperbolic, quasi-pastoral language asserts a superhuman status and power" for the Man of Ross.[48] He is closely akin to Marvell's Lord Fairfax, especially as portrayed in "Upon the Hill and Grove at Bill-borow." Both are heroic, saintly men who have repudiated the outer darkness of the world beyond their walls and have tried to restore the old unfallen perfection to their own domains. Landscape in the *Epistle to Bathurst,* as in Marvell's poem, is treated as emblematic of the man who inhabits it. His perfections (or lack of them) are mirrored in his setting; it, in turn, defines him by possessing (or failing to possess) all the qualities and associations of the ideal landscape, biblical and classical. E. K. Waterhouse's observation that Sir Peter Lely's style of "portrait in a landscape" became a "dominant theme in British painting until the end of the eighteenth century" is corroborated in the sister art of poetry.[49] Pope's literary portraits in a landscape, unlike Lely's, serve a purpose that is ultimately moral rather than decorative. As the Man of Ross's setting proclaims its master's glory, so Timon's domain, with its "huge heaps of littleness," shames its pretentious owner.

Epistle Four, *To Burlington,* follows *To Bathurst,* although it was published first and may have been written earlier. Its scope initially seems narrower, its purpose not as high. Pope's satire is ostensibly directed against men whose tastes rather than their morals are defective. Timon's gargantuan, baroque extravagance is contrasted with Burlington's understated, classical elegance. But again the reader is confronted with the emblematic implications of differing landscapes, and their moral dimension becomes apparent. If he does not follow nature, the estate designer ends by perverting it. Ostentation must be avoided, art concealed, and the integrity of the whole preserved.

> Let not each beauty ev'ry where be spy'd,
> Where half the skill is decently to hide.

48. *Pope's Epistle to Bathurst* (Baltimore, 1960), p. 41.
49. *Painting in Britain, 1530–1790,* The Pelican History of Art (Harmondsworth, Middlesex, 1954), p. 59.

He gains all points, who pleasingly confounds,
Surprizes, varies, and conceals the Bounds.

[ll. 53–56]

The work requires both innate sensitivity to "the Genius of
the Place" and a clear inward vision of the ideal to be ultimately achieved. Intelligence, resourcefulness, and patience are
the marks of a successful creator of his own ideal landscape.

Consult the Genius of the Place in all;
That tells the Waters or to rise, or fall,
Or helps th'ambitious Hill the heav'n to scale,
Or scoops in circling theatres the Vale,
Calls in the Country, catches opening glades,
Joins willing woods, and varies shades from shades,
Now breaks or now directs, th'intending Lines;
Paints as you plant, and, as you work, designs.
Still follow Sense, of ev'ry Art the Soul,
Parts answ'ring parts shall slide into a whole,
Spontaneous beauties all around advance,
Start ev'n from Difficulty, strike from Chance;
Nature shall join you, Time shall make it grow
A work to wonder at—perhaps a STOW.

[ll. 57–70]

In contrast to the qualities both implicitly and explicitly
exalted in the first part of the poem, we are shown the negative
side of the picture. Villario's dissatisfaction with the result of
his ten years of toil and his ultimate preference for a field suggest extremism in the pursuit of the natural and a wrongful
repudiation of the ideal. The forests grown by Sabinus are
destroyed by his son who is equally extremist in his faddish
preference for "one boundless Green." Most of Pope's scorn,
however, is reserved for the mansion and grounds of Timon.
The latter's walled gardens illustrate the artificiality and uniformity that was anathema to the Burlington circle. An inner
emptiness is everywhere reflected and reiterated:

No pleasing Intricacies intervene,
No artful wildness to perplex the scene;

218

> Grove nods at grove, each Alley has a brother,
> And half the platform just reflects the other.
>
> [ll. 115–18]

Instead of a subtle blend of classical line and rococo grace, the "suff'ring eye" beholds an "inverted Nature" in Timon's landscape, punctuated with sterile topiary art, nonfunctioning fountains, and dusty urns. These offensive and unnatural qualities pervade Timon's house as well as his landscape. The owner's shallowness and pride are everywhere mirrored, perhaps with most vivid irony in his chapel:

> On painted Cielings you devoutly stare,
> Where sprawl the Saints of Verrio or Laguerre,
> On gilded clouds in fair expansion lie,
> And bring all Paradise before your eye.
>
> [ll. 145–48]

Remembering the way in which Marvell made comparatively modest Appleton House the emblem of Lord Fairfax, we are struck by the adroit skill Pope employs here to use the form of the country house poem with a new satiric power, revealing its owner's moral impoverishment by the tasteless ostentation of his dwelling.

The poet's Arcadian vision has undergone substantial changes since the early poems. Though it seems muted, even forced, an optimistic anticipation of a restored Golden Age occurs toward the end of the *Epistle to Burlington:*

> Another age shall see the golden Ear
> Imbrown the Slope, and nod on the Parterre,
> Deep Harvests bury all his pride has plann'd,
> And laughing Ceres re-assume the land.
>
> [ll. 173–76]

Pope's vision of the new Golden Age is less certain and more deferred than it was in *Windsor Forest*. It is also a good deal more utilitarian, involving public works like bridges, dams, and better highways. King and nobleman, artist and citizen—all are called upon to contribute their energies and knowledge "to happy Britain." This Augustan age, like the

219

original, evoked from its principal poet conflicting images of urban realities and a vanished pastoral perfection. It was nostalgia for the latter that gave impetus to Pope's derisive and exhortatory lines in the *Epistles*. The Golden Age landscape, originally vivid and decorative in the early poems, has, by the middle of the poet's career, grown into an emblem of England for Pope, one too often desecrated and misinterpreted, but still powerful in its promise.

The Romantic Landscape

While the Arcadian world represented a harmonious order with an ultimately moral significance to Pope, he occasionally made poetic use of another kind of landscape which he expected to have a primarily emotional impact on the reader. This different kind of natural scenery, also highly picturesque, invariably elicited a favorable response from Pope himself; he labeled it "romantic," a word with fairly precise connotations in the eighteenth century.[50]

The most explicit notion of the kind of landscape Pope found romantic comes from one of his letters, written to Martha Blount in August, 1734.[51] It describes a trip by boat to Netley Abbey near Southampton, made with Lord Peterborow. The solitary and inaccessible area, the ivy-covered Gothic ruins, the view of sea, hills, and woods, all stimulated Pope the artist;

50. "The word *romantic* then, from the general meaning of 'like the old romances,' came to be used as a descriptive term for the scenes which they describe, old castles, mountains and forests, pastoral plains, waste and solitary places. In the earlier instances of the adjective the literary reference is more or less explicit; but by the eighteenth century, it had come to express more generally the newly-awakened, but as yet half conscious, love for wild nature, for mountains and moors, for 'the *Woods*, the *Rivers*, or *Sea-shores*,' which Shaftesbury mentions as sought by those who are 'deep in this *romantick* way'" (Logan Pearsall Smith, "The History of Four Words," *Society for Pure English* [Oxford, 1924], XVII, 12; cited in Nicolson and Rousseau, *"This Long Disease, My Life,"* p. 211 n.)

51. For text and commentary, see G. S. Rousseau, "A New Pope Letter," *PQ*, XLV (1966), 409–18.

he spent much of his visit sketching and expressed a wish to
"go another day, & finish my drawings." His letter describes
several of the views which captured his fancy; the following
example is typical:

> When we came to the Shore, we were both struck with the
> beauty of it, a rising Hill very deeply hung with Woods, that
> fell quite in to the Water, & at the Edge of the Sea a very old
> min'd Castle. We were very hungry, but the aspect of the
> Towers, & the high crumbling Battlements, overgrown with
> Ivy, with a Square room in the middle out of which at three
> large arches you saw the Main Sea, & all the windings of the
> Coasts on the Side next us, provoked us first to look in.[52]

The culmination of all previous views is reached in Pope's first
glimpse of the thirteenth-century abbey itself. Approaching
through the woods a half mile away, he was able to view it as a
whole within its setting before focusing on various details: the
cloister, vaulted windows, stone pillars still erect, arches, ivied
walls, and flowers, especially roses, grown almost wild in the
courtyards. Pope and Peterborow dined amid the ruins, having
"found Seats of the Capitals of two Pillars that were fallen,"
and Pope's letter goes on to describe the elaborately wrought
appointments of the abbey church. Reluctantly, at last he
bowed to the necessity of leaving before low tide, "the night
coming on apace, with a beautiful Moon."

The part of Pope's nature that responded intensely to Netley
Abbey's picturesque ruins found poetic expression in two works
published almost twenty years earlier than his excursion with
Lord Peterborow. *Eloisa to Abelard* and *Elegy to the Memory
of an Unfortunate Lady* gain much of their effect from an emphasis on certain scenic details that were to become stereotypical of the sublime landscape, the latter a mélange of Edmund
Burke and Salvator Rosa. Pope's debts to the visual arts include
the work of Rosa; they doubtless also extend to the tenebrists,
especially of the Spanish school, artists like Ribera and Ribalta
whose dramatic chiaroscuro often emphasized the gloomy, even

52. *Ibid.,* p. 411.

221

Plate 13 Ribera, *Penitent Magdalen*   Mas—Art Reference Bureau

morbid religiosity of their canvases (see plate 13) .[53] Like Caravaggio, the tenebrists tried to oppose a sterile, academic classicism that emphasized both rational and linear clarity with an
essentially romantic style which exploited chiaroscuro effects
for their emotional intensity. The Pope who wrote *Eloisa* and
admired Netley Abbey would have felt the appeal of this
Counter Reformation art. Pope was also indebted to literary
sources, to Ovid's *Heroides,* of course,[54] and to the work of
more modern poets like Milton's *Il Penseroso* and Dryden's
fable of "Theodore and Honoria."

The result of this blend of the sister arts is the sort of atmosphere that Gothic novelists and graveyard poets were later
to find indispensable. "What beck'ning ghost, along the moonlight shade/ Invites my step, and points to yonder glade?" So
begins the *Elegy,* with a nocturnal apparition exhibiting her
sword-pierced breast to an understandably distraught admirer.
Eloisa to Abelard makes effective use of many of the same ingredients—tragic love, religion, death (actual or anticipated),
and a passionate woman as the central figure. Pope's landscape
art in both poems is designed to heighten the emotional impact
that these women's fates have upon the reader. Eloisa lan-
guishes in both actual and spiritual darkness. She is a *tenebroso*
Magdalen like Ribera's masterpiece in the Prado, and her
walled convent possesses many characteristics similar to those
Pope was later to single out in his description of Netley Abbey.

> These moss-grown domes with spiry turrets crown'd,
> Where awful arches make a noon-day night,
> And the dim windows shed a solemn light
>
> [ll. 142–44]

53. "There is scarce any picture in Homer so much in the savage
and terrible way as this comparison of the Myrmidons to wolves. It
puts one in mind of the pieces of Spagnolett or Salvator Rosa."
"Observations" on Homer, XVI.xix. Jusepe de Ribera (1591–1652),
called Lo Spagnoletto, was a tenebrist, one of a group of Spanish
painters who experimented with the Caravaggesque technique of
chiaroscuro.

54. "The pictorial Ovid had established in his *Heroides* the tradition of creating sympathetic landscape as a kind of visual accom-
paniment to the emotions" (Hagstrum, *The Sister Arts,* p. 218) .

"Darksom pines," rocks, "wandring streams," hills, lakes, and grottoes surround the convent, ingredients of natural scenery as easily assembled into a serene Claudian vista as a dark, horror-filled Salvatorian one. Pope chooses here to darken his landscape, to heighten a sense of stasis until it becomes a "dread repose," and to position the dominant allegorical figure of "Black Melancholy" in the center of his carefully composed scene.

> But o'er the twilight groves, and dusky caves,
> Long-sounding isles, and intermingled graves,
> Black Melancholy sits, and round her throws
> A death-like silence, and a dread repose:
> Her gloomy presence saddens all the scene,
> Shades ev'ry flow'r, and darkens ev'ry green,
> Deepens the murmur of the falling floods,
> And breathes a browner horror on the woods.
>
> [ll. 163–70]

This brooding landscape almost appears the product of Eloisa's feverish dreams. It is a wilderness whose barrenness and decay haunt her in a recurring image of "the same sad prospect" that mirrors her griefs and dispels her passionate memories of Abelard's love.

> Alas no more!—methinks we wandring go
> Thro' dreary wastes, and weep each other's woe;
> Where round some mould'ring tow'r pale ivy creeps,
> And low-brow'd rocks hang nodding o'er the deeps.
> Sudden you mount! you beckon from the skies;
> Clouds interpose, waves roar, and winds arise.
> I shriek, start up, the same sad prospect find,
> And wake to all the griefs I left behind.
>
> [ll. 241–48]

These obsessive nightmares become in the course of the poem essentially the landscape of Eloisa's tortured mind. They express in pictorial terms her morbidity, despair, and sense of loss; they are metaphorical representations of her painful state. As Thomas Edwards has said, these two "romantic" poems "evoke feeling, so powerfully and directly as to exceed the limits of Augustan poetic procedure." [55] Pope extends his Ovidian form by choosing pictorial passages whose imagery carries the burden of his heroine's powerful feelings. The baroque moments in these poems, like Abelard's soaring heavenward, add to this sense of straining at the limits of a form. The *enargeia* that infuses many passages in *Eloisa to Abelard* has been strikingly apparent to Pope's critics since the eighteenth century, prompting them, in some cases, to suggest painterly analogues.[56]

Finally, in both poems past or future bliss is briefly contrasted with present sorrow by allusions to a Golden Age landscape dramatically opposed to the prevailing Gothic gloom. Eloisa, at one point in the poem, reflects on the life of Abelard and his monks at the Paraclete Monastery, a retreat in the district of Troyes, Champagne, where for a time Abelard's stormy life was relatively tranquil.

> You rais'd these hallow'd walls; the desert smil'd,
> And Paradise was open'd in the Wild.
>
> [ll. 133–34]

When, at the end of the poem, Eloisa anticipates her ultimate resting place at the Paraclete Monastery, a common grave with Abelard, she imagines "two wandring lovers" coming in pilgrimage, "To Paraclete's white walls, and silver springs" (l. 348), there to join hands and weep for the tragic pair interred beneath the "pale marble." There is in this scene a reminder of the inherently opposing ideas of death and the Arcadian perfection of eternal spring, so fascinating to seven-

55. *This Dark Estate,* p. 22.
56. In ll. 303 ff. Eloisa imagines herself lying on a tomb, hearing the voice of a spirit. Says Joseph Warton, "This scene would make a fine subject for the pencil, and is worthy a capital painter." Warton comments on the single lamp illuminating the figure of Eloisa and urges that the putative painter choose the exact *"instant"* when she hears the saint's voice and starts with astonishment. Later (ll. 337 ff.) Abelard's imagined death scene reminds Warton of Domenichino's well-known picture of the dying St. Jerome. See *Essay on the Genius and Writings of Pope,* I, 323, 326.

teenth-century painters. The *Elegy* also offers the suggestion of a paradisal resting place to console the troubled ghost whose passing was unmourned and whose grave remains unmarked.

> What tho' no weeping Loves thy ashes grace,
> Nor polish'd marble emulate thy face?
>
> [ll. 59–60]

The absence of conventional funerary art, sorrowing *putti* or a bust of the departed, will be compensated for by the tributes paid by nature and by heaven.

> Yet shall thy grave with rising flow'rs be drest,
> And the green turf lie lightly on thy breast:
> There shall the morn her earliest tears bestow,
> There the first roses of the year shall blow;
> While Angels with their silver wings o'ershade
> The ground, now sacred by thy reliques made.
>
> [ll. 63–68]

Though Pope was, as we have seen, inclined all his poetic life to make use of Arcadian imagery, his brief excursion into depicting the romantic landscape was not repeated. There is probably some truth to the notion that the mature Pope found visual rather than verbal expression for his tastes in romantic landscape. He chose at Twickenham both in his grotto and that part of the garden memorializing his mother to give vent to the solemn and affecting associations evoked for him by a "shadowy Cave" or an *"Ægerian Grott."*

Pope and the Baroque

While the romantic landscape was associated by Pope with that quality of emotional agitation, even terror, supposedly conveyed by the sublime, the baroque mode often suited his purposes best when the primary emphasis of a poem was to be on vastness and elaborate ornamentation. The cosmic immensities conjured up at the beginning of *The Temple of Fame* and at the end of *The Dunciad* require a canvas as large as Milton's in *Paradise Lost*.

> I stood, methought, betwixt Earth, Seas, and Skies;
> The whole Creation open to my Eyes:
> In Air self-ballanc'd hung the Globe below,
> Where Mountains rise, and circling Oceans flow;
> Here naked Rocks, and empty Wastes were seen,
> There Tow'ry Cities, and the Forests green:
> Here sailing Ships delight the wand'ring Eyes;
> There Trees, and intermingl'd Temples rise:
> Now a clear Sun the shining Scene displays,
> The transient Landscape now in Clouds decays.
>
> [*The Temple of Fame*, ll. 11–20]

In the line following this passage, Pope refers to the view from his vantage point as a "wide prospect," an expression often used in his time to suggest an expanse too vast and undefined to be labeled a landscape proper. Pope's painterly sense led him to handle such prospects in segments, as a series of landscapes, to be viewed successively and often antithetically, juxtaposed in an effective order for contrast or counterpoint. Milton's cosmic vistas are not so ordered; impressions grand but seemingly haphazard succeed each other in a fashion closer to Chaucer's *House of Fame* than to Pope's imitation of the original. Reading the later poet's version, one becomes increasingly aware that it follows a scenic rather than a narrative structure.[57]

The *ut pictura poesis* orientation of the landscape passage above has usually evoked specific reference to Claude from critics focusing attention on the last four lines of the text cited.[58] But Pope is being characteristically eclectic in his style and iconography; though the final couplet is indeed Claudian in its concentration on the evanescent luminosity of the scene being viewed, the rest of the passage suggests other pictorial analogues more strongly. Poussin has a greater inclination than Claude to punctuate his landscapes with architectural motifs. The "intermingl'd Temples" glimpsed amid trees recall the

57. See *Works*, Vol. II, ed. Geoffrey Tillotson, Introduction, p. 222.

58. See, for example, Manwaring, *Italian Landscape in Eighteenth-Century England*, p. 97.

composition of the two Phocion pictures, and the contrast of "Tow'ry Cities" with "Forests green" is common in Poussin's work.[59] Brueghel's "expensive delicate ship" viewed with other sailing vessels from a promontory in *The Fall of Icarus* conveys the same pure visual pleasure as "Here sailing Ships delight the wand'ring Eyes." The desolation of "naked Rocks, and empty Wastes" is hardly likely to have appealed to Claude; such a vista suggests earlier Renaissance masters like Bellini (c. 1430–1516) and Mantegna (1431–1506), each of whom created severely spare, rocky landscapes for their versions of *The Agony in the Garden*, both in London's National Gallery. On the other hand, the view of "The whole Creation . . ./ In Air self-ballanc'd . . ." is more often found in emblem books than in paintings, though Bosch's great triptych, usually called *The Garden of Earthly Delights*, presents when closed a global universe depicting the moment of creation.

Bosch's name admittedly is not one we would ordinarily couple with Pope's; however, their eye for grotesque images which symbolize a distorted, perverted nature is surprisingly similar. Here is Pope's view of a new creation, brought about by the reign of Dulness, presented again in a series of brief landscapes taken from *The Dunciad:*

> The forests dance, the rivers upward rise,
> Whales sport in woods, and dolphins in the skies;
> And last, to give the whole creation grace,
> Lo! one vast Egg produces human race.
>
> [III.245–48]

The macabre visions of Bosch and Brueghel, known perhaps to Pope through engravings, would certainly have appealed both to his satiric sense and his own penchant for fantastic images. In the same section of *The Dunciad*, Pope depicts the Angel of Dulness doing cosmic mischief. Though the obvious debt is to Milton, the exaggerated, almost maniacal impression the scene

59. Anthony Blunt, *Nicholas Poussin*, 2 vols. (New York, 1967), pls. 76, 77. See also pls. 187, 188, 191, 193, 200, 206, 214, 230.

creates recalls frequent pictorializations of Hell and The Last Judgment in Renaissance art throughout Western Europe.[60]

> In yonder cloud behold,
> Whose sarsenet skirts are edg'd with flamy gold,
> A matchless youth! his nod these worlds controuls,
> Wings the red lightning, and the thunder rolls.
> Angel of Dulness, sent to scatter round
> Her magic charms o'er all unclassic ground:
> Yon stars, yon suns, he rears at pleasure higher,
> Illumes their light, and sets their flames on fire.
>
> [III.253–60]

The frequency of words like "flamy gold," "red lightning," "flames," and "fire," combined with images of stars and suns, make this passage blaze like an inferno. Even more dramatically effective is the famous passage which concludes the fourth book. Here light is extinguished as primeval night and chaos return in the wake of Dulness, by now an allegorical presence of such awful power as to dominate utterly even the vast canvas upon which she is depicted exercising her malign influence.

> She comes! she comes! the sable Throne behold
> Of *Night* Primæval, and of *Chaos* old!
> Before her, *Fancy's* gilded clouds decay,
> And all its varying Rain-bows die away.
> *Wit* shoots in vain its momentary fires,
> The meteor drops, and in a flash expires.
> As one by one, at dread Medea's strain,
> The sick'ning stars fade off th'ethereal plain;
>
> [IV.629–36]

The fiery imagery, an invariable element in *The Dunciad*'s cosmic nightpieces, is retained to the end to shine for one futile additional moment before annihilation. Again the personifications—Fancy and Wit—contribute to the baroque artifice of

60. A visual anthology of such paintings may be found in Robert Hughes, *Heaven and Hell in Western Art* (New York, 1968).

Pope's landscape, being themselves a part of it as "gilded clouds" and comets. Baroque as well is the intensity and theatricality of the chiaroscuro in which the forces of light and those of darkness stage their eschatological confrontation.

Though all of the pictorially significant landscapes in *The Dunciad* are cosmic and baroque, this is not equally true of *The Temple of Fame* which is much more varied. Except for the opening passage, discussed above, Pope is content to restrict his prospects to more paintable proportions, retaining, however, an emphasis on baroque vastness when describing the temple itself.

> Four brazen Gates, on Columns lifted high,
> Salute the diff'rent Quarters of the Sky.
>
> [ll. 67–68]

or,

> These massie Columns in a Circle rise,
> O'er which a pompous Dome invades the Skies:
> Scarce to the Top I strech'd my aking Sight,
> So large it spread, and swell'd to such a Height.
>
> [ll. 244–47]

The four faces of the Temple of Fame (each exemplifying a different architecture), its jeweled and ornamented interior, Ripa-like emblems, and portraits of heroic figures like Homer, deserve careful inspection. Geoffrey Tillotson has rightly called *The Temple of Fame* "one of the most massively planned poetic scenae in English poetry." [61] The westward "Frontispiece" contains some mythological landscape scenes in the classical Italian style,

> Here *Orpheus* sings; Trees moving to the Sound
> Start from their Roots, and form a Shade around:
>
> [ll. 83–84]

while the "Eastern Front" pictures Brahmin mystics "deep in desert Woods," calling up ghostly visitations in a moonlight setting romantic as that of *Eloisa to Abelard:*

61. *On the Poetry of Pope*, rev. ed. (Oxford, 1950), p. 55.

230

These stop'd the Moon, and call'd th'unbody'd Shades
To Midnight Banquets in the glimmering Glades;
Made visionary Fabricks round them rise,
And airy Spectres skim before their Eyes;

[ll. 101–4]

The most important single landscape section in *The Temple of Fame* is the view of Zembla, whose crest provides a foundation for "a glorious Pile," the Temple itself, "Whose tow'ring Summit ambient Clouds conceal'd." Zembla's whiteness is compared to "*Parian* Marble"; it is of "Stupendous" size and appears "to distant Sight of solid Stone." This is an almost ecphrastic description; although Zembla is a mountain, not an object of art, Pope emphasizes its vividly pictorial quality by describing it in iconic terms. Its sculptured purity of form and unshadowed brilliance of hue remind one of the alpine mountains of Patenir or Altdorfer, fantastic snowy heights that dwarf men and their habitations, making the pictures in which such mountains occur seem all but technically pure landscapes, nearly devoid of human presence and stretching from earth to sky in one enormous yet delicately molded mass.

So *Zembla's* Rocks (the beauteous Work of Frost)
Rise white in Air, and glitter o'er the Coast;
Pale Suns, unfelt, at distance roll away,
And on th'impassive ice the Lightnings play:
Eternal Snows the growing Mass supply,
Till the bright Mountains prop th'incumbent Sky:
As *Atlas* fix'd, each hoary Pile appears,
The gather'd Winter of a thousand Years.

[ll. 53–60]

The Zembla passage has evoked the critical approbation of literary pictorialists from Pope's day to our own. Predictably, Joseph Warton, who compared it to a painterly passage from James Thomson's "Winter," averred that "a real lover of painting will not be contented with a single view and examination of this beautiful winter-piece, but will return to it, again and again, with fresh delight." [62] Since Pope owed nothing to

62. *An Essay on the Genius and Writings of Pope,* I, 342.

Chaucer's original for these pictorial effects, the poet evidently chose to imitate a work that was potentially pictorial, one in which he might give free rein to satisfying his iconic urge in the description of the Temple and his predilection for landscape in the delineation of its setting. *The Temple of Fame* is a poem of exuberant virtuosity; its reason for being is almost wholly as a vehicle for revealing the range and brilliance of its author's pictorial imagination. Pope's reflections on the pursuit of fame, his pantheon of classical figures, and his wish for "an honest Fame" or none are all traditional; these provide his poem with a suitable theme. Essentially, however, *The Temple of Fame* is as close to art for art's sake as a young Augustan poet could allow himself to come.

Pope's Homer

In 1715, the year in which Pope published *The Temple of Fame,* he also brought out the first four books of the *Iliad* translation. Homer's central place in Fame's temple (with Vergil second-ranked) revealed where Pope stood in the perennial debate over which of the two was the greater epic poet. In just four lines Pope lists the qualities reflected in the *Iliad* that he finds most admirable:

> Motion and Life did ev'ry Part inspire,
> Bold was the Work, and prov'd the Master's Fire;
> A strong Expression most he seem'd t'affect,
> And here and there disclos'd a brave Neglect.
>
> [ll. 192–95]

Such an enthusiastic endorsement of vitality, forceful expression, and fiery boldness again illustrates that Pope's classicism was far from being narrow or stereotypical. The "brave Neglect" echoes the "brave Disorder" of *An Essay on Criticism* and underscores Pope's often reiterated dictum that genius may ignore rules and "boldly deviate from the common Track." Since nature and Homer were found to be the same, an Augustan poet could appreciate Homer's "fire" and "invention" without fearing that he would thereby cease to follow nature.

232

In his preface to the *Iliad* translation, Pope halfheartedly attempts a temperate analysis of Homer's beauties and defects, using the traditional method, but soon decides that Homer's many beauties are his own and his few defects those of his time. Even the analogies Pope uses to discuss the older poet's work unmistakably reveal how congenial he found him.

> Our Author's Work is a wild Paradise, where if we cannot see all the Beauties so distinctly as in an order'd Garden, it is only because the Number of them is infinitely greater. 'Tis like a copious Nursery, which contains the Seeds and first Productions of every kind, out of which those who follow'd him have but selected some particular Plants, each according to his Fancy, to cultivate and beautify. If some things are too luxuriant, it is owing to the Richness of the Soil; and if others are not arriv'd to Perfection or Maturity, it is only because they are over-run and opprest by those of a stronger Nature.[63]

Most often, however, when discussing Homer, it is the painterly rather than the horticultural image that seems to suit Pope best. The preface to the translation provides ample evidence that a good part of what endeared Homer to Pope directly or ultimately derived from his pictorialism. When Homer is praised for his invention, it is usually done in terms that make full use of the *ut pictura poesis* tradition: "he [Homer] not only gives us the full Prospects of Things, but several unexpected Peculiarities and Side-Views, unobserv'd by any Painter but *Homer*." Further, Homer's "expression is like the colouring of some great Masters, which discovers itself to be laid on boldly, and executed with Rapidity." Homeric epithets "are a

63. *Works,* VII, 3. Pope may be indebted to Addison for this landscape imagery. Writing in the *Spectator* (No. 417, 1712), the latter contrasts the *Iliad* and the *Aeneid* in these terms: "Reading the *Iliad* is like travelling through a Country uninhabited, where the Fancy is entertained with a thousand Savage Prospects of vast Deserts, wide uncultivated Marshes, huge Forests, mis-shapen Rocks and Precipices. On the contrary, the *Æneid* is like a well-ordered Garden, where it is impossible to find out any Part unadorned, or to cast our Eyes upon a single Spot, that does not produce some beautiful Plant or Flower."

sort of supernumerary Pictures of the Persons or Things to which they are join'd." And again, "His Similes are like Pictures, where the principal Figure has not only its proportion given agreeable to the Original, but is also set off with occasional Ornaments and Prospects." [64]

Pope was not alone in finding Homer a pictorial poet. Joseph Warton observed that "the Poems of Homer afford a marvelous variety of subjects proper for history-painting." [65] A Frenchman, the Comte de Caylus, attracted the wrath of Lessing (who also attacked Pope) for having published in Paris (1757–58) his work *Tableaux tirés de l'Iliade, de l'Odysée d'Homère, et de l'Enéide de Virgile, avec des observations générales sur le costume.* Caylus found the three great classical epics highly picturesque and did not hesitate to recommend appropriately pictorial scenes to history painters presumably too dull of wit to find their own. For Pope's age nothing was more natural or congenial than to seek out especially visual passages. The reader of Homer in eighteenth-century England appreciated the additional pains Pope took to insure his enjoyment of these sections, among which were the use of an index to the epics' images and descriptions as well as the prolongation of moments of stasis and the heightening throughout the translation of visual details and color words.[66] Often in the "Observations" reference is made to specific painters in the contemporary pantheon whose style seemed to Pope especially well suited to a particular Homeric scene.[67] Pope's method of translation, based on Dryden's, was free enough for him to allow himself to add to his original those "Ovidian beauties" remarked upon, though not disapprovingly, by both Warton and Dr. Johnson. Though, in the century that followed, Pope's "literary artificial manner" met with critical disapproval,[68] his Homer vastly pleased the age for which it was intended.

64. *Works,* VII, 9, 10, 13.
65. *An Essay on the Genius and Writings of Pope,* I, 364.
66. See especially Ault, *New Light on Pope,* pp. 91–95, and Nicolson and Rousseau, *"This Long Disease, My Life,"* pp. 273–80.
67. See, for example, n. 53 above.
68. Matthew Arnold, *On the Study of Celtic Literature and On Translating Homer* (New York, 1883), p. 150. "Artificial" is an epithet often repeated; see pp. 160, 200, 227.

Space permits discussion here of only a few of Pope's superb epic landscapes and the necessary omission of all that is not landscape. Finally, the elaborate attention in both text and notes given to the iconic section in Book XVIII on the Shield of Achilles cannot be dealt with in its entirety. It is here that one becomes most forcibly impressed by the extent of Pope's *ut pictura poesis* orientation. In the "Observations" on the Shield he states three goals: to "Reply to the loose and scatter'd Objections of the Cricks"; to reproduce and comment upon "the regular Plan and Distribution of the Shield," designed by a French artist, Boivin; and to "attempt what has not yet been done, to consider it as a Work of *Painting,* and prove it in all respects comfortable to the most just Ideas and establish'd Rules of that Art." [69] Pope's partisan argument is designed to refute those predecessors of Lessing who found Homer's description of the Shield too crowded with scenes and too filled with episodic action to permit its representation in the visual art.[70]

What can be done in the space that remains is, first, to try to identify the kinds of landscape Pope chose to elaborate and recompose in his translation. J. M. W. Turner's term, "elevated pastoral," is perhaps the most accurate general label to use.[71] Pope's belief that Homer's world showed both man and nature in their earliest, most simple state made the pastoral mode an appropriate one. After all, Paris, a king's son, tended sheep, and Nausicaa, whose father was the great Alcinous, supervised the family laundry. Pope was also aware that parallels had been drawn between Homer's milieu and the biblical pastoralism of much of the Old Testament. It is clear that Pope tried to reproduce a setting that was rural, but not rustic, and ideal, but still natural—one, in short, that would reflect the dignity of its epic origins without ceasing to be appropriately "primitive." Almost invariably Pope preceded each book with

69. *Works,* VIII, 358.

70. For Lessing's criticism of Pope's "Observations" on the Shield and on Boivin's drawing as well, see *Laocoön* (Boston, 1890), chap. 19.

71. Turner, coincidentally, used lines from Pope's *Iliad* for an epigraph to be placed under one of his own landscapes.

a short notation in which he set the scene, as if the whole were to be conceived in terms of a history painting. Viewed thus, his landscapes function as a means of conveying authorial attitudes, emotional nuances, and moral or thematic content. They reinforce the narrative element in the epic while at the same time composing the whole into a unified, visually harmonious design. Of course all of these purposes are not fulfilled in every landscape. Some are very brief and have a more limited role.

An example of landscape used to enhance the emotional impact of a scene may be found in Book X. Ulysses and Diomedes, after a council meeting of the Greeks, have volunteered to scout the Trojan camp by night. Armed, they set forth:

> Thus sheath'd in Arms, the Council they forsake,
> And dark thro' Paths oblique their Progress take.
> Just then, in sign she favour'd their Intent,
> A long-wing'd Heron great *Minerva* sent;
> This, tho' surrounding Shades obscur'd their View,
> By the shrill Clang and whistling Wings, they knew.
>
> [ll. 319–24]

The two pray to Pallas, then proceed more confidently:

> Now, like two Lions panting for the Prey,
> With deathful Thoughts they trace the dreary way,
> Thro' the black Horrors of th'ensanguin'd Plain,
> Thro' Dust, thro' Blood, o'er Arms, and Hills of Slain.[72]
>
> [ll. 353–56]

Pope emphasizes the night scene's Gothic horrors. The Greeks move uncertainly "thro' Paths oblique" obscured by "sur-

---

72. E. V. Rieu's prose translation, reprinted in-the Penguin edition (Harmondsworth, Middlesex, 1958), p. 188, provides this reading of the passages above: "Armed in this formidable manner the pair set out, leaving all the chieftains there. Pallas Athene sent them a lucky omen, a heron close to their path on the right. The night was too dark for them to see the bird, but they heard it squawk. . . . They set out like a pair of lions through the black night, across the slaughter, picking their way among the corpses and the bloodstained arms."

rounding Shades" where the intense darkness makes Minerva's
heron seem at first a more fearful than reassuring manifestation. The morbid furnishings of this tenebrist scene are described as "black Horrors," half perceived and hence doubly
appalling. Pope has transformed "corpses" into "Hills of
Slain," another small detail which increases the somber and
oppressive atmosphere of the landscape. The pithiness of
Homer's original version has been invested with *enargeia* and
a strong dash of the sublime; for a moment Pope has aban-
doned the prevailing "elevated pastoral" landscape for a "romantick" one.[73]

Pope's fondness for night landscapes finds its most notable
expression in the famous "nightpiece" which concludes Book
VIII. Twice as long as Homer's passage, the scene is invested
with an emotional depth and intensity hard to perceive in the
original.

> The Troops exulting sate in order round,
> And beaming Fires illumin'd all the Ground.
> As when the Moon, refulgent Lamp of Night!
> O'er Heav'ns clear Azure spreads her sacred Light,
> When not a Breath disturbs the deep Serene,
> And not a Cloud o'ercasts the solemn Scene;
> Around her Throne the vivid Planets roll,
> And Stars unnumber'd gild the glowing Pole,
> O'er the dark Trees a yellower Verdure shed,

73. The inherent romanticism of Pope's night scene does not
anticipate that of the nineteenth century. Rather its pictorial affinities link it more with the seventeenth century. Besides the tenebrists, one thinks especially of such night landscapes as Jacob van
Ruisdael's (1628/29–82) cemetery pictures, one at the Gemälde-
galerie, Dresden, another in the Detroit Institute of Arts. Marcel
Brion believes that these suggest that "the landscape was being
intensified by a spiritual concept, no longer conceived as an objective reality but as a reflection of the emotional state of the artist"
(*Larousse Encyclopedia of Renaissance and Baroque Art* [London,
1967], p. 259). Norman Callan has compared the night scene to
Rembrandt's *The Night Watch* and suggested that Jervas may have
helped Pope with its visual effects. See "Pope's *Iliad*: A New Document," *Essential Articles for the Study of Alexander Pope*, pp. 595,
608 n.

And tip with Silver ev'ry Mountain's Head;
Then shine the Vales, the Rocks in Prospect rise,
A flood of Glory bursts from all the Skies:
The conscious Swains, rejoicing in the Sight,
Eye the blue Vault and bless the useful Light.
So many Flames before proud *Ilion* blaze,
And lighten glimm'ring *Xanthus* with their Rays:
The long Reflections of the distant Fires
Gleam on the Walls and tremble on the Spires.
A thousand Piles the dusky Horrors gild,
And shoot a shady Lustre o'er the Field.
Full fifty Guards each flaming Pile attend,
Whose umber'd Arms, by fits, thick Flashes send.
Loud neigh the Coursers o'er their Heaps of Corn.
And ardent Warriors wait the rising Morn.[74]

[ll. 685–708]

Pope called this passage "the most beautiful Nightpiece that
can be found in Poetry." [75] If it is, the credit is not all Homer's.
His translator has increased the dramatic chiaroscuro of the
scene until the pictorial quality intensifies our sense of a symbolic relationship between the serenity of the starry heavens
and the tranquil confidence of the Trojan forces around their
watchfires. The dark battlefield is illuminated and warmed for
a brief space. We are taught by Pope, however, to perceive
more in the scene than do the Trojans. The latter do not share

---

74. E. V. Rieu's translation reads as follows: "Thus all night long
they sat, across the corridors of battle, thinking great thoughts and
keeping their many fires alight. There are nights when the upper
air is windless and the stars in heaven stand out in their full splen-
dour round the bright moon; when every mountain-top and head-
land and ravine starts into sight, as the infinite depths of the sky
are torn open to the very firmament; when every star is seen and
the shepherd rejoices. Such and so many were the Trojans' fires,
twinkling in front of Ilium midway between the ships and the
streams of Xanthus. There were a thousand fires burning on the
plain, and round each one sat fifty men in the light of its blaze,
while the horses stood beside their chariots, munching white barley
and rye, and waiting for Dawn to take her golden throne" (pp.
159–60).

75. "Observations," VIII.l.

Plate 14 Elsheimer, *St. Paul on Malta*

our knowledge that this is the high point of their fortunes and that soon the Greek forces will seize and maintain the advantage. The fragility of this moment of stasis is communicated in the picture, wholly original to Pope, of the fires' reflection upon the walls and towers of Troy. It is easy to anticipate in this image the burning and looting of the city which ultimately follows from Troy's defeat. Pope thus plays up the sad and fearful associations that night possesses.[76]

Most interesting technically is Pope's adroit skill in connecting the cosmic landscape of the majestic moon, the circling planets, and the innumerable stars with the guards' watchfires far below. The simile with which the passage began establishes a parallel between stars and fires, but Pope reinforces that relationship by constructing his canvas from the top, that is, from heaven to earth. He lingers especially on the "midground" area of mountain and treetop drenched in moonlight. These are linked with the light reflected in the vales, from which "the Rocks in Prospect rise." The connecting element is the light, beaming from the heavens, repeated in the campfires, and reflected alike in river and plain. The progression of the eye is from light to light and the effect is consciously pictorial. Pope may have seen a work by the Italianate Dutch painter Adam Elsheimer (1578–1610), *St. Paul on Malta* (see plate 14), which uses light in a fashion similar to his own above to unite three planes of a picture—a distant moonlit sky, illumined rocks and trees in midground, and groups of foreground figures caught in the reflected firelight. Rather similarly structured, though a less precise parallel to Pope's nocturnal scene, is another Elsheimer nightpiece, *The Burning of Troy*.[77]

76. See G. S. Rousseau, "Seven Types of *Iliad*," *English Miscellany*, XVI (1965), 156. Rousseau believes that in this passage Pope reveals more affinity to the Graveyard School of poetry than to Homer, an exaggeration, perhaps, but an understandable one. Maynard Mack's discussion of the sense of foreboding in the nightpiece passage points out Pope's debt to Shakespeare's *Henry V* in the lines describing the waiting armies camped the night before Agincourt. See *Works*, VII, Introduction, pp. lv–lvi.

77. Elsheimer was popular in England from 1650 on. John Evelyn mentions his widely known (through Goudt's engraving) *Flight into Egypt*, another subject the artist treated in a night land-

Pope has been called "perhaps the acutest observer of effects of light among the English poets." [78] Such a preoccupation with light, especially with luminous distances in a pastoral scene, has made certain of his poetic passages appear suggestively Claudian to many critics.[79] But it is less a question of Pope imitating Claude than of sharing with him a similarly intense interest in the play of light on a landscape. Nearly always the English poet chooses, for example, to heighten the visual effects of a Homeric sunrise, adding color, compositional detail, and the natural or allegorical personification so characteristic of heroic landscape.

> But when the rosy Messenger of Day
> Strikes the blue Mountains with her golden Ray,[80]
>
> [IX.828–29]

In the original there is no hint of the presence of Aurora, the mythical figure found in so many Renaissance landscape paintings of dawn, preceding Apollo's sun chariot.[81] The first morning light touching the mountaintop is original with Pope, as are the colors, "blue" (perennially the shade used by landscape painters to suggest distance through aerial perspective) and "golden."

scape. See Henry and Margaret Ogden, *English Taste in Landscape in the Seventeenth Century* (Ann Arbor, 1955), p. 139.

78. Mack, *The Garden and the City*, p. 46.

79. See, for example, David Ridgley Clark, "Landscape Painting Effects in Pope's Homer," *JAAC*, XXII (1963), 25–28. Clark writes appreciatively about Pope's Claudian qualities, taking issue with Christopher Hussey who denies a close resemblance between painter and poet. Clark does not try to explain Pope's omission of Claude's name in the "Observations" where it would be natural for him to draw the parallel when commenting on the pastoral scene from the Shield of Achilles or the landscapes of Calypso and Circe. Although other painters' names, potential illustrators of Homeric scenes, flow easily from Pope's pen, he never mentions Claude.

80. Rieu has simply, "But in the first fair light of dawn . . ." (p. 180).

81. See, for example, Guido Reni's *Aurora*, reproduced in Hagstrum, *The Sister Arts*, pl. 24; also Poussin's *Diana and Endymion*, and *A Dance to the Music of Time*, in Blunt, *Nicolas Poussin*, Vol. II, pls. 63 and 127.

> And now from forth the Chambers of the Main,
> Thick clouds ascend, in whose capacious womb
> Arose the golden Chariot of Day,
> And tipt the Mountains with a purple Ray.[82]
>
> [VII.498–501]

Again Homer's brief, economical version has been augmented by the carefully positioned sun god as well as with touches of color—the "golden Chariot" and the "purple" (probably scarlet) shaft of sunrise light.

Basically, most of Homer's similes are representations of natural settings, highly various—snowscapes and seascapes, as well as the more usual fields, floods, and rivers. Pope usually elaborates these, adding pictorial details; he also restructures them until the compositional elements are more harmoniously ordered, as in a painting. It should be reiterated and stressed that he is the first poet we have dealt with who has employed this technique consistently. In one example the rain of stones from Greek catapults falling on besieged Troy is likened to a snowstorm:

> As when high *Jove* his sharp Artill'ry forms,
> And opes his cloudy Magazine of Storms;
> In Winter's bleak, uncomfortable Reign,
> A Snowy Inundation hides the Plain;
> He stills the Winds, and bids the Skies to sleep;
> Then pours the silent Tempest, thick, and deep:
> And first the Mountain-Tops are cover'd o'er,
> Then the green Fields, and then the sandy Shore;
> Bent with the Weight the nodding Woods are seen,
> And one bright Waste hides all the Works of Men:
> The circling Seas alone absorbing all,
> Drink the dissolving Fleeces as they fall.
> So from each side increas'd the stony Rain,
> And the white Ruin rises o'er the Plain.[83]
>
> [XII.331–44]

82. Rieu's version reads, "The Sun, climbing into the sky from the deep and quiet Stream of Ocean, had already lit the fields with his first beams . . ." (p. 142).

83. "By now the stones were falling thick as snowflakes on a winter day when Zeus the Thinker has begun to snow and let men

242

Such a sensitive eye for pure landscape is hard to find among Pope's contemporaries. Except for the rhymed couplet form, the scene above might have been drawn by only one other Augustan, James Thomson. Indeed, a passage from "Winter," first of his *Seasons* poems, shows that Thomson may have viewed Pope's picturesque lines with an attentive eye.

> The keener tempests come: and, fuming dun
> From all the livid east or piercing north,
>   To shed his sacred Light on Earth again,
> A vapoury deluge lies, to snow congealed.
> Heavy they roll their fleecy world along,
> And the sky saddens with the gathered storm.
> Through the hushed air the whitening shower descends,
> At first thin-wavering; till at last the flakes
> Fall broad and wide and fast, dimming the day
> With a continual flow. The cherished fields
> Put on their winter-robe of purest white.
> 'Tis brightness all; save where the new snow melts
> Along the mazy current. Low the woods
> Bow their hoar head; and, ere the languid sun
> Faint from the west emits his evening ray,
> Earth's universal face, deep-hid and chill,
> Is one wild dazzling waste, that buries wide
> The works of man.[84]
>
>   [ll. 223–40]

Like Pope, Thomson constructs his scene from sky to land, working from top to bottom, and noting the gradual progression of the snowfall. The effect on the fields and plains and on the "mazy current" or "circling Seas" is very similar. Even the vocabularies are alike: "fleecy world" and "dissolving Fleeces"

---

see the javelins of his armament; when he has put the winds to sleep and snows without ceasing, till he has covered the high hill-tops and the bold headlands of the coast and the clover meadows and the farmers' fields; till even the shores and inlets of the grey sea are under snow, and only the breakers fend it off as they come rolling in—everything else is blanketed by the overwhelming fall from Zeus's hand" (Rieu, p. 228).

84. From the 1730 version. See *James Thomson, Poetical Works,* ed. J. Logie Robertson.

for the appearance of snow and, most obvious, the echo in Thomson's last two lines of Pope's "And one bright Waste hides all the Works of Men." Thomson appears to have played the painterly game of borrowing motifs from a fellow artist's work.

Elsewhere in the *Iliad*, Pope's use of characteristically Ovidian touches betrays his taste for the decorative embellishment. Such passages set him apart from his contemporary Thomson, whose landscapes more often suggest a quasi naturalism uncongenial to Pope. A good example of this sort of elaborated image may be found in Book XVII, where the death of Euphorbus is likened by Homer to the uprooting of a beautiful tree:

> As the young Olive, in some Sylvan Scene,
> Crown'd by fresh Fountains with eternal Green,
> Lifts the gay Head, in snowy Flourets fair,
> And plays and dances to the gentle Air;
> When lo! a Whirlwind from high Heav'n invades
> The tender Plant, and withers all its Shades;
> It lies uprooted from its genial Bed,
> A lovely Ruin now defac'd and dead.[85]

[ll. 57–64]

Pope has transformed Homer's simile from a parable to a diptych, eliminating the original's narrative progression and substituting two carefully designed landscape views. The first presents the olive tree at the height of its loveliness; the gaiety and grace of Euphorbus are epitomized in the flower-crowned tree's swaying motion. The undefined locale in Homer becomes, in Pope, a *locus amoenus* of pastoral perfection where fountains, verdure, and gentle breezes decorate the "Sylvan Scene." The contrasting picture is dramatically somber. Destroyed by a "Whirlwind," the tree is blasted and withered, transformed into a ruin, "defac'd and dead." One senses that Pope found biblical echoes in Homer's simile, or that he remembered, perhaps, emblematic representations depicting the

---

85. "A gardener takes an olive shoot and plants it in a place of its own where it can suck up plenty of moisture. It grows into a fine young tree swayed by every breeze, and bursts into white blossom. But a gusty wind blows up one day, uproots it from its trench and stretches it on the earth" (Rieu, p. 317).

244

brevity of man's life, before he is, like Euphorbus, cut down in his bloom.

Pope's skill with the *locus amoenus* landscape is illustrated at greater length in the *Odyssey*. An example is Circe and her setting (Book X), where the sorceress "in a woody vale . . ./ Brown with dark forests and with shades around" sits broodingly in the foreground among "tufted trees" that reveal her palace towers in the distance. A more detailed bower is that of Calypso in Book V where, one suspects, Pope's knowledge of Spenser and Milton helped provide the ingredients of his own pictorial *locus amoenus:*

> Without the grot, a various sylvan scene
> Appear'd around, and groves of living green;
> Poplars and alders ever quiv'ring play'd,
> And nodding cypress form'd a fragrant shade;
> On whose high branches, waving with the storm,
> The birds of broadest wing their mansion form,
> The chough, the sea-mew, the loquacious crow,
> And scream aloft, and skim the deeps below.
> Depending vines the shelving cavern screen,
> With purple clusters blushing thro' the green.
> Four limpid fountains from the clifts distill, ⎫
> And ev'ry fountain pours a sev'ral rill,   ⎬
> In mazy windings wand'ring down the hill: ⎭
> Where bloomy meads with vivid greens were crown'd,
> And glowing violets threw odors round.
> A scene, where if a God shou'd cast his sight,
> A God might gaze, and wander with delight!
> Joy touch'd the Messenger of heav'n: he stay'd
> Entranc'd, and all the blissful haunt survey'd.[86]

[ll. 80–98]

86. "The cave was sheltered by a verdant copse of alders, aspens, and fragrant cypresses, which was the roosting-place of feathered creatures, horned owls and falcons and garrulous choughs, birds of the coast, whose daily business takes them down to the sea. Trailing round the very mouth of the cavern, a garden vine ran riot, with great bunches of ripe grapes; while from four separate but neighboring springs four crystal rivulets were trained to run this way and that; and in soft meadows on either side the iris and the parsley flourished. It was indeed a spot where even an immortal visitor must pause to gaze in wonder and delight.

The messenger stood still and eyed the scene. When he had

Most notable in this passage are the colors, the purples of grapes and violets and the lavishly reiterated greens. But also worthy of comment is Pope's enjoyment of the serpentine line of the grapevines screening Calypso's cave and the fountains' "mazy windings" flowing down the hill. Hermes, "the Messenger of heav'n," provides Pope with an observer's eye through which we see the grotto and its environs. The technique is similar to Milton's use of Satan to provide the first aerial glimpse of Eden, but Pope's scene is less haphazard in its arrangement, being controlled by directional words like "without," "around," "aloft," "down," and "round." Hermes' entrancement with the scene matches Pope's own:

> It is impossible for a Painter to draw a more admirable rural Landskip: The bower of *Calypso* is the principal figure surrounded with a shade of different trees: Green meadows adorn'd with flowers, beautiful fountains, and vines loaded with clusters of grapes, and birds hovering in the air, are seen in the liveliest colours in Homer's poetry.[87]

One of Pope's most extended exercises in ideal landscape in the *Odyssey* is the enclosed garden of King Alcinous.[88]

> Close to the gates a spacious Garden lies,
> From storms defended, and inclement skies:
> Four acres was th' alloted space of ground,
> Fenc'd with a green enclosure all around.
> Tall thriving trees confess'd the fruitful mold;
> The red'ning apple ripens here to gold,
> Here the blue fig with luscious juice o'erflows,
> With deeper red the full pomegranate glows,
> The branch here bends beneath the weighty pear,

---

enjoyed all its beauty, he passed into the great cavern" (Rieu, pp. 89–90).

87. "Observations," V.viii. Maynard Mack has pointed out an "imaginative affiliation" which may link Calypso's grotto with Pope's own at Twickenham and partly account, perhaps, for the poet's obvious delight in the Homeric original. See *Works,* VII, Introduction, ccxxiv.

88. See Book VII, 142–81. For Rieu's translation of this passage, see my chapter 1, n. 44.

And verdant olives flourish round the year.
The balmy spirit of the western gale
Eternal breathes on fruits untaught to fail:
Each dropping pear a following pear supplies,
On apples apples, figs on figs arise:
The same mild season gives the blooms to blow,
The buds to harden, and the fruits to grow.
   Here order'd vines in equal ranks appear,
With all th' united labours of the year;
Some to unload the fertile branches run,
Some dry the black'ning clusters in the sun,
Others to tread the liquid harvest join,
The groaning presses foam with floods of wine.
Here are the vines in early flow'r descry'd, ⎫
Here grapes discolour'd on the sunny side, ⎬
And there in autumn's richest purple dy'd. ⎭
   Beds of all various herbs, for ever green,
In beauteous order terminate the scene.
   Two plenteous fountains the whole prospect crown'd; ⎫
This thro' the gardens leads its streams around, ⎬
Visits each plant, and waters all the ground: ⎭
While that in pipes beneath the palace flows,
And thence its current on the town bestows;
To various use their various streams they bring,
The People one, and one supplies the King.
   Such were the glories which the Gods ordain'd
To grace *Alcinous,* and his happy land.
Ev'n from the Chief who men and nations knew,
Th' unwonted scene surprize and rapture drew;
In pleasing thought he ran the prospect o'er,
Then hasty enter'd at the lofty door.

                        [VII.142–81]

The poetic picture of this earthly paradise follows the gorgeously rendered iconic passage describing the palace and its furnishings—the brass walls, golden doors, silver pillars and lintels, the sculptured dogs formed by Vulcan's art, embroidered carpets, and golden statues of boys holding flaming torches. The garden possesses the same decorative opulence that was the palace's most striking feature. Except for the final six lines, this passage was translated by Pope in 1713 and published the same year, later to be incorporated without change into the complete *Odyssey* of 1725–26. It was in 1713 as well that Pope's painting lessons with Jervas began, and the effects of that instruction are apparent in almost every line of the poetic landscape he creates. Pope's version is drenched in color; Homer's greenery and purple-tinged grapes are retained and augmented by tones of red, gold, blue, and black. These colors are sometimes modified by words that increase the intensity of their hue: "deeper red," "richest purple," and Homer's own "for ever green." There is, as well, a strong sense of painterly composition in phrases like "terminate the scene" and "the whole prospect crown'd." The repeated "here," varied occasionally with "there," "this," "that," or "thence," directs the eye insistently and continually to pleasing juxtapositions of color and mass. The rococo windings of the streams, flowing from the two fountains, unite the several planes of Pope's picture and, as in the original, a viewer, Ulysses himself, is positioned at the garden's entrance, indicating a single vantage point from which both reader and epic hero take in the scene. The description of the Garden of Alcinous, said Sir William Temple, is "wholly poetical, and made at the Pleasure of the painter." [89] Pope would certainly have agreed.

Pope's landscape art in the Homer translation culminates in the description of the shield of Achilles. Despite the movement of marchers, plowmen, and dancers, a sense of stasis is maintained by the framing of each scene within its own partition of the shield and by the intuitive apprehension that the movement depicted possesses the kind of eternally frozen quality Keats conveyed in his description of the figures on his Grecian urn. Color is abundant but gold and silver predominate, keeping the reader conscious of the metallic medium with which Pope and Homer worked. Perhaps most remarkable is the sense of unity amid diversity. Contrast and antithesis characterize the individual sections of the shield: a city at peace and one at war, a scene of plowing and one of reaping, the violence of a

89. Albert Forbes Sieveking, ed., *Sir William Temple upon the Gardens of Epicurus, with other XVIIIth Century Garden Essays* (London, 1908), p. 24.

bull torn by lions and the tranquillity of a sheep cote. The dance at the end of the description, however, hints at an icono-graphic meaning as subtle and encompassing as the same motif in Botticelli's *Primavera,* which the engraved illustration in Pope's quarto resembles.[90] Pope's additions to the original also recall Spenser's *Faerie Queene,* Book VI, Canto x, and the sym-bolic significance of the Graces' dance on Mount Acidale.

> Now all at once they rise, at once descend,
> With well-taught Feet: Now shape, in oblique ways,
> Confus'dly regular, the moving Maze:
> Now forth at once, too swift for sight, they spring,
> And undistinguish'd blend the flying Ring:
> So whirls a Wheel, in giddy Circle tost,
> And, rapid as it runs, the single spokes are lost.[91]
>
> [XVIII.690–96]

Taken in its totality, the dance may be Pope's visual metaphor for the *discordia concors* so much a part of his art and age.[92] The diversity and contradictions he dealt with in poetry, re-flecting those he found in life itself, were hard to unify and resolve, especially in a temporal structure. The spatial dimen-sions of painting or landscaping or even the pictorial passages

90. See Edgar Wind, *Pagan Mysteries in the Renaissance,* rev. enl. ed. (New York, 1968), pp. 113–27.

91. Rieu's translation has simply the following: "here they ran lightly round, circling as smoothly on their accomplished feet as the wheel of a potter when he sits and works it with his hands to see if it will spin; and there they ran in lines to meet each other" (pp. 353–54).

92. Fern Farnham's article on the Shield section appears to find in Pope's "ambivalence toward allegory" and ignorance of "pattern" grounds for denying that he perceived much more in the Shield than a series of contrasting pictures. The nature of Pope's additions to Homer's original passage makes such an interpretation debatable. If Pope "misses certain aesthetic values which we of the twentieth century can find in the poem and, particularly, in the Shield pas-sage," surely the appreciation of the dance as a symbolic representa-tion of the *discordia concors* is not one such value overlooked by the poet. See "Achilles' Shield: Some Observations on Pope's *Iliad,*" *PMLA,* LXXXIV (1969), 1571–81.

of his poetry permitted him to suggest "another sort of organization—one concerned with the interrelatedness of parts to form a whole rather than one which works through a mere sequence of parts. This sense of interrelatedness is the final product of successful invention." [93]

Pope's "sense of interrelatedness" enabled him to understand the complementary aspects of opposing styles and prompted him to blend them consistently and successfully in his pictorial landscapes. The regularity of his verse form complements the asymmetry of his images, as Palladian architecture complemented the serpentine windings, concealed bounds, and sudden surprises of the *jardin anglais.* A surprisingly small part of his landscape art may be accurately labeled classical with no qualifying modifier attached. Even in the epics his finest pictorializations seldom arise from translating Claudian ingredients into his own poetic medium until one sees mountain and vale, grove and field balance each other like the two lines of a closed couplet. In poetic form he remained a conservative (though never a reactionary) ; in landscape he was an innovator. His eclectic taste prompted the tenebrist effects of night scenes in which he gave full rein to his fondness for dramatic chiaroscuro; his bower of Calypso exploited the painterly, decorative use of color and his almost omnipresent serpentine line. ("Maze"—or "Mazy," its adjectival form—must be one of Pope's most frequently used words in landscape description.) A feeling for baroque vastness and elaborate ornamentation informs *The Temple of Fame,* while the *Pastorals* reveal Pope's affinity for the graceful and decorative rococo of his contemporaries. Pope's pictorialism resists a single descriptive label; he is, by turns, classical, romantic, baroque, and rococo, flexibly suiting mode to purpose, whether the latter is moral, affective, or decorative. Invariably, however, until the cataclysmic negation of

93. Douglas Knight, *Pope and the Heroic Tradition,* Yale Studies in English, No. 117 (New Haven, 1951), p. 32. Knight is here discussing Pope's use of the *ut pictura poesis* analogies in the introduction and notes of the Homer translation, but his observations are more widely applicable as well.

The Dunciad destroyed his vision of the *discordia concors,* Pope's landscapes attempt to portray an ideal world in which disparate elements may be harmonized and an intrinsic order asserted.

Plate 15 Bassano, *The Earthly Paradise*

⌁ 6 ⌁

James Thomson and Ideal Landscape: The Triumph of Pictorialism

Relatively modest though James Thomson's contribution to English letters is, his influence upon subsequent literary history and upon landscape art is disproportionately significant. In his "Life of Thomson," Samuel Johnson called *The Seasons* a poem "of a new kind," [1] and it has become a critical commonplace to view Thomson and his friend John Dyer as "the godfathers of the picturesque," that durable cult which persisted into the nineteenth century.[2] Marshall McLuhan, who opposes "descriptive" poets to those he labels "picturesque," considers that the "epoch of picturesque experiment and exploration" began with Thomson's *Seasons*.[3] Neverthe-

1. *Lives of the English Poets,* ed. George Birkbeck Hill, 3 vols. (Hildesheim, 1968), III, 285.
2. Mario Praz, *The Romantic Agony;* trans. Angus Davidson (London, 1951), p. 18 n. Praz is reiterating a point made earlier by both Elizabeth Manwaring (*Italian Landscape in Eighteenth-Century England* [London, 1925]) and Christopher Hussey (*The Picturesque* [London and New York, 1927]).
3. "Tennyson and Picturesque Poetry," *Essays in Criticism,* I (1951), 264.

less, it must be emphasized that Thomson's own contemporaries never viewed his poetry as outrageously novel; his colleague Alexander Pope, for example, wrote graciously of the pleasure afforded him by *The Seasons*, taking three copies when it was published by subscription in 1730.[4] Thomson's impact upon later poets is attributable to the pivotal position he occupies in eighteenth-century literature: his work represents both the culmination of the heroic tradition in landscape and an anticipation of the later fully developed picturesque. He shares the extensiveness and conscious elaboration of pictorial elements that characterize his successors, but the nature of his landscapes and the sources from which they derive link him closely to the other Augustans and beyond them to poets of the previous century like Milton and Dryden.

Joseph Warton, like most of Thomson's critics, had serious reservations about his diction, but his admiration for the poet's fidelity to natural phenomena is echoed even by such stalwarts of the Romantic movement as Wordsworth and Hazlitt. Thomson's passion for verisimilitude did not, of course, conflict with an equal passion for the ideal, for a nature that was elevated and dramatized as well as "true." As Warton observed, "The scenes of Thomson are frequently as wild and romantic as those of Salvator Rosa, varied with precipices and torrents, and 'castled cliffs,' and deep vallies, with piny mountains, and the gloomiest caverns." [5] If Warton found his work comparable to Rosa's, Thomas Twining, in an essay on Aristotle's *Poetics* written in 1789, perceived parallels between Thomson's landscapes and those of Claude Lorrain. Pondering the failure of Greek poets to "describe the scenery of nature in a picturesque manner," Twining attributes their lack of fully developed landscape poetry to the dearth of landscape painters in Greece. He alleges that "those beauties were not heightened to them [the Greek poets], as they are to us, by comparison with painting—with those models of *improved* and

4. Austin Warren, *Alexander Pope as Critic and Humanist,* Princeton Studies in English, No. 1 (1929; reprint ed., Gloucester, Mass., 1963), pp. 263–64.

5. *An Essay on the Genius and Writings of Pope,* 2 vols. (London, 1806), I, 41–42.

selected nature, which it is the business of the landscape painter to exhibit. They had no Thomsons, because they had no Claudes." [6] Continuing on, Twining appears to anticipate E. H. Gombrich's theory that a taste for landscape painting precedes any deep appreciation for natural landscape among viewers who are not themselves artists.[7] Describing the effect of natural landscape on the cultivated viewer, trained by exposure to painted ideal landscapes, Twining observes that "such beauty does imitation reflect back upon the object imitated." [8]

In view of such a response it is hard to quarrel with Patrick Murdoch's assertion that Thomson taught others how to look at nature. After the publication of "Winter," first of *The Seasons* poems, Murdoch remarked that everyone marveled "how so many pictures, and pictures so familiar, should have moved them but faintly to what they felt in his descriptions." [9] A similar tribute survives in a poem, "To Mr. Thomson on His Seasons," written by James Delacour in 1734. Delacour argues that Thomson's nature actually exceeds its original in vividness; the ideal surpasses reality.

> Beneath thy touch description paints anew,
> And the skies brighten to a purer blue;
> Spring owes thy pencil her peculiar green,
> And drown'd in redder roses summer's seen:
> While hoary winter whitens into cold,
> And Autumn bends beneath her bearded gold.[10]

Thomson's invariable, unremitting use of personification has been criticized, but it is characteristically Augustan and contributes significantly to the organization of his landscape

6. Cited in Manwaring, *Italian Landscape,* p. iii.

7. See "The Renaissance Theory of Art and the Rise of Landscape," in *Norm and Form* (London, 1966).

8. Manwaring, *Italian Landscape,* p. iii.

9. Murdoch's account of the poet's life and writing is available at the beginning of volume I of the first collected edition of Thomson's *Works,* 2 vols. (London, 1762). For the above quotation, see I, vii.

10. Cited in Ralph Cohen, *The Art of Discrimination* (Berkeley, 1964), pp. 194–95.

compositions.[11] Winter, for example, is not simply a season, but a harsh deity presiding over an abjectly demoralized world. He has an emblematic, Ripa-like quality recognizable in figures representing the seasons in illustrations by J. Clark and B. Picart for the nonsubscription edition of 1730.

> See, Winter comes to rule the varied year
> Sullen and sad, with all his rising train—
> Vapours, and clouds, and storms.
>
> [ll. 1–3]

Winter is "the father of the tempest" who is "wrapt in black glooms," and his presence in the natural world sheds an "influence malign." Since uninhabited landscape was in Thomson's day still both rare and unappreciated, the poet's personifications populate his verbal canvases, implicitly revealing "human attitudes" [12] and directing the reader's response to the scene portrayed.

Thomson's poetic pictures stressed natural scenery heightened by associations both emotional and aesthetic. Their creator had had his own vision sharpened by the great landscape artists of sixteenth- and seventeenth-century Italy, and he was able to transmit to his readers that insight into the ideal pictorially as well as poetically.

11. Says Mario Praz: "That the heroic, rather than the natural, landscape was Thomson's real source of inspiration is proved by his use of personifications as the focal point of the scene." See *Mnemosyne* (Princeton, 1970), p. 12. The same point was made earlier by Jean Hagstrum. See *The Sister Arts* (Chicago, 1958), pp. 257, 259.

12. Ralph Cohen, "Thomson's Poetry of Space and Time," *Studies in Criticism and Aesthetics, 1660–1800,* ed. Howard Anderson and John S. Shea (Minneapolis, 1967), p. 178. Also frequent in Thomson's poetic landscapes are sculpturesque figures (like Musidora in "Summer") who provide an elaborate, often theatrical focal point for one of his scenic vignettes. Examples of such stylized human statuary have been noted by Alan Dugald McKillop (*The Background of Thomson's Seasons* [Minneapolis, 1942], pp. 70–71) and Jean Hagstrum (*The Sister Arts,* p. 249).

He summed up in his imagery the main achievements made in landscape-painting from the late 16th-century onwards. He was fascinated by the Venetian harmonies, the mannerist perspective taken from a high point of vision, Claude's spread of golden light (developed perhaps from Elsheimer's landscape of mood, but using a direct gaze into the sun), Poussin's complex constructions, Salvator Rosa's romanticising of the wilds. (Thomson had his predecessors like Dyer, but made the decisive advance.) [13]

The Landscape of The Seasons

The emphasis upon natural description in Scottish poetry has been offered as one explanation for Thomson's choice of subject in "Winter," especially since, by his own admission, he was familiar with such exercises in the genre as his friend Robert Riccaltoun's *A Winter's Day*. The differences between Thomson's *Seasons* and the nature poems of his countrymen, however, are more pervasive and important than their superficial similarities. Thomson's poem attempted, for one thing, to encompass the heroic strain. It is, as O. B. Hardison has suggested, "a particularly clear example of nature poetry with epic pretensions." [14] If Thomson, characteristically, lapsed at times into prosiness or burlesque, his faulty control of the poem's tone does not vitiate his high intent. His diction, often exotic or obscure, is consciously Miltonic and designedly Vergilian; scores of echoes of *Paradise Lost* and the *Georgics* mingle with coinages of his own, though the effect can often be more inflated than majestic.[15] A. D. McKillop, applying the term *baroque* to Thomson's style at its most ornate, did not intend the label to be a complimentary one; [16] it implies the same reservations

13. J. M. W. Turner, *The Sunset Ship,* ed., with an essay, by Jack Lindsay (London, 1966), p. 15.

14. *The Enduring Monument* (Chapel Hill, N.C., 1962), p. 86.

15. Otto Zippel's critical edition of *The Seasons* (Berlin, 1908) lists these allusions to Vergil, Milton, and other poets. See pp. xxxi–xl.

16. *The Background of Thomson's Seasons,* p. 6.

about Thomson's poem that Dr. Johnson had voiced in his biographical sketch of Thomson:

> His diction is in the highest degree florid and luxuriant, such as may be said to be to his images and thoughts "both their lustre and their shade"; such as invests them with splendour, through which perhaps they are not always easily discerned. It is too exuberant, and sometimes may be charged with filling the ear more than the mind.[17]

If Thomson's elaborate diction set him apart from the mass of his fellow nature poets, the pictorial method of his description further proclaimed his originality. The Argument, or Table of Contents, which precedes the sections of *The Seasons* is filled with items like "Flowers in prospect," "A landskip of the shepherd tending his flock," "A view of an Orchard," and many other such instances of the poet's scene-by-scene organization of his poem.[18] The old "catalogue" style, a series of landscape details described in sequential but essentially haphazard order, lacked any pretense to unity and made no attempt to combine particulars into a finished composition. Such a style characterized Scottish nature poetry,[19] and there are passages in *The Seasons* which show that Thomson was not entirely free of the faults inherent in this descriptive mode himself. He remained addicted to the prospect view, a panorama often too expansive to be labeled a landscape in the technical sense and one which encouraged an enumerative approach. Such breadth of vision is not wholly detrimental to the poetic impact of *The Seasons;* it tends, when effective, to reinforce the heroic dimension of the poem. Thomson's cosmic landscapes cannot match Milton's in grandeur, but they possess a total impact greater than the

17. *The Lives of the English Poets,* III, 300.
18. Ralph Cohen has observed that Thomson differentiates among four kinds of scenes: landscape, "an inclusive term for a rural scene observed from ground level"; prospect, "an extended view from a height"; vista, "a view between rows of trees"; and view, "a general term for that which is observed by the eye or mind." See *The Unfolding of the Seasons* (Baltimore, 1970), p. 172 n.
19. Stopford A. Brooke, *Naturalism in English Poetry* (New York, 1920; reprint, 1964), p. 40.

combination of pictorial details which provide their ingredients. Hazlitt has rightly hailed this aspect of Thomson's art:

> Thomson is the best of our descriptive poets: for he gives most of the poetry of natural description. Others have been quite equal to him, or have surpassed him, as Cowper for instance, in the picturesque part of his art, in marking the peculiar features and curious detail of objects;—no one has yet come up to him in giving the sum total of their effects, their varying influences on the mind. He does not go into the *minutiæ* of a landscape, but describes the vivid impression which the whole makes upon his own imagination; and thus transfers the same unbroken, unimpaired impression to the imagination of his readers. The colours with which he paints seem yet wet and breathing, like those of the living statue in the Winter's Tale.[20]

The prospect view is not invariable in Thomson. Often it precedes or prepares for a scene of rural life (sheep-shearing, haying) in which he concentrates on the "foreground" of his poetic landscape, filling it with as many details as a Flemish genre study. An anonymous critic writing in an Irish journal, *The Flapper,* in 1796 compared passages of Thomson's nature poetry to "highly finished paintings of the Flemish school." [21] Nonetheless, the careful maintenance of Vergilian dignity and the pervasive Miltonic diction almost invariably combine to elevate Thomson's "Flemish" artistry and ally it with a more classical and ideal mode.

Thomson's landscape art has most generally, and more properly, been compared to Claude Lorrain's, and Thomson himself has been dubbed "the Claude of Poets." In *The Seasons,* however, his pictorializations are usually what might be con-

20. "On Thomson and Cowper," Lectures on the English Poets, *Works,* ed. P. P. Howe, 21 vols. (London, 1930–34), V, 87. C. E. deHaas has also stressed Thomson's preference for the "general" landscape, one that includes "mountains and valleys, forests and brooks, under different atmospheric conditions, so that his poem consists of a series of pictures" (*Nature and the Country in English Poetry* [Amsterdam, 1928], p. 102).

21. Cited in Cohen, *The Art of Discrimination,* p. 178.

veniently and accurately labeled pre-Claudian, seldom approximating the idyllic pastoralism and poetic luminosity that characterize the work of Claude—and add so effectively to the magical atmosphere of Thomson's own *Castle of Indolence.* Since Elizabeth Manwaring's pioneering study of Italian landscape in eighteenth-century English poetry, we have formed the unhistorical habit of looking back at Thomson retrospectively from the vantage point of the later picturesque. As a result, we have, at times, imprecisely attributed to him stylistic qualities more consonant with the fully developed art of a slightly later period of landscape painting. Though Claudian moments occur in *The Seasons,* a more consistent and exact comparison of its landscapes can be made by examining them in conjunction with the work of, among others, Claude's own predecessors and models, Paul Brill (1554–1628) and the mysterious, elusive Adam Elsheimer (1578–1610).[22]

The artistic background of these two painters, like Thomson's own, included a strong tradition of focusing directly upon observed nature, of depicting in lovingly realistic terms the beauty and variety of northern landscapes. Their heritage in the treatment of a traditional subject like the seasons was work resembling that of Peter Brueghel the Elder whose earthy, vital harvest scene in *The Harvesters* (see plate 6) was of a wholly different mode from that of Nicolas Poussin. Like Thomson, however, Brill and Elsheimer rejected this naturalistic approach to landscape most familiar to them for a style that was elevated and classical. Like Thomson, they left their homeland, choosing to practice their craft in surroundings more conducive to the nurturing of their talents. But combined with the Roman suavity acquired by these Flemish artists there remained that fidelity to the "landscape of fact" which was the hallmark of their artistic forebears. So too with Thomson. The transplanted Scotsman's Augustan elegance, which he acquired in London, transmutes but does not wholly conceal the rural poet's debt

22. The development of Claude's art from that of northern painters who settled in Rome, specifically Brill and Elsheimer, has been pointed out by, among others, Michael Kitson. See "The Relationship between Claude and Poussin in Landscape," *Zeitschrift für Kunstgeschichte,* XXIV (1961), 142–62.

to his own rugged countryside and its simple people.[23] Brill, Elsheimer, and Thomson were pioneers in their fields, exploring the possibilities of a newly developed genre whose full potential would be realized more clearly and consistently by others. These, their successors, were ready to absorb the original visions inherent in the transitional landscape art of the three innovators who tentatively and gradually assimilated the new ideal mode and reconciled it with the familiar and more naturalistic. Though the parallel does not seem to have been remarked before, Thomson's landscapes in *The Seasons* are much more comparable to the earlier work of Brill and Elsheimer in a number of particulars than they are to the finished, consciously articulated style of Claude. Certain techniques of the two northern painters can be used to isolate important characteristics of Thomson's landscape art.

From Paul Brill, Thomson may have learned, though perhaps not directly, a technique which distinguished that artist's work from his fellows and much influenced the style of his successors. Brill, well known in England from the early seventeenth century, was credited by Edward Norgate in *Miniatura* (1625, enlarged 1649) with perfecting a method of achieving the effect of distancing in a landscape by making the contrast between light and shadow progressively less striking as the viewer's eye moves from foreground to background (see plate 16). Norgate describes Brill's innovation as follows:

> In a word, the most generall and absolute rule and vniversally to be observed in landscape was taught mee by the most excellent Master in this kind now dwelling in Rome, Paulo Brill, whose delightfull workes are many of them extante in print. . . . His observation was only this, that a good workeman must be suer ever to place light against darke and darke against light. His meaning was that the only way to remove the ground, and to extend the prospecte farr off was

23. Martin Price has stressed that the "gritty fidelity to natural fact, which we find again in Wordsworth, underlies Thomson's ecstasies." Comparing Thomson to Constable, Price remarks that both are "filled with a natural piety that watches for the revelation that lies in the minute natural process." See *To the Palace of Wisdom* (New York, 1965), pp. 357–58.

Plate 16 Brill, *The Death of Procris*

by apposing light to shadowes, yett soe as euer they must loose theyre force and vigoure proportionably as they remoue from the eye, and the strongest shadowes euer nearest hand, and (as they caule it) on the first ground.[24]

Thomson appears to have absorbed Brill's lesson well. In the following passage, deeply shadowed woods dominate his landscape's foreground and middleground with the same variance in hue that is a striking feature of so many Brill landscapes.[25] The dark woods, in turn, give way to a bright background of sky and cloud which expresses "a certayne aereall Morbidezza, as Paulo Brill caules it, or dilicatt softenes"; [26] Thomson's lines are from "Autumn."

> But see the fading many-coloured woods,
> Shade deepening over shade, the country round
> Imbrown; a crowded umbrage, dusk and dun,
> Of every hue from wan declining green
> To sooty dark. These now the lonesome muse,
> Low-whispering, lead into their leaf-strown walks.
> And give the season in its latest view.
>   Meantime, light shadowing all, a sober calm
> Fleeces unbounded ether; whose least wave
> Stands tremulous, uncertain where to turn
> The gentle current; while, illumined wide,
> The dewy-skirted clouds imbibe the sun,
> And through their lucid veil his softened force
> Shed o'er the peaceful world.
>
>   [ll. 950–63]

Later Claude was to adapt Brill's technique of using darker elements in his painting's foreground to frame the delicate expanse of pale sky that lit up its distance. Claude, however, tended to use a single tree, or, at most, a clump of two or three

24. Cited in Henry and Margaret Ogden, *English Taste in Landscape in the Seventeenth Century* (Ann Arbor, 1955), pp. 10, 172.

25. For instance, besides plate 16, the one, titled simply *Landscape*, in the Borghese Gallery, and another, also titled *Landscape*, in the Musée des Beaux-Arts, Algiers, reproduced in the *Larousse Encyclopedia of Renaissance and Baroque Art*, pl. 603.

26. Ogden and Ogden, *English Taste in Landscape*, pp. 10, 172.

as side screens, whereas Brill, like Thomson after him, usually preferred forest depths that extended for some distance into his picture and often dominated the foreground.

Both Brill and Thomson are capable of employing "violent chiaroscuro" [27] to strengthen the impact of dramatic moments. This chiaroscuro, combined with the "tension and movement" characteristic of Thomson's "best landscapes," [28] can be compared on the purely pictorial level to a painting like Brill's *Martyrdom of Two Dominicans* (Borghese Gallery, Rome). In this work a sunlit patch of meadow, like a floodlit stage, provides the focal point for the murder being enacted. Sudden, violent motion is suggested in one figure's running posture and another's arm, lifted to strike. All around, the darkly shadowed woods are utterly still. The painterly contrasts between light and shadow and between stillness and movement resemble those same effects in Thomson's stag-hunt scene in "Autumn." The following lines describe the culmination of the pursuit, the stag at bay, and the moment of his death:

> He bursts the thickets, glances through the glades,
> And plunges deep into the wildest wood.
> If slow, yet sure, adhesive to the track
> Hot-steaming, up behind him come again
> The unhuman rout, and from the shady depth
> Expel him, circling through his every shift.
> He sweeps the forest oft; and sobbing sees
> The glades, mild opening to the golden day.
>
> [ll. 435–42]

At length the exhausted, fearful stag is set upon by the dogs who have penetrated the dark peace of the forest, once his refuge.

> the growling pack,
> Blood-happy, hang at his fair jutting chest,
> And mark his beauteous chequered sides with gore.
>
> [ll. 455–57]

27. This phrase was applied to Thomson's landscapes by Martin Price. See *To The Palace of Wisdom*, p. 361.
28. *Ibid.*, p. 357.

Thomson, whose response to blood sports was as negative as
Oscar Wilde's, though much less witty, is not too distracted by
moral indignation to forget to heighten the pictorial and dramatic qualities of this scene by focusing upon the reiterated
light/dark motif of the stag's "chequered sides," blood-streaked.
Tension and movement in Thomson are again used, repetitively and effectively, in the fairly elaborate storm scenes of
each season which form one of the poem's unifying patterns.

Brill also shared with Thomson a fondness for the prospect
view, combining it with other kinds of landscape scenery. The
northern painter's taste for the panoramic undoubtedly derived
from the landscape styles of his predecessors, Peter Brueghel
and Joachim Patenir. Through Brill, an appreciation for
larger, more extended views passed into Italian landscape painting. Brill successfully demonstrates in one medium what Thomson illustrates later in another, that "the varying of the prospect
is a method of observing the diversity of nature," [29] dramatizing
its contrasting elements, and suggesting its multiplicity, all to
be controlled within the artist's unified structure. Such paintings as those by Brill provide a precedent from the visual arts
for the structure of a passage like this one, again from "Autumn," that relies upon a complex pattern, emphasizing contrast and multiplicity. Not only do dark and light predictably
yet effectively complement each other, but enclosed and open
space, vale and plain, shaggy wood and manicured garden are
arranged in ordered, pleasing juxtaposition.

> Oh! bear me then to vast embowering shades,
> To twilight groves, and visionary vales,
> To weeping grottoes, and prophetic glooms;
> Where angel forms athwart the solemn dusk,
> Tremendous, sweep, or seem to sweep along;
> And voices more than human, through the void
> Deep-sounding, seize the enthusiastic ear.
> Or is this gloom too much? Then lead, ye Powers
> That o'er the garden and the rural seat
> Preside, which, shining through the cheerful land

29. Cohen, *The Unfolding of The Seasons*, p. 125.

In countless numbers, blest Britannia sees—
Oh! lead me to the wide extended walks,
The fair majestic paradise of Stowe!

[ll. 1030–42]

Without some understanding of the impact upon classical Italian painting of the work of Paul Brill and his predecessors, Thomson might have achieved in his varied canvas a less balanced pictorial effect, producing instead an imitative, second-rate version of Milton's scenes in *Il Penseroso* and *L'Allegro*.

The landscapes of Claude's other model, Adam Elsheimer, offer at least one useful clue to the essentials of Thomson's pictorial view of nature. It may well have been Elsheimer who was most instrumental in impressing upon Claude the importance of light in an atmosphere,[30] and Thomson too is ever preoccupied with its changing effects and various manifestations—dawn, sunset, moonlight, the intermittent sunlight of a cloud-filled sky, the lightning flashes that fitfully illuminate a storm-darkened landscape. Not all of his inspiration in these celebrations of light derive from any one source; they come in part from literature and science as well as from the visual arts. His debt, for example, to Milton, as everyone has recognized, is considerable, and it is most strikingly apparent in the apostrophe to light in "Summer," which recalls Milton's incomparable invocation in *Paradise Lost,* Book III.

Prime cheerer, Light!
Of all material beings first and best!
Efflux divine! Nature's resplendent robe,
Without whose vesting beauty all were wrapt
In unessential gloom; and thou, O Sun!
Soul of surrounding worlds! in whom best seen
Shines out thy Maker! may I sing of thee?[31]

[ll. 90–96]

30. See Kenneth Clark, *Landscape into Art* (Boston, 1961), pp. 51–52, and Germain Bazin, *Baroque and Rococo Art,* trans. Jonathan Griffin (New York, 1964), pp. 108, 142–43.
31. Equally Miltonic is a later passage; see ll. 175–84..

Thomson's paean moves from mystical preoccupations to cosmic ones, though he is far more interested than was Milton in fairly precise astronomical observations and the diffusion and refraction of light in different atmospheres, such as clouds, fog, or storms. His debt to Newton in this area has been carefully analyzed by Marjorie Nicolson.[32] Obviously light, and especially its primary source, the sun, often prompted Thomson to spiritual or scientific responses that were not always pictorial as well. But the poet of *The Seasons* was a less than systematic or even consistent thinker, and mixed with his exalted concepts of light as a symbolic manifestation of the Divine Light are other images that are pictorial rather than philosophical. Here he reminds us of several painters in his classical pantheon, but most strikingly of Adam Elsheimer.

In Thomson's moonlight landscapes especially, an underlying romanticism threatens at times to obscure his poem's dominant classical mode. Night presents the poet with an opportunity to create a landscape of mood, one in which an intensity of light may blaze forth more theatrically for the darkness with which it is surrounded. He much resembles Elsheimer whose Roman technique failed to dissipate his northern romanticism. The latter tendency found an outlet in his night pieces which reflect that preoccupation with nocturnal beauty so pervasive in both the poetry and the painting of the early seventeenth century. His popularity in England extends back to the early seventeenth century when at least thirteen paintings attributed to Elsheimer were in the great collections of Charles I, Arundel, and Buckingham. Edward Norgate praised his work highly, and Inigo Jones paid him the compliment of adapting the moonlight setting of the painter's *Flight into Egypt* for his scenery for Davenant's *Luminalia* in 1638.[33] His work circulated widely in prints which Thomson may well have seen. The following passage from "Winter," describing a sunset and an almost simultaneous moonrise, capitalized on

32. *Newton Demands the Muse* (Princeton, 1946; reprint, 1966), pp. 48–54.
33. Ogden and Ogden, *English Taste in Landscape,* p. 31.

the sense of disequilibrium intrinsic to a scene wherein several bodies of light compete for dominance. The irregular movement and shifting points of focus are reminiscent of the three planes of light which structure the composition of Elsheimer's *St. Paul on Malta* (see plate 14), discussed in the previous chapter.

> When from the pallid sky the Sun descends,
> With many a spot, that o'er his glaring orb
> Uncertain wanders, stained, red fiery streaks
> Begin to flush around. The reeling clouds
> Stagger with dizzy poise, as doubting yet
> Which master to obey; while, rising slow,
> Blank in the leaden-coloured east, the moon
> Wears a wan circle round her blunted horns.
> Seen through the turbid, fluctuating air,
> The stars obtuse emit a shivering ray;
> Or frequent seem to shoot athwart the gloom,
> And long behind them trail the whitening blaze.
>
> [ll. 118–29]

Most strikingly like Elsheimer's style is the emphasis on diffused light, revealed in "fiery streaks" and "shivering ray." The stars that "trail the whitening blaze," half obscured by clouds, are especially characteristic of paintings like *St. Paul on Malta* or the nocturnal *Flight into Egypt,* attributed to Elsheimer and engraved by Goudt.[34] Thomson, like Pope, obviously associates night scenery with the sublime, and his whole landscape is designed to evoke an emotional response (most notably in the personifications of the clouds and heavenly bodies) that attunes one to the mood he is trying to communicate, one of bleak loneliness and mystery. A storm is about to break, and the foreboding and tension expressed by the night sky are matched on earth by images of a "withered leaf," a "wasted.taper," and a "crackling flame." Helping to connect the two planes, sky and earth, are the birds, seeking shelter from the storm about to burst upon them.

34. This engraving is reproduced in *ibid.,* pl. 102.

But chief the plumy race,
The tenants of the sky, its changes speak.
Retiring from the downs, where all day long
They picked their scanty fare, a blackening train
Of clamorous rooks thick-urge their weary flight,
And seek the closing shelter of the grove.
Assiduous, in his bower, the wailing owl
Plies his sad song. The cormorant on high
Wheels from the deep, and screams along the land.
Loud shrieks the soaring hern; and with wild wing
The circling sea-fowl cleave the flaky clouds.

[ll. 137–47]

The apprehensive movement and plaintive cries of the birds combine with the other images of tense expectation, until a cumulative impact is reached with the fierce, sudden onset of the storm. And when it is spent, with almost as dramatic swiftness as it began, the mood changes to one of meditative serenity.

Another night landscape emphasizing subtle chiaroscuro and the movement of light is this one from "Summer," which attempts to pictorialize an evanescent moment before the light changes and the mood alters:

Among the crooked lanes, on every hedge,
The Glow-worm lights his gem; and, through the dark,
A moving radiance twinkles. Evening yields
The world to Night; not in her winter robe
Of massy Stygian woof, but loose arrayed
In mantle dun. A faint erroneous ray,
Glanced from the imperfect surfaces of things,
Flings half an image on the straining eye;
While wavering woods, and villages, and streams,
And rocks, and mountain-tops that long retained
The ascending gleam are all one swimming scene,
Uncertain if beheld.

[ll. 1682–93]

After a few lines devoted to "Sweet Venus . . . the fairest lamp of night," Thomson continues:

As thus the effulgence tremulous I drink,
With cherished gaze, the lambent lightnings shoot
Across the sky, or horizontal dart
In wondrous shapes—by fearful murmuring crowds
Portentous deemed.

[ll. 1699–703]

It is not to be wondered that Thomson's name is invariably associated with painters who shared his fascination for light on landscape—Elsheimer, Claude, Turner. Like them he tends to concentrate on those times of day or evening—sunrise or twilight—when light paints the landscape with ever shifting nuances, revealing shadows precariously captured at almost the instant they fade and are defined anew.

Thomson's debt to Elsheimer may well have been indirect, of course. Besides influencing Claude, Elsheimer had an effect upon the landscapes of his friend Rubens and of another friend in Rome, Pieter Lastman, who became Rembrandt's teacher. By whatever route they came to Thomson, it is clear that these seventeenth-century paintings of night, suffused with romantic feeling and emphasizing the sublime mood engendered by the nocturnal setting, evoked a sensitive response from this pictorial English poet who often chose to depict the night landscape in his own medium.

A different, more classical handling of light occurs in other parts of *The Seasons* and can be exemplified in the following passage from "Summer." Here Thomson's landscape more resembles Guido Reni's than Adam Elsheimer's, its foreground filled with mythological deities representing forces in nature. In the lines cited below, Thomson has allowed his own personifying tendency free rein in order to portray the sun as a monarch whose diurnal progress is reflected in all nature:

But yonder comes the powerful king of day
Rejoicing in the east. The lessening cloud,
The kindling azure, and the mountain's brow
Illumed with fluid gold, his near approach
Betoken glad. Lo! now, apparent all,
Aslant the dew-bright earth and coloured air,
He looks in boundless majesty abroad,

> And sheds the shining day, that burnished plays
> On rocks, and hills, and towers, and wandering streams
> High gleaming from afar.
>
> [ll. 81–90]

Despite the abundant and nicely discriminated effects of the play of light upon the various ingredients of this early morning setting, preeminence is given to the sun himself, a power whose kingly presence predictably dominates the heroic landscape Thomson has created. When, some lines later, this figure is sketched more precisely with the attending personages who make up his train, the reader is expected to recall Renaissance paintings of Apollo in his chariot.

> round thy beaming car,
> High seen, the Seasons lead, in sprightly dance
> Harmonious knit, the rosy-fingered hours,
> The zephyrs floating loose, the timely rains,
> Of bloom ethereal the light-footed dews,
> And, softened into joy, the surly storms.
>
> [ll. 120–25]

Persuasive evidence exists that Thomson may have been thinking of a specific painting, Guido Reni's *Aurora*.[35] But such is the eclecticism of *The Seasons* that a coolly classical landscape like that above may exercise its decorative appeal in one section of the poem, while elsewhere quite another kind of visual impact is sought and obtained.

Thomson's response to light is more discriminating and varied than his use of color which tends to be, more often than not, fairly conventional though appreciative. He takes a sensuous pleasure in the rich multiplicity of hues to be found in jewels ("Summer," ll. 140–59) or a rainbow ("To the Memory of Sir Isaac Newton," ll. 102–18), but he does not ordinarily seize upon opportunities to fill his rural canvases with colors other than the predominant green and brown of earth and the meticulously differentiated blues of sky. There is enough evidence of the poet's discerning eye and sophisticated color sense

35. See Hagstrum, *The Sister Arts*, pp. 259–61.

to lead us to assume that what restrained Thomson was fidelity
to nature and a disinclination to heighten decorative elements
overmuch. Given the chance to describe an orchard in blossom
viewed from an eminence, the poet's eye does not fail.

> And see the country, far-diffused around,
> One boundless blush, one white-empurpled shower
> Of mingled blossoms; where the raptured eye
> Hurries from joy to joy, and, hid beneath
> The fair profusion, yellow Autumn spies.
>
> ["Spring," ll. 109–13]

And, in a floral passage also from "Spring," Thomson describes
"The yellow wall-flower, stained with iron brown" (l. 533).
"Winter," quite properly, is drawn in almost unrelieved tones
of gray, black, or brown against the white of snow and ice. The
affinity of ice for dazzling reflections of light is exploited by
Thomson, who also likes the peculiarly blue cast of frost and
snow under the austere illumination of a winter's day. "Summer" achieves some splashes of color in those selections celebrating exotic tropic lands; in "citron groves," for example,
Thomson notes "the lemon and the piercing lime,/ With the
deep orange glowing through the green" (ll. 664–65), but his
bookish sources betray him into repetitive, seemingly mechanical allusions to "the green serpent" or the crocodile "cased in
green scales."

One hindrance to a colorful palette is the frequency of the
poet's prospect view which inevitably concerns itself less with
details of hue and more with contrasting forms and the composition of structural masses into a pictorially integrated whole.
These landscapes reveal Thomson's concern with the larger
contrasts of light and shadow, vale and hill, or even with
textures—roughness and irregularity juxtaposed with smooth,
manicured surfaces. A good example can be excerpted from
Thomson's lengthy description of Hagley Park in "Spring."

> Meantime you gain the height, from whose fair brow
> The bursting prospect spreads immense around;
> And, snatched o'er hill and dale, and wood and lawn,
> And verdant field, and darkening heath between,

And villages embosomed soft in trees,
And spiry towns by surging columns marked
Of household smoke, your eye excursive roams—
Wide-stretching from the Hall in whose kind haunt
The hospitable Genius lingers still,
To where the broken landscape, by degrees
Ascending, roughens into rigid hills
O'er which the Cambrian mountains, like far clouds
That skirt the blue horizon, dusky rise.

[ll. 950–62]

Thomson here is working in the grand manner, complimenting George Lyttelton by emulating "the generalized public prospects of the Carracci landscape tradition" [36] rather than encompassing a more intimate, less formal landscape. To some readers of Thomson, perhaps unfamiliar with Carracci, the landscape above has seemed too extensive to be pictorial. Thomson's Augustan readers, however, would not have considered it so, and they would have applauded the adaptation of this recognized subgenre to a view of Lyttelton's estate. Quite properly Thomson has muted the affective impact of color (except for "verdant field" and "blue horizon"), choosing to work instead with a combination of baroque space and classical line, thus emulating the style of the Bolognese eclectics.

Such stylistic versatility is almost as marked in Thomson as in Pope when one looks only at the landscapes and not at the overriding didacticism and moral sententiousness that provide, in the later versions of his poem, a certain homogeneity of tone to help unify the diversity of scene. *The Seasons* does not function like a picturesque poem, alternating passages of the Salvatorian sublime with others of Claudian beauty. That sort of formula for landscape poetry operates only after the mid-eighteenth century when heroic landscape degenerates into the more familiar picturesque mode. One can look back at Thomson from the vantage point of the late eighteenth century and

36. This phrase is E. K. Waterhouse's. See *Italian Baroque Painting* (New York, 1962), p. 34. Thomson's art collection included Carracci prints.

273

pluck out scenes that appear to have been inspired by Rosa or Lorrain, but too often, we suspect, Thomson's own contemporaries would have drawn different artistic parallels from our own.

Elizabeth Manwaring has, for example, called the passage quoted above "Claudian," focusing probably on the last two lines.[37] Mountains rising in a luminous distance were almost invariable in a landscape with any depth; they did not originate with Claude, however, but went back to early northern art like that by Patenir and Altdorfer. With no more detail on the quality of light in such a passage, it is not specifically enough characterized to be labeled Claudian with any assurance.

Another passage from "Summer" called Claudian by a distinguished Thomson scholar [38] is the following:

> Around the adjoining brook, that purls along
> The vocal grove, now fretting o'er a rock,
> Now scarcely moving through a reedy pool,
> Now starting to a sudden stream, and now
> Gently diffused into a limpid plain,
> A various group the herds and flocks compose,
> Rural confusion! On the grassy bank
> Some ruminating lie, while others stand
> Half in the flood and, often bending, sip
> The circling surface. In the middle droops
> The strong laborious ox, of honest front,
> Which incomposed he shakes; and from his sides
> The troublous insects lashes with his tail,
> Returning still. Amid his subjects safe
> Slumbers the monarch-swain, his careless arm
> Thrown round his head on downy moss sustained;
> Here laid his scrip with wholesome viands filled,
> There, listening every noise, his watchful dog.
>
> [ll. 480–97]

The habit of associating with Claude's work almost any idyllic pastoral scene that is composed by Thomson in a picturesque

37. *Italian Landscape in Eighteenth-Century England,* p. 104.
38. See Patricia Meyer Spacks, *The Varied God: A Critical Study of Thomson's The Seasons,* University of California Publications in English, No. 21 (Berkeley, 1959), pp. 102, 105.

manner may arise, again, from extensive reading in the landscape poetry of the later eighteenth century and the association
of Thomson with that tradition, as one born out of time.
Thomson is still viewed as more atypical of his age than the
admitted originality of *The Seasons* warrants. The passage
cited is really not at all Claudian. The affectionate realism
with which the animals are depicted should cause us to agree
rather with Joseph Warton's estimation: "A groupe worthy
the pencil of Giacomo da Bassano." [39] Bassano's domestic animals, a prominent feature of his landscape art, have an earthy,
individualized flavor like Thomson's ox in the scene above (see
plate 15). Just such an ox, indeed, may be seen in the foreground of Bassano's *The Grape Harvest* (Doria Pamphili,
Rome).[40] On the other hand, the pose of Thomson's swain,
"his careless arm/ Thrown round his head on downy moss sustained," evokes Poussin's *Narcissus and Echo* (Louvre), where
Narcissus, dead or dying, lies in such a posture, attended by
Cupid and a grieving Echo. The graceful positioning of the
sculpturesque form of Narcissus was widely copied by other
painters from Poussin's original. Thomson, once again, is dis-
playing his eclecticism in choosing the ingredients for his
landscape sketch with a characteristically catholic taste, mingling echoes of Bassano's style with a borrowed attitude from
Poussin. It was not his only debt to Poussin whose combination
of Vergilian gravity, ideal landscape, and human forms molded
like antique statues must have exercised a great appeal for
Thomson. The four paintings of the Seasons (see plates 1–4),
especially *Summer*, as Jean Hagstrum points out, contain a
number of "striking parallels to Thomson." [41] We have, in the
previous chapter, examined similarities of theme and treatment
between Poussin and Pope; Thomson's response to Poussin

39. *An Essay on the Genius and Writings of Pope*, I, 44.
40. This painting is reproduced in the *Larousse Encyclopedia of
Renaissance and Baroque Art*, pl. 422.
41. Hagstrum, *The Sister Arts*, p. 251 n. Thomson in "Summer"
retells the biblical story of Ruth and Boaz; his narrative of Lavinia
and Palemon takes place against the background of the countryside
at harvest time. Especially evocative of the details of the Poussin
painting are ll. 151–66.

links him once again to contemporary tastes in the visual arts. Too much emphasis has also been placed upon Thomson's Rosa-like moments. Certainly he consciously strove for the sublime, but his sources for the natural sublime owe more to the English tradition of Dennis and Addison than they do to Rosa. The sublime was fashionable partly because it helped to elevate the poetry of natural description by incorporating into it a moral as well as an emotional dimension. Such a concept of the sublime motivates Thomson to write to David Mallet, advising his friend about his *Excursion:* "My idea of your Poem is a description of the grand works of Nature raised and animated by moral and sublime reflections; therefore before you quit this earth you ought to leave no great scene unvisited." [42] Included in great scenes are such natural disasters as volcanic eruptions, storms at sea, and earthquakes. There is ample evidence that Thomson followed his own advice in *The Seasons,* especially in "Summer" and "Winter" where the poet uses spectacular if remote locales, taken from travel books, to vary the more regular and familiar landscape of Britain. One such celebrated scene is Thomson's picture of sharks following a slave ship helplessly buffeted by winds and waves in a tropical storm. C. B. Tinker remarked that the intensity of the scene's visualization might have inspired Turner's *Slave Ship.*[43]

> Increasing still the terrors of these storms,
> His jaws horrific armed with threefold fate,
> Here dwells the direful shark. Lured by the scent
> Of steaming crowds, of rank disease, and death,
> Behold! he rushing cuts the briny flood,
> Swift as the gale can bear the ship along;
> And from the partners of that cruel trade
> Which spoils unhappy Guinea of her sons
> Demands his share of prey—demands themselves.
> The stormy fates descend: one death involves
> Tyrants and slaves; when straight, their mangled limbs

42. Cited in Marjorie Nicolson, *Mountain Gloom and Mountain Glory* (New York, 1963), p. 333.
43. See *Painter and Poet* (Cambridge, Mass., 1938), pp. 151–52.

Crashing at once, he dyes the purple seas
With gore, and riots in the vengeful meal.

["Summer," ll. 1013–25]

Thomson's storm scenes have been called his "specialty." He consistently achieves in them the sublime effects that elicited the admiration of eighteenth-century readers. That he deliberately affected the sublime can be seen by an examination of "the poetic criteria of his 1726 preface" as well as by his frequent choice of "material which his time had labeled automatically sublime." [44]

Thomson employs the sublime for purposes primarily moral, even sacramental, that is, for its mystical, revelatory potential. Like Pope he is aware of the powerful emotional responses evoked by the sublime in nature, but unlike Pope (except in parts of *The Temple of Fame* and the fourth *Dunciad*) his design in using the sublime is seldom to stimulate a largely affective reaction. The powerful feelings of awe and fear aroused by these passages theoretically induce a receptive state of mind, ready for the philosophical or moral truths ultimately forthcoming. These truths are concerned with nature and man's place in it, often with Thomson's vision of Britannia, a Whiggish and less mystical version of Blake's restored Albion. Here art and nature, commerce and agriculture flourish in concert; the vision of a new Golden Age, the dream of Restoration wit and Augustan satirist alike, is updated with a new progressivism. Thomson's utopian theme is clearly defined in both *Liberty* and *The Castle of Indolence,* but *The Seasons,* despite its successive revisions or perhaps because of them, attempts to explore too many disparate scientific and philosophical areas to permit the clearcut articulation of a single central theme. The

44. Spacks, *The Varied God,* pp. 78–79. Spacks notes that John Holmes's *Art of Rhetorick,* 1739, analyzed the ingredients of Longinian sublimity, using *The Seasons* "as text and illustration." Christopher Thacker has also argued that Thomson's storm scenes, especially that of "Winter," illustrate the "revolution in attitudes" in the early eighteenth century toward the pleasing terrors aroused by storms. See " 'Wish'd, Wint'ry, Horrors': The Storm in the Eighteenth Century," *Comp. Lit.,* XIX (1967), 36–57.

use of landscape as a metaphor rather than just a setting, its importance in *The Seasons* as "a medium more than a site," [45] sometimes results in ambiguity, even in some contradiction between tenor and vehicle. The optimistic message in the "Hymn" that nature's seasonal variety shows forth God's glory and essential benignity forms a curious coda to a poem which, in its emphasis on the natural sublime, has often focused upon the apparently whimsical cruelties which nature's God visits upon his subjects. The impact of "Winter" is overwhelmingly grim, and even "Summer" includes the slave ship and Amelia's death by lightning. Patricia Meyer Spacks has censured Thomson's "apparent unwillingness or inability to face consistently the major philosophic problems he suggests," especially the problem of evil.[46] Such inability may be traced to a conflict between Thomson the landscape artist and Thomson the increasingly didactic and conventional moralist.

Ralph Cohen has suggested that descriptive poetry like Thomson's tends "to stress the 'discors' of *concordia discors* and to minimize the reconciliation of extremes." [47] A striving after novelty, a need to exhibit the variety and multiplicity of nature may be accompanied by the poet's assertion of an overriding harmony, but the vivid evidence of "discors" in *The Seasons* may outweigh the statement of faith in "concordia," especially for non-eighteenth-century readers. In "Winter," Thomson retains the framework of his landscape imagery to make such a statement, imagining the favorable effect of retirement and meditation on his own perceptions and those of his friends.

> Hence larger prospects of the beauteous whole
> Would gradual open on our opening minds;
> And each diffusive harmony unite
> In full perfection to the astonished eye.
> Then would we try to scan the moral world,
> Which, though to us it seems embroiled, moves on

45. See Price, "The Sublime Poem: Pictures and Powers," *Yale Review*, LVIII (1969), 210.
46. *The Varied God*, p. 34.
47. *The Art of Discrimination*, p. 147.

In higher order, fitted and impelled
By wisdom's finest hand, and issuing all
In General good.

[ll. 579–87]

Such an utterance is characteristic enough of eighteenth-century poetry; one need only cite Pope's *Essay on Man*. But the harmony that Thomson is able to perceive in "larger prospects" is an evanescent vision, too fragile to outlast the repetition of striking close-up views of a more realistic, less sentimental nature. In an interesting discussion of the problems inherent in landscape poetry that moves from description to moralization, Alan Roper asserts that "the two values" involved may not be "fully coincident." A likely result is "the existence in the poem of two syntaxes, one descriptive, one moral." [48] This kind of difficulty is at the root of Thomson's *Seasons,* especially in its final revisions of 1744 and 1746.

These revisions are an important index for revealing Thomson's intellectual growth. Professors McKillop, Spacks, and Cohen have analyzed the poet's increased absorption with philosophical, moral, and scientific concerns, and the consequent diminution of purely descriptive emphasis in *The Seasons.* The decline of emphasis on the pictorial, however, cannot be attributed to Thomson's repudiation of his painterly approach to landscape. Some of the later emendations and additions are among his most visually striking passages; the lines on Hagley in "Spring" and on sheep-shearing in "Summer" were first inserted into the 1744 edition. Rather the difference is one of proportion; as the poem swelled to its final extensiveness, the majority of the additions represented Thomson the moralist, not Thomson the poetic painter of heroic landscape. When the didactic strain was made to flow, as a meditative corollary, from a vividly realized landscape scene, the former

48. *Arnold's Poetic Landscapes* (Baltimore, 1969), p. 67. Roper's book, though focusing on Arnold, refers at several points to Thomson's *Seasons.* Roper suggests that "the Augustans and Victorians share a strongly objective sense of nature and landscape as something to be reflected upon, examined for evidence of transcendent truth, or used as the correlative of a mood" (p. 8).

was able to borrow vigor and a measure of conviction from the latter. When, however—and unfortunately this second case is more common—the moralization appears gratuitously inserted, when its pedestrian, even platitudinous tenor seems imposed upon the landscape format rather than derived from it, Thomson's poem is obviously weakened. In "Winter," for example, later versions present, substantially unchanged from the 1730 edition, the spectacular, Zembla-like ice mountains looming fearfully over terrified sailors in arctic waters which epitomize the intractable elements in a savage land. Thomson's landscape, so structured, is a powerful and vivid exercise in the sublime whose impact is lessened by a later, nonpictorial addition:

> Thence winding eastward to the Tartar's coast,
> She sweeps the howling margin of the main;
> Where, undissolving from the first of time,
> Snows swell on snows amazing to the sky;
> And icy mountains high on mountains piled
> Seem to the shivering sailor from afar,
> Shapeless and white, an atmosphere of clouds.
> Projected huge and horrid o'er the surge,
> Alps frown on Alps; or, rushing hideous down,
> As if old Chaos was again returned,
> Wide-rend the deep and shake the solid pole.
>
> [ll. 902–12]

Continuing on to paint the desolate surroundings at greater length, Thomson concludes by pointing out that the bleakness of the terrain has bred a correspondingly uncivilized race of inhabitants, gross and animalistic.

In the 1744 edition, however, a thirty-seven-line passage in praise of Peter the Great was inserted into the poem at this point, introduced by a rhetorical question designed to provide a transitional bridge: "What cannot active government perform,/ New moulding man?" The Czar's accomplishments are duly recited, accompanied by interjections ("Immortal Peter! first of Monarchs!" and "The wonder done! behold the matchless prince!") which fail to punctuate Thomson's moral tale with the sense of urgency and dramatic excitement they are clearly intended to convey. A substantial decline in poetic force is inevitable; the landscape is sustained by its own power, but Thomson cannot breathe a corresponding measure of life into his digression on Peter the Great. Such a pattern continues, unfortunately, to mar the effectiveness of Thomson's pictorialist skill in *The Castle of Indolence,* where an allegorical rather than a historical bringer of civilization, the Knight of Art and Industry, wreaks even greater aesthetic havoc upon Thomson's landscape.

At the end of *The Seasons,* we are left with Thomson's varied gallery of rural scenes, painted with immense technical skill, in the style and with the staple ingredients of sixteenth- and seventeenth-century classical art, and rejuvenated by the poet's own informed love of nature. These scenes sustain the poem, providing nearly all of its memorable moments, but Thomson sadly did not trust their power to stand alone, perhaps because of the low estate of descriptive poetry in his age. Ironically, he weakened his poetic edifice while thinking he buttressed it, by adding verbose, moralistic passages of physico-theology, undigested bits of scientific lore, and the less than incisive reflections of an often undisciplined mind. *The Seasons* showed how effectively poetry "appropriated landscape as a means of evoking and defining states of mind," [49] but Thomson the pictorialist failed too often to put sufficient trust in the power of his own art.

The Castle of Indolence

Published in 1748, the last year of his life, Thomson's *Castle of Indolence* recapitulates in some particulars the developmental growth of *The Seasons.* We are familiar with its beginnings as a literary jest, "little more than a few detached stanzas" of affectionate burlesque written to commemorate Thomson's diverse but congenial circle of friends.[50] It swelled into an alle-

49. Marshall McLuhan, "The Aesthetic Moment in Landscape Poetry," *English Institute Essays,* 1951, ed. Alan S. Downer (New York, 1952), p. 171.
50. See *Works,* ed. Murdoch, I, xiv.

gory of the conflict between Indolence and the Knight of Art
and Industry, covering two cantos and composed of about one
hundred and fifty Spenserian stanzas. Moral and philosophical
considerations increasingly occupied Thomson's attention as
he revised his poem: primitivism versus progress, contemplative
retirement versus strenuous activity. The result of these accretions, as scholars since Thomson's own time have agreed, is a
poem of markedly uneven quality in which disparate tones
are conjoined, jocosity vying with high seriousness; larger questions are unconvincingly answered, if they are answered at all;
and the poetic structure wavers among three alternatives, the
pictorial, narrative, and didactic-logical.[51]

Out of this mélange can be salvaged some of Thomson's finest
pictorializations as well as iconic passages that illustrate his
absorption with the landscape form and his familiarity with
some of its most notable practitioners. The Castle itself is a
palace of art, composed in the same genre as Pope's more elaborately detailed *Temple of Fame,* but stressing even in its
decorative furnishings the landscape motif. Its tapestries
(I.xxxvi–xxxvii) illustrate pastoral myths of the Golden Age,
"Such as of old the rural poets sung/ Or of Arcadian or Sicilian
vale." There, "Reclining lovers, in the lonely dale" occupy the
foreground, "While flocks, woods, streams around, repose and
peace impart." Alternatively, other wall hangings depict equally
pastoral scenes from the Old Testament:

> What time Dan Abraham left the Chaldee land,
> And pastured on from verdant stage to stage,
> Where fields and fountains fresh could best engage.
> Toil was not then. Of nothing took they heed,
> But with wild beasts the silvan war to wage,
> And o'er vast plains their herds and flocks to feed:
> Blest sons of nature they! true golden age indeed!
>
> [I.xxxvii]

---

51. The neoclassical poet regularly employed these "alternative
methods of ordering his materials." See Hagstrum, *The Sister Arts,*
p. xviii.

Subject and treatment recall Giorgione rather than medieval tapestries; [52] Thomson's archaisms, like Spenser's own, are relatively superficial and do not extend beyond minor alterations in vocabulary to reflect a genuine understanding of medieval art. Essentially, Thomson's pantheon remains unchanged from *The Seasons*, but he more obviously anticipates the later picturesque in his debt to Claude and Salvator whose landscape styles contribute in essential ways to the visual impact of the setting for the Castle in Canto I and that of Selvaggio, the Knight's father, in Canto II. Claude's and Salvator's landscapes are specifically conjured up in the section in Canto I which describes the paintings that decorate the Castle's walls. This stanza (xxxviii) immediately follows those on the tapestries.

> Sometimes the pencil, in cool airy halls,
> Bade the gay bloom of vernal landskips rise,
> Or Autumn's varied shades imbrown the walls:
> Now the black tempest strikes the astonished eyes;
> Now down the steep the flashing torrent flies;
> The trembling sun now plays o'er ocean blue,
> And now rude mountains frown amid the skies;
> Whate'er Lorrain light-touched with softening hue,
> Or savage Rosa dashed, or learnèd Poussin drew.

The presence of "learnèd Poussin" in this triumvirate gives evidence again of Thomson's prevailing classicism.[53] After 1750 a

52. The reclining lovers and their surroundings (flocks, woods), as well as the mood of "repose and peace," suggest Giorgione's well-known *Fête champêtre* in the Louvre. Biblical pastorals in Giorgione's oeuvre include *The Testing of Moses* and *The Judgment of Solomon*, both in the Uffizi, Florence. Both paintings provide an extensive and idyllic landscape background, as does Giorgione's *The Golden Age* (National Gallery, London) which depicts the "blest sons of nature" undisturbed by "wild beasts" nearby.
53. The lengthy subtitle of George Turnbull's *A Treatise on Ancient Painting* (London, 1740) suggests Poussin's stature in Augustan England by beginning with the following: "To which are added some Remarks on the peculiar Genius, Character, and Talents of Raphael, Michael Angelo, Nicolas Poussin, and other Celebrated Modern Masters; and the commendable use they made of the ex-

reference to Poussin seldom meant Nicolas, the intellectual; it referred to his brother-in-law, Gaspard Dughet (1615–75), who took the more illustrious surname of Poussin to boost his slender reputation and to lend a borrowed luster to his graceful but superficial landscape paintings. With Claude, he enjoyed a vogue in England that eclipsed his uncle's during the age of sensibility and the early years of the Romantic period.

The iconographical hints in the stanza cited prove that Thomson was familiar with the contrasting styles of Claude and Salvator. With the exception of the third line whose reference to Autumn may be designed to recall the *Seasons* series, none of the landscapes enumerated seems characteristic of Nicolas Poussin. Certainly the line about "the gay bloom of vernal landskips" and that describing the play of light from "the trembling sun" upon the "ocean blue" should be attributed to Claude. The "black tempest," "flashing torrent," and "rude mountains" may be confidently assigned to Salvator Rosa. As Samuel H. Monk has shown, once "the distinction between the sublime and the beautiful was firmly established, Salvator's landscapes became the example of the one and Claude's of the other." [54] Thomson's lines quoted above anticipate that distinction, too often tritely reiterated during the latter half of the century.

Besides the reference to Lorrain, Rosa, and Poussin, one other painter, Titian, is mentioned by Thomson. The very dreams of the Castle's inhabitants, we are told, take place in a landscape setting, an Elysium like Titian's earthly paradises, embellished with voluptuous beauties reclining on beds of flowers.

> And hither Morpheus sent his kindest dreams,
> Raising a world of gayer tint and grace;
> O'er which were shadowy cast Elysian gleams,
> That played in waving lights from place to place,
> And shed a roseate smile on nature's face.
> Not Titian's pencil e'er could so array,

quisite Remains of Antiquity in Painting as well as Sculpture. . . ." Among subscribers listed were Jonathan Richardson and James Thomson.

54. *The Sublime* (Ann Arbor, 1960), p. 194.

So fleece with clouds the pure ethereal space;
Ne could it e'er such melting forms display,
As loose on flowery beds all languishingly lay.

[I.xliv]

Titian's Venuses and his Danae are usually posed reclining in the foreground of a painting which employs an extended landscape view, often seen through a window, in the background. Clouds in the *Danae* are especially fine, and Titian almost invariably displays in his landscapes a virtuoso skill with the manipulation of light and shadow that would have recommended him to one as conscious of chiaroscuro effects as Thomson.

Since the Castle's actual setting, described in the beginning of Canto I, superimposes a dream-vision quality on the already idealized ingredients of the heroic landscape, it bears a close resemblance to the dream landscape of the Castle's sleeping inhabitants above.[55] The "world of gayer tinct and grace," the "waving lights" and contrasting shadows, the fleecy clouds and "pure ethereal space" all suggest that "real" landscape, as well as this one, sleep induced. Indeed, the parallel is even closer when we are told that the "listless climate" with its "sleep-soothing groves" and beds of poppies (I.ii–iii) produces a trancelike state in all the inhabitants of the Castle. Such a magical atmosphere combined with unalloyed pastoral perfection has evoked Claude to more than one critic.[56] Thomson's

55. Patricia Meyer Spacks notes this dream-vision quality but argues that Thomson's landscape of Indolence though vivid is "rarely visual," mostly because Thomson has chosen to emphasize the emotional rather than the visual qualities in his landscape. Conversely, the very effectiveness of this landscape derives, I believe, from Thomson's care in allowing the reader's emotional response to arise out of the initial and predominant pictorial stimulus. See Spacks, *The Poetry of Vision* (Cambridge, Mass., 1967), pp. 46–47, 49, 89.

56. To William Hazlitt, Claude's landscape was unreal, "as if all objects were become a delightful fairy vision"; to Sir Joshua Reynolds, as well, Claudian settings suggested a "fairy land." These reactions are cited in Jean H. Hagstrum, "The Sister Arts: From Neoclassic to Romantic," in *Comparatists at Work*, ed. Stephen G. Nichols, Jr., and Richard B. Vowles (Waltham, Mass., 1968), p. 184.

Castle of Indolence is, in mood and style if not in every iconographical detail, a perfect literary parallel to Claude's *Landscape with Psyche and the Palace of Amor* (Courtauld Institute, London), more familiarly known as *The Enchanted Castle*.

Stanzas ii–vii describe the setting for the Castle and may be Thomson's most highly skilled and elaborate exercise in ideal landscape. This passage is composed like a painting; in stanza ii the reader is positioned to "see" the prospect before him. His attention is drawn to the figure of the Wizard and to the general features of the terrain. After this initial impression Thomson directs the reader's eye to details in the landscape's three planes—foreground, midground, and background—moving in orderly succession from one to the next in stanzas iii, iv, and v. In stanza vi the eye is allowed to lose itself in an expanse of summer sky before being pulled back in stanza vii to the Castle in midground and forward again to the Wizard seated beneath a palm tree in front of the Castle, enchanting the pilgrims with his song. This circular structure of the scene approximates quite accurately the manner of viewing a seventeenth-century landscape composed in three planes and designed to lead the eye from one plane to the next (see plate 17).[57] In order to examine Thomson's technique more closely, the relevant stanzas (ii–vii) are quoted below:

> In lowly dale, fast by a river's side,
> With woody hill o'er hill encompassed round,

57. Kenneth Clark has, for example, summarized Claude's "underlying scheme of composition" as follows: "This involved a dark *coulisse* on one side (hardly ever on two), the shadow of which extended across the first plane of the foreground, a middle plane with a large central feature, usually a group of trees, and finally two planes, one behind the other, the second being that luminous distance for which he has always been famous, and which, as we have seen, he painted direct from nature. Much art was necessary to lead the eye from one plane to the next, and Claude employed bridges, rivers, cattle fording a stream and similar devices; but these are less important than his sure sense of tone, which allowed him to achieve an effect of recession even in pictures where every plane is parallel" (*Landscape into Art*, p. 64).

Plate 17 Domenichino, *St. George and the Dragon*

A most enchanting wizard did abide,
Than whom a fiend more fell is nowhere found.
It was, I ween, a lovely spot of ground;
And there a season atween June and May,
Half prankt with spring, with summer half imbrowned,
A listless climate made, where, sooth to say,
No living wight could work, ne carèd even for play.

Was nought around but images of rest:
Sleep-soothing groves, and quiet lawns between;
And flowery beds that slumbrous influence kest,
From poppies breathed; and beds of pleasant green,
Where never yet was creeping creature seen.
Meantime unnumbered glittering streamlets played,
And hurlèd everywhere their waters sheen;
That, as they bickered through the sunny glade,
Though restless still themselves, a lulling murmur made.

Joined to the prattle of the purling rills,
Were heard the lowing herds along the vale,
And flocks loud-bleating from the distant hills,
And vacant shepherds piping in the dale:
And now and then sweet Philomel would wail,
Or stock-doves plain amid the forest deep,
That drowsy rustled to the sighing gale;
And still a coil the grashopper did keep:
Yet all these sounds yblent inclinèd all to sleep.

Full in the passage of the vale, above,
A sable, silent, solemn forest stood;
Where nought but shadowy forms were seen to move,
As Idless fancied in her dreaming mood.
And up the hills, on either side, a wood
Of blackening pines, ay waving to and fro,
Sent forth a sleepy horror through the blood;
And where this valley winded out, below,
The murmuring main was heard, and scarcely heard, to flow.

A pleasing land of drowsyhed it was:
Of dreams that wave before the half-shut eye;
And of gay castles in the clouds that pass,
For ever flushing round a summer sky:
There eke the soft delights, that witchingly

Instil a wanton sweetness through the breast,
And the calm pleasures always hovered nigh;
But whate'er smacked of noyance, or unrest,
Was far far off expelled from this delicious nest.

The landskip such, inspiring perfect ease;
Where INDOLENCE (for so the wizard hight)
Close-hid his castle mid embowering trees,
That half shut out the beams of Phoebus bright,
And made a kind of checkered day and night.
Meanwhile, unceasing at the massy gate,
Beneath a spacious palm, the wicked wight
Was placed; and, to his lute, of cruel fate
And labour harsh complained, lamenting man's estate.

Stanza ii begins with "virtually a Spenserian formula for landscape," as A. D. McKillop has shown.[58] The trackless wood, enchanted castle, and the wizard are recognizable romance staples also, coming perhaps from the Italian poets as well as from Spenser.[59] There is evidence, however, that Thomson is thinking in painterly as well as literary terms; the valley, though sunny, is "with summer half imbrownd," giving the suggestion of a darker shading. In stanza iii, as Thomson focuses the reader's gaze on the foreground of his picture, the stasis achieved in his description is underscored by the somnolent stillness of the land of Indolence. The "sleep-soothing groves, and quiet lawns between," "flowery beds," "poppies," and "beds of pleasant green" are all devoid of any "creeping creature." The only parts of the foreground scene in motion are the "unnumbered glittering streamlets" that "hurlèd everywhere their waters sheen," reflecting the sunlight in the glade.

The play of light is especially noticeable in this stanza. The

58. *James Thomson, The Castle of Indolence and Other Poems,* ed. Alan Dugald McKillop (Lawrence, Kan., 1961), p. 16. McKillop cites two examples from *The Faerie Queene*: "Down in a Dale forby a River's side" (VI.iii.29.6) and "Down in a Dale, hard by a Forests side" (I.i.34.2).

59. Among Thomson's books, listed in the 1749 Sale Catalogue, were the works of Dante, Ariosto, and Tasso (G. C. Macaulay, *James Thomson* [London, 1908], p. 74).

glitter and motion of the streamlets, which contrast so markedly with the absolute stillness of all else, rivet the reader's attention on this part of the landscape, becoming the foreground's focal point. Once again, as in *The Seasons,* Thomson employs a certain amount of motion in the composition of his landscapes. Like Claude, he also expends much artfulness in moving the reader's eye on to the middle plane of his landscape. A poet has the advantage over a painter of being able to use the sense of sound. Thomson, having focused on the streamlets' appearance, now describes their "lulling murmur" and, in stanza iv, connects this sound with those heard farther away. We make the transition to the landscape's midground, therefore, by an auditory rather than a visual device which continues to work well for Thomson. The forest background, which dominates stanza v, is introduced smoothly by noting first (in stanza iv) the sound of nightingale and stock-dove, heard but too far away to be seen. The forest itself, at the edge of the valley, provides the necessary dark contrast to Thomson's largely sunny landscape as well as a foreboding counterpoint to the cheerful brightness of the valley. The contrast of light and shadow is emphasized by the movement of the trees which has the same effect as the motion of the streamlets, though somber instead of gay. These two elements in an otherwise stationary scene stand out and become dominant in the planes of the landscape they occupy.

The vista opens out even further in stanza vi to achieve the luminous distances of Claudian skies. The dreamy motif persists with cloud castles anticipating the real Castle's description in stanza vii. The "flushing . . . summer sky" brings back the light, so that now Thomson's composition achieves dramatic contrast with the light-dark-light sequence of foreground, middle ground, and background. The Castle's position, "mid embowering trees" that half exclude, half admit the light and produce "a kind of checkered day and night," underscores this light-dark pattern. The latter has, of course, a symbolic as well as a pictorial function, helping to develop the theme of reality versus unreality; the dark forest will become the setting for Selvaggio and the Knight, but the Castle in its sunny valley will prove as insubstantial as the cloud castles above it.

The precise effects of the opening landscape scene do much more in Canto I than set the stage and evoke the dreamy atmosphere. Through imagery, Thomson conveys his ambivalent feelings about his paradise of Indolence and artfully sustains a rather complex view of it until Canto II. The perniciousness of Spenser's Bower of Bliss is always clearcut, following the traditions of Renaissance poets who used the motif of the enchanted garden. Thomson, however, was a son of the eighteenth century and familiar, therefore, with retirement literature extolling withdrawal from worldly concerns as a positive virtue. The grotesque scenes glimpsed by the pilgrims in the Mirror of Vanity (I.xlix–lv) satirize spendthrifts, pedants, and politicians with a vigor that is quite Popean, and the Knight himself, when his work is done, retires to "a farm in Deva's vale."

The farm recalls Shenstone's Leasowes, highly praised by Thomson, whose suggestions for its further embellishment were designed to blend it into the surrounding terrain in a more picturesque manner. Otherwise, exclaimed the admiring poet to Shenstone, "You have nothing to do . . . but to dress Nature." [60] So, too, the Knight's task is simply to assist nature.

> As nearer to his farm you make approach,
> He polished nature with a finer hand;
> Yet on her beauties durst not art encroach;
>
> > [II.xxviii]

The farm is itself a work of landscape art:

> Still, as with grateful change the seasons pass,
> New scenes arise, new landskips strike the eye,
> And all the enlivened country beautify:
> Gay plains extend where marshes slept before;
> O'er recent meads the exulting streamlets fly;
> Dark frowning heaths grow bright with Ceres' store;
> And woods imbrown the steep, or wave along the shore.
>
> > [xxvii]

The Knight bears a more than passing resemblance to Pope's Man of Ross, and his farm would have suited the squire of Twickenham very well.

60. *James Thomson, Letters and Documents*, ed. Alan Dugald McKillop (Lawrence, Kan., 1958), p. 185.

More old-fashioned artistically is Thomson's picture of a Scottish shepherd who occupies not an eighteenth-century *ferme ornée* but the baroque canvas of a heroic landscape crammed with allegorical presences.

> As when a shepherd of the Hebrid Isles,
> Placed far amid the melancholy main,
> (Whether it be lone fancy him beguiles,
> Or that aerial beings sometimes deign
> To stand embodied to our senses plain)
> Sees on the naked hill, or valley low,
> The whilst in ocean Phoebus dips his wain,
> A vast assembly moving to and fro;
> Then all at once in air dissolves the wondrous show.
>
> [I.xxx]

Joseph Warton exclaimed, "What an exquisite picture has Thomson given us," referring to this stanza,[61] and it is indeed of the type that stimulated readers in that age to create a vivid tableau of a few details that may strike us as meager or vague.

Obviously the variety that characterized *The Seasons* is also apparent in the pictorializations of *The Castle of Indolence*. Thomson at times employs the emblematic mode, most effectively in his portraits of Beggary and Scorn in Canto II. Beggary especially appears to have been copied in all particulars from an old emblem book, reprinted, like that of Caesar Ripa in 1709, for Augustan readers. He is placed in the Inferno-like landscape of Indolence after the Knight has dispelled its illusion. Eden becomes "a desert wild" or, elsewhere, "a joyless land of bogs," "a gray waste," or a frozen tundra peopled by corpses or specters.

Contributing to our impression of Thomson's almost over-facile eclecticism are exercises in the sublime that owe an initial debt perhaps to Salvator Rosa but verge upon the grotesque. When the Knight waves his wand to return the Castle and its setting to reality, illusions are dispelled with grisly vividness.

> Sudden the landskip sinks on every hand;
> The pure quick streams are marshy puddles found;

---

61. *An Essay on the Genius and Writings of Pope,* I, 348.

On baleful heaths the groves all blackened stand;
And, o'er the weedy foul abhorrèd ground,
Snakes, adders, toads, each loathly creature crawls around.

And here and there, on trees by lightning scathed,
Unhappy wights who loathèd life yhung;
Or in fresh gore and recent murder bathed
They weltering lay; or else, infuriate flung
Into the gloomy flood, while ravens sung
The funeral dirge, they down the torrent rolled:

[II.lxvii–lxviii]

Thomson's instinct for making his landscapes communicate the essentials of his poetic meaning is, as we have seen, an almost invariably successful device. In this poem, however, like *The Seasons,* a breakdown in the pictorial form results in a serious artistic failure. When narrative (the Knight's birth, upbringing, and exploits) or preachment (the bard's lengthy song in praise of honest toil) is allowed in Canto II to distort the poem's structure, slow its pace, or dull the delicacy of its allegorical fancy, *The Castle of Indolence* rapidly loses its enchantment over us. Only in Canto I does the pictorial structure enable the poem to progress in a series of generally effective scenes occasionally marred by abrupt and extreme changes in tone. Thomson's unevenness prevented him from developing into the major poet he might have become had he adhered to his resolve of being the portrait painter of nature. In a letter written from Paris in 1731, Thomson revealed the true bent of his poetic vocation, but in the years that passed he too often lost sight of it.

Travelling has long been my fondest wish, for the very purpose you recommend, the storing one's imagination with ideas of all-beautiful, all-great, and all-perfect Nature. These are the true *materia poetica,* the light and colours, with which fancy kindles up her whole creation, paints a sentiment, and even embodies an abstracted thought.[62]

62. Cited in Macaulay, *James Thomson,* p. 34.

It is as a poet of nature, not as a philosopher or a sage, that Thomson claims a place in English letters. On this point there is universal agreement, though Ralph Cohen has taught us a greater esteem for the poet's intellectual growth as reflected in *The Seasons* than we, in this century, have generally accorded him. A degree of vagueness still persists when we attempt to isolate and describe those qualities that characterize Thomson's view of external nature. That view is implicit in his pictorialism. Clearly his models are heroic and ideal, not naturalistic. Thomson can no longer be considered a precursor to Wordsworth, an anachronism partially redeeming the barrenness and aridity of Augustan poetry. But he is still associated far too frequently with the picturesque movement of the later eighteenth century. While juxtapositions of Claudian beauty and Salvatorian sublimity do occur in *The Castle of Indolence,* they are designed to recapitulate, on the level of image, the thematic conflicts on which Thomson focuses in the poem. These contrasting passages should not be cited as typical of his work as a whole, nor do they ever threaten to degenerate into the stereotyped formula repetitively used by minor poets of the latter half of the century. Thomson is "picturesque" only in the sense that he composes his scenes of nature "like a picture." The narrower meanings of the term are of later derivation and cannot be applied retrospectively to the poet of *The Seasons.*

The Seasons is Thomson's major work, a poem whose evolution spanned almost his entire career. It reflects his preoccupations both intellectual and aesthetic over a twenty-year period. So various are its scenes of rural life that it is possible to find and extract from its context a particular passage to illustrate almost any style. Looked at more generally, however, *The Seasons* reveals itself as typical of the age that produced it. Its originality cannot be denied, but its inspiration and pictorial sources are largely unchanged from those of Thomson's contemporary, Alexander Pope. The decorative rococo and baroque styles assume a greater importance in Pope's work because his landscapes tend to be representative of more traditional poetic subgenres—the pastoral, the estate poem. Thomson's *Seasons* was not such a recognized type, so of necessity he became more of an innovator, but only in his methods, not in his sources.

Evidence suggests that these sources are largely pre-Claudian. Thomson, while first writing *The Seasons,* was learning to reconcile his northern heritage and his love of rugged natural terrain with the new landscape architecture coming into vogue and with the traditional artistic pantheon he learned to appreciate during the time of his pictorialist apprenticeship in London. He was not yet ready to assimilate the fully realized Claudian ideal, or to trade his own varied poetic canvases for the notably less diverse pastoral vistas portrayed by Claude. The parallels to Elsheimer and Brill have been pointed out and need not be restated except to stress that Thomson appears to have solved certain problems in depicting landscape (the prospect view, diffused lighting) and used certain techniques (aerial perspective, chiaroscuro effects) in ways strikingly similar to the methods used by Elsheimer and Brill. Finally his ability to elevate the landscape of fact into the heroic mode resembles that of the two Northern painters and such Italians as Bassano, a circumstance that helps to explain his appeal to later poets who found his landscapes more natural and less artificial than those of Pope.

Thomson's unique but limited talents were stimulated to best advantage by the time and place in which he was fortunate enough to exercise them. His work gave an added impetus to the landscape movement in both the verbal and the visual arts until his educative influence on his successors came to be out of all proportion to his own stature as a poet.

Conclusion

$\mathcal{G}$enerally we are accustomed to the richness of English nature poetry even though we are still discovering aspects of
its complex genealogy and mapping areas of its varied terrain
whose precise boundaries persistently elude us. Remembering
how few civilizations have reacted appreciatively to landscape,[1]
we are stimulated into attempting to assess the local causes of
this relatively unusual cultural phenomenon and the influences
which have operated upon it. Though this survey of landscape
poetry from Marvell to Thomson covers only about one hundred years, it is a crucial segment of a larger whole and one
that has been often ignored or misinterpreted. It would be
well, at the conclusion of this study, to summarize important
points and to evaluate the meaning of the changes that occurred in the poetry of natural description between 1650 and
1750.

1. Only three cultures out of Arnold Toynbee's list of about
twenty-six—the Indian, European, and Chinese—have responded
to nature with any aesthetic appreciation. See J. D. Frodsham,
"Landscape Poetry in China and Europe," *Comp. Lit.*, XIX (1967),
193.

Before discussing descriptive techniques, we should give priority to thematic considerations. What concepts and attitudes lie at the heart of English landscape poetry of this period? Surely among the most constant is the view of England as Eden, a durable ideal but one rendered fragile by civil war and continuing religious and political strife. Marvell's anguished cry in the mid-seventeenth century could as easily be Pope's a hundred years later:

> What luckless Apple did we tast,
> To make us Mortal and The Wast?
> ["Upon Appleton House," ll. 327–28]

If nostalgia for that prelapsarian garden helped give impetus to poetry celebrating the joys of retirement, a sense of sin or an abiding restlessness was as potent a force as any angel with a flaming sword in effecting other expulsions. Marvell could not remain sequestered at Nun Appleton, Thomson turned against his land of Indolence, and Pope's Twickenham became less a refuge than a fort from which he thundered forth at Walpole and the powers of darkness. Milton's Eden was a private religious vision which sustained the Puritan poet in his last years of disillusionment and old age, while Dryden's earthly paradise was precariously restored only in the first exuberant years after the return of Charles II. Mixed with the dream of Eden was that of the lost Golden Age which might come again with Astraea's return, banishing war, injustice, and the uglier urban realities. It is remarkable that the poets of a supposedly pragmatic and rational time should maintain such an abiding hope in the possibility of reversing the natural evolutionary process by trading bitter experience for lost innocence. But the image of the earthly paradise is as flexible as it is evanescent, both biblical and classical accretions rendering it an adaptable vehicle for other poetic variations on the theme of what constitutes man's felicity.

Pastoral traditions and the ingredients of the *locus amoenus* setting have combined to make love a frequent consideration in landscape poetry. Cynicism conflicts with the ideal, and, more often than not, the negative view appears to prevail.

Woman, at least as a sexual partner, must often be excluded from the new Eden if it is to endure. The implications of chastity associated with the *hortus conclusus* motif can engender ambivalent attitudes toward sex, and the powerful tradition of the Renaissance epic with its enchantress who more resembles Circe than Eve militates against the depiction of amorous idylls in pastoral retreats. A distaste for carnal pleasures or disillusionment with them is reflected especially in Marvell's poetry, but a decided wariness is apparent as well in Pope's *Pastorals* and in Thomson's *Castle* whose *locus amoenus* is peopled by a group resembling an Augustan gentlemen's club. Marvell's cruel Juliana even more than Milton's Eve testifies to the persistence of discord in the closest and most basic of human relationships —even in Eden. Unless he dwells in it alone, forswearing woman's fickle or dangerous charms, the unchanging perfection of the *locus amoenus* landscape may end by mocking the rural swain, refusing to become an emblem of his inevitable cosmic alienation. Ironically, ideal landscape often serves as a paradoxical metaphor for man's discontent both with his environment and with his fellow creatures, until, finally, he must escape his earthly paradise or even destroy it like Marvell's Damon the Mower and Thomson's Knight of Art and Industry.

Obviously the ideal landscape of Eden or of the Golden Age represents a complex of fundamental ideas, melancholy as well as joyful in its imagery. Eternally unchanging but constantly renewed, it stimulates man's immortal yearnings but appears to deny them.[2] Its stress upon rural simplicity possesses a compelling attraction for those who cannot extricate themselves from a world of increasing urban complexity. But if the ingredients of the ideal landscape can be manipulated to represent a rosy dream of a new Arcadia, they also can be employed

2. Morchard Bishop notes a "tomb-haunted" quality and a preoccupation with death in Arcadian motifs appearing in Italian Renaissance poetry. See "The Natural History of Arcadia," *The Cornhill Magazine,* CLXVI (1952–53), 84–85. We have noted the same theme reiterated in seventeenth-century landscapes by Poussin, Guercino, and Castiglione. It is interesting to observe how this preoccupation with death persists in the poetry of Pope and Thomson.

to reveal graphically to us the tragic gulf between present imperfection and an ideal forever unattainable. Because so many of these implicit meanings touch upon man's deepest preoccupations, the image of the garden or earthly paradise is enlarged powerfully into myth and has implications for us, both conscious and unconscious, possessed by no other symbol.

The imagery of ideal landscape changes very little from age to age, but within the period covered by this study it reveals some interesting variations. Besides the well-documented growth in appreciation for mountains and other "sublime" aspects of nature, the most notable change is a tendency toward expansion. Marvell's *hortus conclusus* grows into Thomson's *ferme ornée.* The omnipresent bower of the Renaissance epic yields to the prospect view of the Augustan poem. The motif of enclosure often endures but becomes disguised; boundaries—in actual landscapes as well as in literary ones—reveal themselves more subtly. A fence gives way to a ha-ha, the concealed ditch which kept an eighteenth-century gentleman's cattle from intruding into his parlor. If Lord Fairfax's walls at Appleton were built to "restrain the World without," Lord Burlington's park at Chiswick was designed to blend imperceptibly into the surrounding countryside. The less visible barriers are at least as efficient as "the undergrowth/ Of shrubs and tangling bushes" that surrounded the Garden of Eden and failed to discourage the trespassing Satan. The latter, however, illustrates another characteristic of the ideal landscape that undergoes modification during the century we have surveyed.

We have stressed that for all its artifice—emblematic motifs, allegorical presences, baroque movement, or mazelike rococo windings—ideal landscape possesses an intrinsic quality of naturalism. Art functions as nature's handmaiden, not her peer, and the two in concert produce a unified impression designed to render visual evidence of the *discordia concors.* While the nature imitated by poet and painter in this genre is a heightened, generalized version of reality rather than *la vraie nature,* the valued principles of variety and contrast were increasingly employed in English poetry throughout the late seventeenth and early eighteenth century to insure against blandness and monotony. Pope's "brave disorder" is controlled, but it is real. His naturalism is not less effective for having been carefully contrived. Dryden works less surely to balance baroque élan with classical restraint; when he succeeds, as in "Anne Killigrew," the effect is dazzling but slightly unconvincing. The landscapes are those of a city dweller who has come to nature through art and Vergil. Thomson's nature, on the other hand, remains the Scotland of his boyhood, transmuted into heroic landscape by his exposure in maturity to the arts of painting and landscape gardening. He too synthesizes disparate elements in his poetry, but less surely than does Pope, often allowing a homely or sentimental detail to strike a discordant note in a landscape designed to maintain the desired balance between the classical and the naturalistic. To make the series of hunting landscapes in "Autumn" culminate in the tavern scene would be an acceptable tactic had Thomson's pictorial models been Northern instead of Italian, but they were not, and his overall design is flawed in consequence.

In proceeding to a final evaluation of the degree and kind of literary pictorialism in the poetic landscapes analyzed in this study, certain judgments seem unmistakably clear. First, there is ample evidence of a growing awareness of landscape painting among English poets from the mid-seventeenth century on. There is also an increasing inclination for them to accept and utilize the concept of *ut pictura poesis,* applying its principles first to the choice of details and later to the descriptive methods employed in designing their own verbal landscapes. Depictions of the *locus amoenus* or *hortus conclusus,* for example, reveal in the later seventeenth century a marked interest in the visual for its own sake and an appreciation of a new and different (to the English) pictorial style, the baroque. The effect may often be inconsistent in the work of Milton, but it is also unexpectedly powerful, which leads us to a second point. The pictorial element in landscape poetry between 1650 and 1750, while at first tentative, unskilled, and intermittent in the poets studied, becomes, by the end of that period, sophisticated, deliberate, and all-pervasive. Milton may be reacting to a whole cultural context—Italy in the age of the baroque—when he delineates a cosmic landscape; Pope and Thomson later respond quite consciously to specific stimuli—to the chiaroscuro of "Spagno-

301

lett" or to a torrent dashing over a precipice drawn by "savage Rosa." Dryden's intermediate position makes him keenly sensible to the effect of certain compositional elements but much less sure about their proper spatial arrangement than the Augustans were. His landscapes are seldom composed like pictures, but they are filled with pictorial ingredients, all common to heroic landscape: light and shade, trees, water, and hills, and allegorical personifications who inhabit the ideal enclaves he depicts.

In English poetry the dominant mode after 1650 was classical baroque. Its visual particulars derived in part from the eclectic style of the Carraccis and included some aspects of the work of a stylistic conservative like Poussin as well as the more typical baroque canvases of an artist like Rubens. We have noted the impact of the baroque on Milton's epic poems and on the work of Dryden. But it should be stressed that Andrew Marvell, a transitional figure, makes extensive use of the emblematic imagery that appealed to the metaphysical poets of the earlier seventeenth century. After Marvell we watch the emblematic almost disappear; only a few examples of the style remain in the work of Pope and Thomson, and these tend either to be restricted to a decorative element (*The Temple of Fame*) or to be semiserious exercises in the grotesque (*The Castle of Indolence*). The emblematic no longer possesses the moral impact of visual allegory in an abbreviated form that was its function in Marvell's pictorial landscapes.

Among the English poets, baroque expression was always tempered to some degree by a disinclination to forsake classical forms completely. Both Milton and Dryden exhibit a tendency to adapt either style to their poetic purposes or, especially in the majority of Dryden's work, to achieve an adroit blend of the two styles. Typical of this sort of English aesthetic compromise is the Augustan response to the reassertion of the classical spirit. This "neoclassicism" resulted not in rigorous purism as in France but in an eclecticism reflected in the work of both Pope and Thomson. Pope tames the baroque extravagance of Dryden in his own *Messiah* but still uses it. He knows when to be "romantick" and can achieve powerful emotional effects in a "nightpiece," like the foray of Diomedes and Ulysses in the

Iliad translation. He can, as easily, affect the charm and playfulness of the rococo and does so in the *Pastorals*.

Such an eclectic spirit was furthered by the impulse in this age to synthesize polarities in all the arts, architecture and gardening as well as poetry and painting.[3] The Palladian manor house surrounded by the twisting, curving lines of the *jardin anglais* has already been cited as the most appropriate visual metaphor for Augustan taste. When its style is successful, Thomson's *The Seasons* is a poetic equivalent of that harmonious mingling of styles that are intrinsically opposed. It can artfully combine the new naturalism with the older stylistic characteristics and aesthetic attitudes of ideal landscape. In the main, however, Thomson lacks both Pope's versatility and his artistic tact; too often the former's attraction to the natural landscape coexists uneasily with his propensity for baroque decoration or the theatrical sublime. Thomson's disequilibrium reflects his transitional position and helps explain his influential effect upon landscapists in both of the sister arts of the succeeding age. It is to be hoped that we are immune to the infection of the picturesque, that dubious but fashionable genre into which ideal landscape was to degenerate in the second half of the eighteenth century. For us, able to take advantage of the perspective of time, it is Pope, the pictorial virtuoso, who best illustrates "the indispensability of landscape as a technique for managing the aesthetic moment in poetry." [4] Reading him, we all too briefly recapture the vision of Eden and suffer again with him the poignancy of its loss.

3. For a discussion of this synthesizing tendency in art and in landscape, see Nikolaus Pevsner, *The Englishness of English Art* (Harmondsworth, Middlesex, 1964), p. 24, and Christopher Hussey, *English Gardens and Landscapes, 1700–1750* (London, 1967), pp. 13–14.
4. Marshall McLuhan, "The Aesthetic Moment in Landscape Poetry," *English Institute Essays*, 1951, ed. Alan S. Downer (New York, 1952), p. 168.

Index

In this index 48 f means separate references on pp. 48 and 49; 48 ff means separate references on pp. 48, 49, and 50; 48–50 means a continuous discussion. *Passim,* meaning "here and there," is used for a cluster of references in close but not consecutive sequence (for example, 13, 14, 16, 17, 20 would be written as 13–20 *passim*).